The Strategy of the Spirit?

The Strategy of
the Spirit?

Peter Hocken

eagle
Guildford, Surrey

British Library Cataloguing in Publication Data. A catalogue
record for this book is available from the British Library.

Published by Eagle, an imprint of Inter Publishing Service (IPS) Ltd,
St Nicholas House, 14 The Mount, Guildford, Surrey GU2 5HN.

Typeset by Palimpsest Book Production Limited, Polmont,
Stirlingshire
Printed by Caledonian International Book Manufacturing, Glasgow

ISBN No: 0 86347 191 9

Contents

Part V: The Issues and the Challenges

Foreword

As the millenium approaches, many Christians have felt that there needs to be a renewed effort to increase understanding and unity among Christians of the different Churches and traditions. This book by a Catholic theologian deserves, in my opinion, to be seen as a major contribution towards understanding and unity. It follows on Peter Hocken's previous books, especially *One Lord One Spirit One Body* and *The Glory and the Shame*, which were deeply appreciated.

Peter writes with great perception as a theologian with an immense historical knowledge of the revival movements of recent centuries, as well as of the contemporary scene. He identifies four streams which have developed mainly outside the historical Churches: The evangelical, the Holiness, the Pentecostal and the charismatic. His main theme is that these streams should not be seen as being in opposition to the historic Churches, especially the Catholic and the Eastern Churches. They should be regarded as complementary. He rightly says that the Holy Spirit is working in both the historic Churches and the streams, and that they need each other.

To try to build an ecumenical bridge between evangelical-Pentecostal–charismatic churches and fellowships on the one side and the historic Churches, especially the Catholic Church, on the other, is a most daunting task, which will be criticised and ridiculed as utopian by many on both sides. But it is surely the main task awaiting the ecumenical movement today, a task in which the Catholic Charismatic Renewal has a special role to play, as the present Pope has publicly recognised.

It is so easy for many Catholics and other Christians from

the historic Churches simply to regard the Pentecostal–
charismatic churches and fellowships as being unbalanced,
fanatical, sectarian, and for many of them to regard
the historic Churches, especially the Catholic Church,
as dead Churches which have betrayed the Lord, so
that the task of overcoming the mountains of prejudice
which exist on both sides requires much patience and
perseverance. This book is a very remarkable attempt
to explain each side to the other and to move towards
an authentic reconciliation, without compromising the
author's beliefs, as an orthodox Catholic priest.

The urgency of this task can be seen from the numerical
situation. The Catholic and Eastern Churches are by
far the largest bloc of Christians in the world, while
the evangelical–Pentecostal–charismatic churches and
fellowships are in many places the rapidly expanding
section of the Christian world. So increasingly, Christians
in the near future will be in one or other of these two
groups. And it is often between these two groups that
there is most misunderstanding and hostility.

The chapter in this book on the relevance of Israel
is a particularly powerful one. Reading it made me
still more aware of the sinful attitudes and acts of
Christians towards the Jews over the centuries. Peter
the Venerable, the Abbot of Cluny (1092–1156), wrote
of the Jews: 'God wishes them not to be killed or wiped
out but to be preserved in a life worse than death,
in greater torment and humiliation than the fratricide
Cain.' Christians are now, thank God, increasingly aware
in their attitude towards the Jews that 'the gifts and the
calling of God are irrevocable' (Romans 11:29). The Jews
remain a chosen people with a unique vocation which is of
vital importance for the whole of humanity. Peter Hocken
points out that 'the greatest credit for Christian recovery
of the on-going place of Israel in God's purposes belongs
to the evangelicals'.

Peter Hocken has long been a promoter of spiritual
ecumenism, which Vatican Two described 'as the soul
of the whole ecumenical movement'. This ideal lies very
much behind all Peter Hocken's work as a theologian

and historian. In his chapter on repentance he makes a
very powerful plea for collective repentance – Christians
repenting of their abominable treatment of the Jews and
repenting of their hostility and disunity in their relations
with each other. Surely he is right in thinking that there
will not be much progress towards unity until there is
much more repentance.

Then he goes on to make a very interesting proposal:
Could not Christians, following the Jewish example of
Yom Kippur, set aside a day each year as a day of repentance, especially repentance for the Christian treatment
of the Jews and for Christian disunity? It is greatly to be
hoped that this suggestion will be taken up by others, for
I think it could be of much importance.

Benedict M. Heron O.S.B.

PART I

A NEW SITUATION AND OPPORTUNITY

Introduction

The subject of this book, the relationship between the Churches and the life-streams (evangelical, Holiness, Pentecostal and charismatic) follows naturally as an extension of my previous studies concerning the charismatic and the Pentecostal movements.[1] It was my doctoral dissertation *Streams of Renewal* on the origins and early development of the charismatic movement in Great Britain[2] that had led me into historical studies as the necessary springboard for theological reflection on a contemporary work of the Holy Spirit. To understand the significance of a movement of revival or renewal, it is necessary to examine how it began and developed.

It was through the dissertation that I was first confronted with the phenomenon of the new charismatic Churches, then called the House Churches. Keeping abreast of the ebb and flow of charismatic currents has kept before my eyes the remarkable growth and spread of the new Churches across the world. Invitations to present papers on Pentecostalism and the new Churches at continental-level meetings held by the Catholic Church on New Religious Movements gave me further incentive to explore this subject and its implications for the Catholic Church.[3]

My growing contact with Youth With A Mission (YWAM) also served to stimulate my thinking and my prayer in this area. The growing desire of people in YWAM to collaborate with the Roman Catholic Church in awakening the faith of young Catholics and training them as disciples and evangelists demonstrated both the difficulties and the potential of positive relationships between Church and stream.

The importance of this subject has also been brought

home to me by pastoral contacts. On the one hand, when
I visit new charismatic church groups, I always meet
some former Catholics. More recently, however, I find
that some of them are modifying their opposition to
the Church they left and one or two decades later are
coming to appreciate some of its strengths. On the other
hand, I occasionally meet, mostly at Catholic charismatic
conferences, people who have returned to the Catholic
Church after a period in a new charismatic church; these
are generally very grateful for what they received there,
but they were led back by a yearning for the eucharist and
for a more liturgical pattern of worship. However, these
returnees mostly experience a frustration over the pau-
city of strong biblical teaching in the Catholic parishes,
and long to have the strengths of both sides. I also meet
Catholics, whose faith has been brought to life through
the charismatic renewal, occasionally in a new church
setting, and who are torn between their attachment to the
Catholic Church and the vitality they have experienced
elsewhere. Improved relations and co-operation between
the old Churches and the new has an important potential
to alleviate these pastoral problems.

Accepting the Challenge and Addressing the Puzzle

This book addresses the challenge that the life-streams
that have arisen in evangelical Protestantism and the
historic Churches, especially the Roman Catholic Church,
pose to each other. One of the first challenges is to know
each other better. For prejudice thrives on ignorance,
and on the stereotypes that opponents typically cherish
of the other side. Thus the first half of the book presents
a short history of the life-streams and renewing currents
in the Churches, especially the Roman Catholic Church,
in modern times.

The later part of the book seeks to articulate the
particular challenges that the two sides present to each
other. Many convinced evangelicals and other-stream
participants on the one hand and many convinced Roman

Catholics on the other, will have difficulty even accepting that there is a challenge that the Spirit of God is presenting in this interaction. For them, the other side is simply apostate or heretical, beyond the pale. I invite any readers tempted to react in this way to consider the following puzzle, which I believe faces both the Roman Catholic and the evangelical Protestant.

For the Roman Catholic the puzzle is why the stream-forms of Christianity, that are non-sacramental, outside all historic succession, non-ecclesial in the Catholic sense of church, have so much vitality, and represent the fastest-growing patterns of Christian faith in almost all parts of the world. For the evangelical and the Pentecostal, the puzzle is why the Roman Catholic Church, that seems to them to represent so much that is not biblical, is so orthodox in its confession of Christ, of the Trinity, of Christian moral principles, and manifests a capacity to resist the inroads of moral relativism that Churches of more recent vintage do not seem to possess.

These two puzzles that each side presents to the other do not make sense within our habitual patterns of mutual rejection. They only make sense if the Spirit of God is at work on the other side in a way that we have not yet recognized. It is my hope that this book will contribute to a larger and more inclusive vision of God's work and purpose that sees how the rise of the new streams and the renewal of the historic Churches are complementary not opposed, however little we yet understand of how they fit together.

I write as a convinced and committed Roman Catholic. I believe in the faith professed by the Church to which I belong, and I believe that the Church needs constant renewal through the power of the Holy Spirit. Indeed, I am convinced that a real trust in the Spirit's guidance of the Church frees Catholics to be able to recognise humbly and generously the work of the same Spirit among all those who confess Jesus as Lord and Saviour, and who desire to make him known and loved. My prayer is that the Catholic Church, together with the other 'mainline' Churches will receive the grace of the Lord to see this

contemporary situation, not simply in negative terms as
a problem with an enemy to be fought, but as a challenge
first to ourselves, to a depth of renewal that alone can
truly further the Lord's purpose for all his people.

I should mention that I have used the upper case for
Church when referring to Church bodies at the national
and international level, and the lower case for local
congregations. I have used the Revised Standard Version
for all biblical citations unless otherwise marked.

Peter Hocken
January 1996

Chapter One

Signs of a Coming Together

In April 1994, a group of prominent evangelicals and Catholics in the United States issued a joint declaration 'Evangelicals and Catholics Together' (ECT). Although this statement has met with some sharp criticism, almost entirely from the evangelical side, the fact of its existence and the eminence of its signatories indicate that a significant realignment is taking place in the Christian world. A subsequent book *Evangelicals and Catholics Together: Toward a Common Mission*, edited by Charles Colson and Richard John Neuhaus,[1] reprints the statement and provides an extensive commentary. The rebuttal of evangelical objections to ECT by one signatory, Dr James Packer, confirms the extent of this sea-change, not least by the staunch Evangelical-Reformed reputation of its author.[2]

Throughout the history of Evangelical Protestantism, Roman Catholicism has been seen as posing a constant threat to the purity of evangelical faith. While the fierce and abusive polemics of previous centuries between evangelical Protestants and Roman Catholics have generally quietened down, deep suspicions towards each other have remained on both sides. However, the last thirty-five years since Pope John XXIII and President Kennedy, have seen many influences contributing to a reshaping of mentalities. Mark Noll describes the evolution of this relationship, particularly in the North American context, in his contribution to the Colson-Neuhaus book.[3]

As the Roman Catholic Church has entered the ecumenical debate, much of the evangelical world has tended to become more and more disenchanted with ecumenism. While accusations of active persecution of Protestants in

overwhelmingly Catholic countries have decreased since
the Catholic acceptance of religious freedom at Vatican
Two, real relationships in these lands have often been
slow to develop. Catholic acceptance of ecumenism has
led in places like Latin America to a sharp distinction
between the mainline (respectable) Churches that do not
proselytize and that participate in the ecumenical movement (Anglicans, Lutherans, Presbyterians, Methodists)
and those who proselytize and whose Christian character
is not recognized. These evangelical and Pentecostal
proselytizers are then denounced as 'sects' and are not
properly distinguished from groups like the Mormons,
the Jehovah's Witnesses and the Unification Church.

Against this background, the 1994 evangelical–Catholic declaration, made as it was by several respected leaders in both traditions has to be taken seriously as a sign
of change. The text indicates that this limited but highly
significant consensus has been spurred and motivated by
the growing assault on historic Christian orthodoxy and
on traditional moral principles, not only within society
but also among Christians. The staunchest opposition to
abortion, to euthanasia and to the acceptance of homosex-
uality has in fact come from the Roman Catholic Church,
especially its leadership, and from the evangelical and
Pentecostal–charismatic sectors. As many committed
Christians in the Western world seek to oppose legislation authorizing and even promoting such practices,
historically rejected as incompatible with the Christian
revelation, they cannot avoid noticing who are their
friends and supporters and who oppose and even ridicule
them. So evangelicals and Catholics have found themselves protesting together outside abortion clinics, praying together before the Supreme Court in Washington,
working together to oppose permissive legislation.

The declaration 'Evangelicals and Catholics Together'
clearly comes out of a decade or more of this shared
experience. The main drafters, Richard John Neuhaus
and Charles Colson, are widely known as strong and
uncompromising opponents of moral relativism and all
decline from objective biblical standards. This coming

together has not been merely pragmatic. There have been signs for some years of a growing evangelical awareness of the need for clear Christian thinking in the face of modern moral decline, and some recognition that the Catholic tradition possesses a wealth of resources for such a combat. Many evangelicals have had for some years a love for the writings of C. S. Lewis, the Anglican Christian apologist of a more Catholic tendency. More recently, their enthusiasm has spread to the heritage of the rumbustious Catholic 'convert', G. K. Chesterton. Lewis and Chesterton are revered and promoted in many evangelical and even Pentecostal circles today because they present, perhaps more than any conservative Protestant authors, a 'no nonsense' defence of Christian faith and its supernatural character, that in no way apologizes for confident affirmation of God and Christ. Rather, they went on the offensive against all modernizing reductionism, and are being discovered now as a breath of fresh air by Christians choked by a fog of ridicule and unbelief.

At the same time as growing secularization and relativism have been helping evangelicals and Roman Catholics to discover one another, several other forms of rapprochement have been taking place. Evangelical and Pentecostal groups have always emphasized vigorous evangelism, and have sought to send out missionaries to all parts of the world to proclaim the gospel. Inevitably, they have been faced with the challenge of inculturation, of how the one eternal gospel can be expressed in the terms of the many different cultures and languages of the world. While the most conservative and most fundamentalist groups are less open to the re-thinking that authentic inculturation demands, there are an increasing number of evangelicals, who are sensitive to this challenge, and who are aware of extensive Catholic grappling with this issue.

There are also signs of several inter-confessional or para-church groups in the evangelical–Pentecostal worlds that are re-thinking their traditional stances towards the Roman Catholic Church. In the past, such agencies took for granted that Catholics were not real Christians and were simply objects for their evangelistic efforts.

Sometimes, they gave the impression that saving Catholics from 'the darkness of popish superstition' was more
wonderful than the conversion of mere pagans.

Campus Crusade for Christ was one of the first evangelical organizations to sense the possibilities in the
post-Vatican Two Catholic Church of helping Catholics
to receive the gospel and to preach it within the Catholic
world. Poland was in many ways the laboratory for these
first experiments in evangelical–Catholic co-operation on
directly spiritual and religious matters. Its overwhelming
Catholic majority presented a problem to the Campus
Crusade missionaries. To evangelize Poles out of the
Catholic Church was to distance them from their history
and culture. Was this really the right goal for evangelical
missionaries in a country where the Catholic culture still
provided a bulwark against the onslaught of atheistic
Communism? The strength of the Polish Catholic resistance to the common Communist enemy also put Poland
in a different category than the 'Catholic' countries of
Latin America, where there was no common enemy and
a weaker Catholic piety.

Youth With A Mission (YWAM) has been another
inter-confessional agency to re-think its attitude and its
policy regarding Roman Catholics. As a group strongly
influenced by Pentecostal–charismatic patterns, YWAM
saw a growing number of young Catholics attending
their courses and joining their staff. They were also in
contact with several Catholic charismatic groups that
were looking for practical teaching on evangelism and the
training of future leaders. Over a period of years, YWAM
has come to accept as a legitimate option a collaboration
that helps Catholics to come to a living faith in Jesus
within their own Church.

YWAM has adopted a notably unselfish stance in
encouraging Catholic adaptation of its training materials and methods, and more recently the staunchly-
evangelical Navigators have begun to discuss the possible
adaptation of their formation programmes and published
materials for Catholic use. This is of course a much
more difficult and controversial area than collaboration

on moral issues. It touches the sensitive question of co-operation in evangelism, and the possibility of forms of joint proclamation of the gospel.

The difficulties here are considerable, as is indicated by the different terminology used by both sides: 'evangelism' by the Protestants and 'evangelization' by the Roman Catholics. The Catholic terminology is certainly more recent than the Protestant, for distinct discussion of 'evangelization' rather than simply missionary work is itself a fruit of the Vatican Council, and in particular of Pope Paul VI's inspiring letter *Evangelii Nuntiandi* of 1975. The Catholic preference for 'evangelization', while no doubt containing an element of distancing from evangelical usage, expresses a concern for an ongoing process of transformation through the gospel that begins with individual conversion but then extends to whole societies and cultures. Yet even with these differences and difficulties, various forms of collaboration in proclaiming the gospel together have been emerging. The sphere for such experimentation has been almost exclusively the charismatic renewal. The role of the charismatic renewal in evangelical–Catholic rapprochement and the reasons for it will be examined in a later chapter.

The evidence for new patterns of evangelical and Catholic co-operation and dialogue around the world is naturally scattered and uneven. This was seen very clearly at the World Evangelical Fellowship and at Lausanne II at Manila, although evangelicals from Latin America were much less open to contacts with Catholics. In Ireland, a group of Catholics, mostly lay people, who call themselves 'Evangelical Catholics' have formed to defend the Catholic orthodoxy of fundamental evangelical convictions. Their leaflet 'What is an Evangelical Catholic?' has been circulated to Protestant church leaders in Ireland, and has provoked much discussion. Their organization, the Evangelical Catholic Initiative, is now sponsoring meetings between Catholics and evangelical Protestants across Ireland, a fact of particular significance and topicality in an island that has known serious sectarian strife and violence.

Another surprising development bridging the evangelical and the Catholic worlds is the rise of what is being called the 'Convergence Movement'. This movement represents a new interaction between three currents: the charismatic, the Evangelical–Reformed and the Liturgical–Sacramental. Among the first shapers of such convergence thinking was the group of men from Campus Crusade for Christ, led by Peter Gillquist, who left to form the Evangelical Orthodox Church, later mostly integrated into the Antiochene Orthodox Church as the Evangelical Orthodox Mission. Another catalyst was Robert Webber of Wheaton College, an Episcopalian, who articulated the convictions of many former evangelicals who were discovering the depth and beauty of liturgical worship. A more recent and perhaps more spectacular expression of this Convergence movement has been the foundation of a new denomination, the Charismatic Episcopal Church, initially spearheaded by some former Pentecostals and independent charismatics, who like Gillquist were seeing the limitations of free-flowing worship and the vagaries of charismatic teaching, while discovering the riches of the Fathers of the Church and of the ancient liturgical traditions of worship. The Charismatic Episcopal Church has been expanding at a remarkable rate, aided by the accession of some Episcopalian charismatics, who had grown weary in the battle for Christian orthodoxy within the Episcopal Church in the United States.

These developments in relationship between the ancient Churches, Roman Catholic and Eastern Orthodox, and the world of evangelical Protestantism both demonstrate an important new opening in the Christian world and point to the enormous potential benefits and blessing if these forms of co-operation and interaction were to become more widespread. This book will examine the background history, the issues and the potential in improved relations between evangelicals, Pentecostals and charismatics on the one hand and the historic Churches, particularly the ancient Churches of East and West on the other.

PART II
A HISTORY OF REVIVAL

Chapter Two

The Evangelical Stream

T he Christian world of the late twentieth century is familiar with the firm faith and vigorous witness of evangelical Christians. Even though scholars sometimes have difficulty defining evangelicalism and who counts as evangelical, all agree that evangelicalism is a major Christian phenomenon spanning many denominations.

My interest in evangelicalism for the purpose of this book lies in its being a Christian stream that is not identical with or reducible to Church affiliation. To be an evangelical is to subscribe to certain convictions and priorities, which in turn play an important role in the Christian identity of their holders. Evangelicalism is the first of these 'non-ecclesial' streams, in which stream participation is not dependent on Church affiliation and is often seen as more important.

The evangelical stream grew out of the evangelistic revivals of the 1730s and 1740s. It is from this association between revival and evangelism that evangelicalism received its strongly activist character, and acquired an aggressive confidence that has been maintained through periods of derision or dismissal.

The Beginnings of Evangelicalism

The period between 1727 and 1743 saw an explosion of revivalistic preaching and a missionary dynamic of enormous significance for the Christian faith. It was in the summer of 1727 that the fire of Pentecost came upon the Moravians at Herrnhut in Saxony under the leadership of Count Nicholas von Zinzendorf (1700–1760). It was around the same time that the Methodist societies

with the Wesley brothers, John (1703–1791) and Charles
(1707–1788), were formed at Oxford, and stirrings of
revival were being felt in New England. In 1738, John
Wesley was transformed through his 'heart-warming
experience' of the Lord, following his encounters with
the Moravians. The fires of revival were also burning in Wales, with the preaching of Howell Harris
(1714–1773), Daniel Rowland (1713–1790) and Howell
Davies (1716–1770). The early 1740s then saw what
became known as the Great Awakening in New England,
in which the figure of Jonathan Edwards (1703–1758) was
particularly prominent, both as preacher and interpreter.

The person who more than any other embodied the
origins of evangelicalism was George Whitefield (1714–
1770). In 1739 Whitefield, who had been ordained an
Anglican priest, took the radical step of preaching in the
open-air, first in Bristol and then in London. His open-air
'pulpit' became a major rival to other public attractions,
drawing vast crowds irrespective of Church affiliation.
He was the first preacher to captivate both the British
and North American publics. In England, Whitefield's
bold venture in the open-air was quickly followed by
John Wesley. While Wesley's emphases were every bit
as evangelical as Whitefield's, he was always much more
than an evangelical, a fact that explains the difficulty of
simply subsuming the later Methodist Church under an
evangelical heading.

In this ferment of revival, something decisively new
was emerging. How new only the hindsight of more than
two centuries can fully show, for this was in fact the
beginning of currents or streams of life that came to
have a certain independence from the historic Churches.
These events of the period 1727–1743 represent the
birth of the evangelical stream, that was to prove to
be the first of these currents of new life spanning the
denominations. The later streams, likewise not identifiable with or restricted to the historic Churches, of
the Holiness movement (from the mid-nineteenth century),
the Pentecostal movement (from the early twentieth century) and most recently the charismatic movement (from

the 1950s and 1960s) will be examined in subsequent
chapters.

The Characteristics of Evangelicalism

Evangelical Christians typically describe themselves as
doughty defenders of the Protestant Reformation, and
the modern heirs of Luther, Calvin, Latimer, Ridley,
Cranmer and Knox. Why then is it that reputed historians of evangelicalism, such as David Bebbington, locate
its beginnings in the 1730s? It is because the combination
of convictions and emphases characteristic of evangelicalism represent a distinctively modern mutation of Reformation principles. The beginnings of evangelicalism
represented at least three elements: (a) an outpouring of
divine grace; (b) a distinctively new historical epoch with
extensive social and cultural change; and (c) a taking up
of preparatory elements and re-shaping them to mediate
the outpouring of God's grace within the modern setting.
Thus this new stream of life has at least three components
corresponding to these three elements: (a) spiritual; (b)
socio-cultural; (c) reformist.

The new socio-cultural situation of the first half of the
eighteenth century included the coming of the Enlightenment in the realm of philosophy and ideas; the beginnings of the Industrial Revolution, particularly in Great
Britain, and the beginnings of a market economy in the
New World; a degree of religious exhaustion in Europe
after the religious wars of the previous two centuries.
These changes had widespread repercussions on the
lives of vast numbers of people on both sides of the
North Atlantic. In Europe, there was the beginnings of
population mobility with the flight of many peasants to
the growing industrial cities; in colonial America, there
was the transformation from a world of barter to a market
economy.

There was also a close link between the Enlightenment
emphasis on reason and the religio-social exhaustion following the wars of religion. For if the major branches of
Christianity could only fight one another, social peace and

concord had to be based on something other than religion. The inability of the Churches to relate creatively and to seek reconciliation contributed not only to the flight to human reason but also to aspirations for spiritual revival detached from the heart of Church life.

The preparatory elements taken up and transmuted into the new evangelical gestalt were Pietism, especially in Continental Europe, and Puritanism, especially in New England. Pietism had arisen in the world of German Lutheranism, as a protest against arid intellectualism and outward formalism in religion. Spearheaded by Philipp Jakob Spener (1635–1705) and August Hermann Francke (1663–1727), Lutheran pietism emphasized heartfelt devotion to Jesus, rooted in the experience of personal conversion from sin. It also involved an element of 'separation' though primarily within the official Church, leading to the formation of 'small churches within the Church' (*ecclesiolae in Ecclesia*).

The doctrinal background of Anglo-American evangelicalism came from the Puritans. Bebbington has singled out 'conversionism, activism, biblicism and crucicentrism' as the consistent elements in evangelicalism[1]; in other words, they were active zealous believers who emphasized conversion, the Scriptures and the cross. He notes that of these four, activism was new with the Evangelicals. Thus, there had been no missionary work in the time of the sixteenth and seventeenth-century Puritans, an astonishing fact often unrecognized by modern evangelicals. But the evangelical emphasis on the unique work of Christ on the cross and the all-sufficiency of Scripture was inherited from the Puritans.

A New Response to a New Situation

The newness of evangelicalism cannot be adequately understood without reference to the newness of the socio-cultural situation in the eighteenth century. The challenges of the Enlightenment, the Industrial Revolution, and the changing economies of Northern Europe and the American colonies under God's grace triggered new responses that were both distinctively modern and notably effective.

The advent of open-air preaching, already mentioned, was one decisive factor in this birth-process. Although Howell Harris had begun to preach in the open air in Wales in 1735, it was Whitefield, followed by John Wesley, who transformed this public ministry into a major tool for evangelism. This was not simply a matter of changed locations for preaching and worship. It was a taking of the gospel to the people; Wesley for example regularly preached to the most deprived among the new urban poor drawn to the manufacturing towns and cities of industrial Britain. It was also a move away from Church control, drawing hearers from the entire population, overcoming the separations between Establishment and Dissent. The evangelical movement also had a strong element of declericalization in its origins: open-air preaching soon led to lay preachers not sanctioned by Church authority. Thus, John Wesley developed a system of lay preachers for the Methodist Societies, authorized and vetted by Wesley himself, but not recognized by the Anglican bishops, several decades before the secession of the Methodists to form a new denomination.

This new lay participation represented a significant change from mainline Reformation Protestantism up to that time. The Lutheran and Reformed traditions had emphasized the preaching of the Word of God by an educated ministry, officially ordained and commissioned. This emphasis was in direct response to one of the major complaints at the Reformation, namely the ignorance of the Catholic clergy. So, the role of the ordained minister in the major Protestant Churches was reinforced. Although the Presbyterian pattern of government provided a protection against ministerial tyranny through the institution of lay elders, their role was administrative, not teaching. The idea of lay preaching and teaching was as foreign to the major Protestant Churches as it was in the Roman Catholic Church of that period.

The lay dimension to evangelicalism undergirds its

egalitarian character. The clericalism of the established
Church worlds, even including the Puritan ministers
of New England, was part of hierarchically ordered
societies, in which birth and education were powerful
indicators of status. The nature of revival, which over-
flows the boundaries of class, education and commerce, is
essentially egalitarian, impacting the masses, and giving
every believer a sense of dignity and of destiny in the
Kingdom of God.

Another major difference between Puritanism and
evangelicalism lay in the understanding of assurance
of salvation. Whereas for the Puritans, assurance was
a grace at which the most earnest might arrive, for the
evangelical, assurance was the normal sign of authentic
conversion. Spiritually, this assurance was the fruit of visibly powerful revivals of faith. This conviction of assured
salvation gave the evangelicals their characteristic note
of confidence in evangelism and service, that indeed
underlay their activism, in contrast to the more intro-
spective piety of the Puritans. This new confidence of the
evangelical Christian must have had some relationship to
the spirit of the age, the confidence in human reasoning,
knowledge and discovery that marked the Enlightenment
and the scientific discoveries that fed the Industrial Revolution. In America, it blended in with the confidence that
characterized the New World with all the opportunities
it offered for entrepreneurial initiatives and skills.

Although the history of evangelicalism involves a constant battle against the inroads of liberal rationalism into
theology and biblical exegesis, evangelicals were themselves children of the Enlightenment. Biblical interpretation became more influenced by the patterns of science
and logic to the detriment of mystery, symbol and typology. The scientific model in which each object of study
has its unitary explanation tended to produce an evangelical exegesis of the Bible that saw only one level
of meaning in each text and assumed that this one
meaning was obvious and easy to determine. In this
respect evangelical interpretation of the Scriptures came
to acquire a distinctively modern flavour in tune with the

new scientific methods and with contemporary Common Sense philosophy, but further removed from the thought worlds of the biblical era and the early Church.

Its Development

The evangelical stream has flowed continuously since the 1730s. As has been remarked, it developed through revivalistic preaching and through outpourings of divine grace that surpassed the impact of even the most anointed preaching. These movements of outpouring were usually preceded by an intensity of prayer for revival.

Britain
One strand in this evangelical awakening was the work of John Wesley and the rise of the Methodist Societies that later became Methodist denomination(s). Another strand was the fruit of the preaching of George Whitefield on both sides of the Atlantic. Like Wesley, Whitefield reached many who did not belong to the Established Church, but unlike Wesley, Whitefield had less regard for particular Church affiliation. With his Calvinist theology, he remained close to the Welsh leaders, whose societies like the Wesleyan Methodists remained within the Established Church, until persecution led to the separation of the Calvinistic Methodists in 1795. Another strand in British evangelicalism was the rise of evangelical clergy and parishes within the Church of England that had nothing to do with the Methodist societies. Early leaders here were Henry Venn of Huddersfield (1725–1797), Thomas Scott (1747–1821) and John Newton of Olney (1725–1807), the former slave runner and author of the hymn *Amazing Grace*. The evangelical banner was then taken up in the next generation by Charles Simeon of Cambridge (1759–1836) and later by John Charles Ryle (1816–1900), the first Anglican bishop of Liverpool.

North America
In America, the emergence of evangelical religion is more complex. The first Great Awakening of 1740–1743 had

the effect in New England of the Puritan heritage being transformed into evangelical patterns that won over the greater part of the Presbyterian and Congregational Churches. The evangelical stream received fresh impetus from the Second Great Awakening in the last years of the eighteenth century and the first years of the nineteenth. While the patterns of evangelical revival in the older states from New England to Pennsylvania were more restrained, revival scenes on the west-moving frontier in Kentucky and Tennessee were more dramatic, impacting the poor, the illiterate and the lawless. It is in this period that we can see the first foundations of what in the twentieth century has become known as the 'Bible belt' and the close association between religious and civic independence, biblical literalism, American patriotism, and evangelical religion.

It would seem that evangelical preaching accompanied by visible manifestations of the Spirit made the first significant impact on the negro slaves. This was the first time that the slaves with their African heritage recognized any real affinity with the 'white man's religion'. This evangelical penetration of the African-American peoples, which produced its own blend of evangelical doctrine and African ritual behaviour, began with the Great Awakening of the 1740s, but reached far greater numbers in the Cane Ridge revival of 1803.

The democratic tenor of the new nation did not sit easily with the Calvinist doctrine of election, while its entrepreneurial spirit favoured human initiative. American Methodism, already the most revivalist denomination, holding Wesley's Arminian views on free will, blazed the trail for what came to be the evangelical emphasis on making decisions for Christ. It was perhaps inevitable that a Reformed preacher would arise who would schematize the conditions for producing revival and who would modify the inherited Calvinist teaching on election. This man was Charles G. Finney (1792–1875), a former lawyer, whose *Lectures on Revival of Religion* had an immense influence on both sides of the Atlantic.

Finney's influence shaped the pattern of evangelical

preaching campaigns, increasingly called 'revivals', and contributed significantly to modern evangelical emphases, particularly what we might call 'do-it-yourself revival'. In other words, Finney heightened what Bebbington has called the 'activism' of evangelical Christians: in organizing prayer for revival, in holding campaigns and crusades, in establishing prayer benches and altar calls, in people coming forward to confess their faith in Christ. In this, Finney was clearly harnessing the American talent for organization and 'getting results' to the sphere of evangelism and conversion.

In its first century from the time of Wesley, Whitefield and Edwards, the evangelical stream generally professed a post-millennial eschatology; that is, they believed in ongoing revivals gathering an increasing harvest, which would usher in an epoch of divine blessing under the rule of Christ that would correspond to the millennium of Revelation 20. This is one of the areas in which the evangelical stream has changed most. For during the period between 1875 and 1925, much of the evangelical world, particularly in the United States, adopted the pre-millennial views first taught by John Nelson Darby (1800–1882), one of the founders of the (Plymouth) Brethren, and then popularized by the Scofield Bible.[2] This pre-millennial dispensationalism taught a literal thousand-year reign of Jesus on earth, following the rapture of the saints.

This eschatological shift radically changed the attitude of evangelical Christians to the future of this world and to the possibilities of social betterment on this earth. The relative optimism of Jonathan Edwards was replaced by a pessimism that saw little value in efforts at social amelioration in a world consigned to judgment and destruction. The Church can only await her rapture, and seek to augment the number of those who will be saved.

The Fundamentalist Battle

The switch to a pre-millennial eschatology was part of the rise of fundamentalism, that was the reaction of much of the evangelical world to the liberal biblical criticism that was gaining ground in the universities and in the mainline Protestant denominations. The history of evangelicalism in the twentieth century has been strongly marked by the debate on fundamentalism, and on the authority and the inerrancy of Sacred Scripture.

Twentieth-century evangelicalism was initially much marked by the fundamentalist–modernist controversies that raged most fiercely in the 1920s. It appeared inititally that evangelicalism had emerged much weakened from this battle, and that the mainline Protestant Churches had prevailed over and against conservative minorities. After the end of World War II, many evangelicals, particularly the more educated, sought to distance their evangelical commitment from the shortcomings of fundamentalism, while still maintaining a conservative stance on biblical criticism and the authority of the Word. This trend was manifest in the formation of the National Association of Evangelicals (1943), the founding of Fuller Theological Seminary (1947), the impact of Billy Graham (1918–) as an evangelist with a worldwide ministry, the influence of Harold Ockenga (1905–1985) and Carl Henry (1913–) and the launching of *Christianity Today* (1956).

The emergence of what at first was called 'neo-evangelicalism' led the evangelical stream in North America out of a sterile phase of doctrinal confrontation and helped it to rediscover its essential link with spiritual revival. As a result, the evangelical movement in all its diversity has largely distanced itself from the most sectarian and narrow forms of fundamentalism, a differentiation expressed in the gap between the more representative and mainline National Association of Evangelicals and the separatist American Council of Christian Churches.

The resurgent evangelicalism of the second half of the twentieth century has generally been a populist phenomenon, not unrelated to forms of cultural and political conservatism, particularly in the United States. Despite its strong disapproval of relativist trends in morality, modern evangelicalism has found it difficult to become a counter-cultural force; very important in this respect was the work and influence of Francis A. Schaeffer (1912–1984), the American founder of L'Abri fellowship in Switzerland, who more than anyone else galvanized evangelicals into the 'pro-life' cause. More recently, there has been significant evangelical self-examination on the weakness of intellectual and theological life within North American evangelicalism.

An important expression of the evangelical stream at world level was the International Congress on World Evangelization held at Lausanne, Switzerland in 1974. The honorary chairman, Billy Graham, wrote that 'Lausanne burst upon us [evangelicals] with unexpected significance and power.'[3] The 15-article Lausanne Covenant drawn up and almost unanimously endorsed at this congress expresses evangelical convictions concerning evangelism, the world and the Church. A second 'Lausanne Congress' was held at Manila in the Philippines in 1989.

By the 1990s, it is clear that there has been a strong evangelical resurgence in almost all parts of the world. The factors contributing to this upsurge must include: the influence of Billy Graham's crusades; the increasing domination of the Protestant mainline – particularly its pastoral and theological leadership – by liberal tendencies that provoke increasing concern at the grass roots; the prevalence of a principled conservatism over against an ideological fundamentalism; the rise of reputable evangelical institutions of learning; the spread of the charismatic movement (from the 1950s) and its later impact on the evangelical world (from the 1980s).

In this history of over 250 years, the evangelical stream represents a current of Christian life and vitality that refuses to be wholly absorbed into the structures of Churches and denominations. While many Christians with evangelical convictions have also had a strong attachment to their ecclesial and/or confessional heritage, evangelicals have typically recognized their affinity with each other. This openness to collaboration and desire for mutual recognition led to the formation of the Evangelical Alliance in Britain in 1846, and the National Association of Evangelicals in the United States in 1943.

Chapter Three

The Holiness Stream

In the nineteenth century, a new stream generally known as the Holiness movement arose within evangelicalism. It has been followed in the twentieth century by two further streams, the Pentecostal and the charismatic. We will examine these new streams in turn. There are varying views of the relationship between these later streams and evangelicalism, especially concerning the Pentecostals and the charismatics. What is clear is that these three streams of later origin have an identity of their own, and that, like the earlier evangelical stream, they are first of all streams of new life and only subsequently gave rise, in varying degrees, to new denominations. In this chapter, we will look at the Holiness stream.

The Holiness movement arose in the mid-nineteenth century. It could be said to have been in gestation from the 1830s and to have burst forth in the 1860s and 1870s. It differed from previous evangelical revivalism in its focus on the issue of holiness or sanctification. The main impetus for this quest came from American Methodists, who were concerned that John Wesley's teaching on entire sanctification was being lost in American Methodism. Leading figures here were two sisters, both Methodists, Phoebe Palmer (1807–1874) and Sarah Lankford (1806–1896), who in 1835 started a Tuesday meeting for the Promotion of Holiness in the Palmer home in New York City. Mrs Palmer sought total consecration to Jesus Christ, and an assurance of the Lord's acceptance of this self-offering. In early 1837, she prayed: 'O may I never rest till I have the witness of the Spirit, that my heart is the temple of an indwelling God, and have the full confidence that Christ reigns supreme on the throne of my affections, bringing every thought into obedience to himself.'[1] This she knew in a decisive experience in July of that year.

Phoebe Palmer's message has been called an 'altar theology', based on the text, 'the altar sanctifieth the gift'. Christ is both the sacrifice for sin and the altar on which the life of the consecrated Christian is laid. Her teaching was simple, radical and practical, presenting three steps of entire consecration, faith and testimony.

Another current in the Holiness stream in North America, that also developed in the 1830s, came from Charles Finney, and Asa Mahan (1799–1889), both from Oberlin College in Ohio. Finney, well-known as a successful revivalist and as a teacher on revivals of religion, represented what one historian has called 'the Methodization of the Calvinistic wing of the revival tradition'.[2] Finney broke with the Calvinist insistence on the total inability of human beings to contribute to God's work of revival and conversion. His writings expounded the conditions for spiritual revival to occur and how Christians can prepare for it. When Finney moved to Oberlin in the 1830s, the emphasis on faith-co-operation with God was channelled into a concern for sanctification. This current, often known as Oberlin perfectionism, caused holiness ideas to spread beyond Methodist circles, particularly among the Presbyterians.

Both the Methodist Holiness current and Oberlin perfectionism developed within an optimistic vision for society. The Oberlin teachers integrated evangelistic, holiness and social concerns more strongly than the Palmer circle, though both were abolitionists on the slavery issue; they also favoured the advancement of women in society and in the Church. Phoebe Palmer played a major role in imparting a strongly lay character to the holiness revival. Through her many friendships and her acquaintance with prominent figures in society, in education and in social concern, she brought the message of sanctification outside the walls of the church and into the centres of social influence.

A link between the Methodist and the Oberlin strands was provided by William E. Boardman (1810–1886), a Presbyterian who was introduced to the experience of entire sanctification by the Palmers in 1842. It was Boardman who coined the term 'Higher Christian Life' to express sanctification in a non-Wesleyan terminology, and his book of that title (1858) became one of the most influential writings in the Holiness stream. The revival in New York City in 1858 had begun in Hamilton, Ontario in late 1857 during a visit by Phoebe Palmer, and this gave renewed impetus to holiness themes. Its largely lay leadership helped to spread its inter-denominational character. The Palmers began a four-year stay in Europe in the midst of the 1859 Revival that especially touched the outlying parts of the British Isles.

A major new phase in the Holiness stream in the United States began after the civil war with the formation of the Association for the Promotion of Holiness, and its organization of national Holiness camp meetings, the first of which gathered 10,000 people to Vineland, New Jersey in the summer of 1867. For the next thirty years at least, the summer camp meetings, which represented a reinvigoration of an existing American institution, much used by the first generation of Methodists, flourished and made the Holiness issue a more populist cause. As a result of the success of the national camp meetings, scores of state, regional and local Holiness organizations were formed.

In the first years of the Holiness Association, the Holiness stream remained almost entirely a phenomenon of the northern states. It was seen in the South as an essentially northern development, especially in view of the close association of Holiness themes with opposition to slavery. This separation was made easier by the division of the Methodist Church on the slavery issue (1844). This geographical concentration slowly began to change in the 1870s, when the southern Methodist bishops encouraged the Holiness movement, and by the turn of the century the Holiness movement had become a major force in the southern states, aided also by

the Wesleyans and Free Methodists. It represented an
upsurge of populist religious sentiment among the rural
and poorer people, as the mainline Protestant denominations, especially their leaders and institutions, steadily
climbed the social scale.

The national organization, which later came to be
known as the National Holiness Association, was at the
outset a Methodist body, and it sought to promote holiness within the overall framework of Methodist church
life. Many of the local organizations, however, soon took
on the character of Holiness missions, seeking to spread
the message to believers of all denominations. Over the
remaining decades of the nineteenth century, the links
of the Holiness stream with official Methodism steadily
decreased – caused both by lack of encouragement and
even some condemnation from the Methodist bishops
and the increasingly critical and separatist stance of
many Holiness groups. As early as 1860, two reform
groups expelled from the Methodist Episcopal Church
had formed the Free Methodist Church, which embraced
the doctrine of entire sanctification. Further tensions
arose within the Methodist Episcopal Church, South, as
to whether itinerant Holiness preachers required the
agreement of local pastors; one prominent case involving
Henry Clay Morrison (1857–1942) led to the preacher's
expulsion and subsequent reinstatement. Such opposition to the Holiness message severely weakened the
loyalty of Holiness people to the Methodist Episcopal
Churches. Thus the 1880s and 1890s saw the formation
of several new Holiness denominations, such as the
Church of God (Anderson, Indiana), the bodies that later
coalesced into the Church of the Nazarene, and those
that in 1922 formed the Pilgrim Holiness Church.[3] By
the end of the century, the National Holiness Association
that had begun with the aim of sustaining the Holiness
message within Methodism was almost entirely outside
the Methodist Episcopal Churches.

Another consequence of the spread of Wesleyan-type
Holiness teaching in the southern states was its first
significant impact among African-American Christians,

mostly among Baptists. Their acceptance of Wesleyan
teaching created tension in their Baptist churches, and by
the turn of the century most of the sanctified among the
African-Americans had seceded into new black Holiness
denominations. While many of them became Pentecostal
following the Azusa Street revival of 1906, the Holiness
message retained a strong appeal among the African-
American people, whether or not they embraced the
Pentecostal movement.

Keswick

Particularly from the 1850s, the Holiness stream saw
constant interaction between Britain and the United
States. The Holiness stream in Britain was developing
in the annual Mildmay conferences begun in 1856, and
was much stimulated by the Methodist William Arthur's
book, *The Tongue of Fire* (1856), that was widely read on
both sides of the Atlantic. These indigenous roots were
aided by visits from North Americans: the Palmers spent
four years in the British Isles (1859–1863) and Charles
Finney also made a visit in 1859, and the Pearsall Smiths
in 1873–1874. Holiness conferences at Broadlands in
Hampshire, at Oxford and at Brighton paved the way
for the annual Keswick conventions, the main expression
of the British Holiness movement from their inception
in 1875.

The early leadership of the Keswick conventions came
from Anglican evangelicals. In its first generation, the
key figures were the founder and Vicar of Keswick,
Canon T. D. Harford-Battersby (1822–1883), Evan Hopkins
(1837–1918), H. W. Webb-Peploe (1837–1923) and Handley
Moule, later Bishop of Durham (1841–1920). The focus
of Keswick was on personal sanctification just as single-
mindedly as in the American Holiness currents. However, with its strong Anglican Evangelical component,
it insisted on a solid theological basis and an avoidance
of enthusiastic extremes. For this reason, there was a
conscious concern to provide a different basis for holiness
teaching from the 'Christian perfection' of John Wesley.

The Methodist contribution to the Keswick stand of the Holiness stream was always small, and the pattern of Holiness teaching that emerged was based more on Calvinist than on Wesleyan theology. Thus the Keswick teaching favoured the language of 'the overcoming' or the 'victorious' life, and opposed the doctrine found in some Wesleyan circles of the possibility of 'sinless perfection'. The Keswick teaching was that in this life the Christian is always contending with the sinful nature, the flesh principle, but that through faith-union with the work of Jesus on the cross, it is possible for the Christian to live a life of victory over sin.

Within a decade, there were some non-Anglican speakers at Keswick including the South African Reformed leader Andrew Murray (1829–1917), the Scottish Presbyterian J. Elder Cumming (1830–1917) from 1883 and the English Baptist F. B. Meyer (1847–1929) from 1887. Women were not allowed to address the Convention, though prominent women Holiness teachers like Jessie Penn-Lewis (1865–1927) were regular attenders at Keswick and spoke to women's circles in the afternoons.

Holiness Currents on the European Continent

The Holiness stream also had a major impact on German Protestantism. Robert Pearsall Smith took his holiness teaching from England to the Continent in 1875, and received a particularly warm welcome in circles where the Pietist influence had remained strong. The German movement developed differently from the forms in the English-speaking world, for the most part continuing the Pietist pattern of small group fellowships within the state church. It emphasized fellowship (giving rise to its German designation as *Gemeinschaftsbewegung*), evangelism of the masses and entire sanctification. The German movement became more organized than in other lands through the formation of the Gnadauer Verband in 1888.[4]

An important figure on the European continent was Otto Stockmayer (1838–1917). Stockmayer was powerfully impacted at one of the Oxford conferences, and

in 1878 he resigned his free-church pastorate to open
a healing and retreat centre in Switzerland. A regular
speaker at Keswick, Stockmayer became the main link
between the Holiness currents in Britain, Germany and
Switzerland. He was noted both for his advocacy of divine
healing (on this he influenced Andrew Murray) and for his
strong assertion that sanctification was in preparation
for the return of Jesus and the marriage feast of the
Lamb. There was also a Holiness current in the French
Reformed world through the person of Theo Monod, who
had been influenced during the Pearsall Smiths visit to
France.

Further American Developments

Anglo-American co-operation continued, particularly with
the visits of the American evangelist, D. L. Moody
(1837–1899), who had a transforming sanctification experience in 1871, not long before his first campaigns in Great
Britain. It was Moody who effectively introduced the
Keswick type of holiness teaching to the United States
through his Northfield conventions in New England,
begun in 1880. This 'higher life' teaching was also
espoused by A. B. Simpson (1843–1919), the founder
of the Christian and Missionary Alliance.

The spread of Keswick-type holiness teaching in the
United States sharpened the contrast between Wesleyan-
type and Calvinistic-Reformed teachings on sanctification. This contrast had been present between the
Palmer–Arthur teaching and that of Oberlin, but those
had both been more northern groupings, united on social
issues such as slavery. Now the contrast was between
the more sophisticated Keswick-type teaching, appealing
to people in the North with some degree of education
and the 'eradicationist' type teaching of the Holiness
groupings mostly detaching themselves from mainline
Methodism. The latter were found more in the Mid-West
and frontier-situations, where camp meetings attracted
less genteel congregations.

The Keswick teaching was more subtle and appealed

to more educated seekers. The Wesleyan Holiness strand, calling sinners to sinless perfection, was more popular and reached the 'blue-collar' public. While the common language of holiness was used, there were considerable differences in ethos and teaching between the two strands. The popular strand, which evoked little echo in Europe, reflected the evangelical attack on the vices of the expanding American frontier, where holiness was closely associated with the taming of nature in the raw, and the total renunciation of alcohol, gambling, violence and dancing.

The Holiness stream was drastically affected by the rise of the next stream, the Pentecostal movement. In the first full generation of the Holiness movement before the beginnings of Pentecostalism, there had been a steady rise in Pentecostal imagery and language. By the 1880s and 1890s, Holiness people commonly taught a post-conversion 'baptism of the Spirit', understood in terms of entire sanctification. Several of their publications and organizations had the word 'Pentecost' in their title. Thus, the Holiness stream proved to be a fertile seed-ground for the new Pentecostal stream that broke forth in the first decade of the twentieth century. When the Pentecostal movement erupted in the United States from 1906, the Holiness stream was seriously divided over what was often seen as the 'tongues' issue. The Holiness stream continued, though with a diminished extent and influence, and modified by its suspicions of Pentecostal elements.

An important strand continued longer within the southern Methodist tradition. Henry Clay Morrison, though often in contention within his Church, always remained a minister of the Methodist Episcopal Church, South. A mass evangelist of Holiness persuasion, he founded the *Pentecostal Herald* around 1890, and in 1910 became president of Asbury College in Wilmore, Kentucky, where he founded Asbury Theological Seminary in 1923. Both institutions played an important role in preserving the Holiness witness within the Wesleyan and Methodist traditions.

Missionary Impact

The Holiness stream has had a pronounced impact on missionary work. While it stressed 'entire sanctification', it also emphasized total surrender to the will of God. It was this sacrificial giving for God's work that spurred the strong missionary thrust in Holiness circles. Two unrelated Taylors were the major missionary pioneers within the emerging Holiness current: the American Methodist Bishop William Taylor (1821–1902) and J. Hudson Taylor (1832–1905), the British founder of the China Inland Mission. William Taylor, an energetic preacher of entire sanctification, had a more immediate impact in many countries serving in India (1870–1875), in Latin America (1877–1884) and in Africa (1884–1896). Hudson Taylor's faith philosophy and dedication has perhaps had the more lasting influence on missionary practice through the faith missions, of which the China Inland Mission was the first.[5] The faith missions, many of which focused on small well-defined areas in Africa, were strongly influenced by Holiness teaching, especially in their early years. D. L. Moody's campaigns gave rise to many missionary calls, including those of the 'Cambridge Seven' in 1885, among whom was C. T. Studd (1860–1931), who later founded the World Evangelization Crusade (WEC).

Other mission societies with a strong Holiness message were the World Gospel Mission, founded in 1910 by the National Association for the Promotion of Holiness, and the Oriental Missionary Society. There was also a pronounced Holiness influence in the East African Revival of the 1930s and expressed particularly in the Rwanda Mission. The revival was marked by strong conviction of sin: one missionary spoke of 'the greatest fruit of the Revival, deep oneness and fellowship with the Africans. We found that when once we had repented and in some cases asked forgiveness for our prejudice and white superiority, a new realm in relationships was entered into which altered the character of all our work.'[6]

The Holiness movement in the twentieth century

is expressed in several relatively small but vigorous denominations as well as in segments within larger churches. These denominations include (in the United States) the Wesleyan Church; the Free Methodist Church; the Church of God (Anderson, Indiana); the Church of the Nazarene. The Wesleyan Theological Society, founded in 1965, gathers scholars from all these Holiness churches together with United Methodists associated with Asbury Theological Seminary.

In Britain, the Keswick conventions have continued, though with some emphases and terminology affected by its aversion to Pentecostal enthusiasm. One synthesis of Keswick teaching summarized its themes under five headings: the Exceeding Sinfulness of Sin, the Way of Cleansing and Renewal, the Life of Full Surrender, the Fullness of the Holy Spirit, and the Path of Sacrifice and Service.[7]

The Holiness stream has continued to be a source of deeper spiritual writings, whether by way of reprints of earlier authors such as Andrew Murray, or by way of new books, as, for example, those of A. W. Tozer (1897–1963), of Ruth Paxson, of Os Guinness and of Roy Hession, whose book, *The Calvary Road*, has been widely read. Holiness-type teaching has also been widely disseminated through the writings of a Chinese teacher, who spent the last twenty years of his life in Communist gaols, Watchman Nee (–1972).

Chapter Four

The Pentecostal Stream

Like the evangelical and Holiness streams, the Pentecostal stream was a fruit of spiritual aspiration and Spirit-led revival. It was not in its origins a set of doctrinal positions, but an irruption of new life associated with distinct emphases and characteristics. These emphases do of course have doctrinal implications and theological content. But the movement or stream is not simply defined or determined by a particular doctrine.

The emphases and characteristics that constitute Pentecostalism as a distinct stream represent a fusion of (1) the preaching and experience of a post-conversion baptism in the Spirit; (2) the exercise and manifestation of spiritual gifts, with many Pentecostals attaching a particular initiatory importance to the gift of speaking in other tongues; (iii) full bodily and vocal expression of the presence and power of the Spirit in worship and ministry. The experience of this gift in baptism in the Holy Spirit was understood as a twentieth-century Pentecost, given for a final spurt of vigorous evangelism to reach all peoples before the fast-approaching return of the Lord.

Historians of Pentecostalism commonly single out two events as foundational in its emergence. The first was the minor outbreak of speaking in tongues at Topeka, Kansas in early 1901 at a small school led by Charles F. Parham (1873–1929). The second is the revival that began in 1906 at the Azusa Street mission in Los Angeles, led by an Afro-American, William J. Seymour (1870–1922). Parham's main contribution was the association between baptism in the Spirit and speaking in tongues; so that he is the father of the widespread Pentecostal doctrine, found for example throughout the Assemblies of God, that speaking in tongues is the necessary initial evidence of baptism in the Spirit. But Azusa Street provided the spiritual explosion that propelled this new stream across all the continents of the globe within the short space of two years. It was at Azusa Street that there was the astonishing spectacle of black and white believers mingling and ministering without regard to racial divisions. The spiritual dynamic coming from Azusa Street was surely connected with this initial racial harmony, and the fusion of elements from African-American slave religion with the evangelical and Holiness traditions of the white believers.

Unlike the beginnings of the evangelical and Holiness streams, which first arose within historic Protestant traditions, Azusa Street was in effect 'outside the city'. This 'fringe' dimension in Pentecostal origins made it more of a lower-class phenomenon in its distinctive ethos than its stream predecessors, an aspect expressed in the title *Vision of the Disinherited*.[1] Though the Azusa Street mission in its first months was affiliated with Charles Parham's Apostolic Faith Mission, itself Parham's own creation, this link was ended after Parham's racially-biased denunciation of their 'animal' behaviour.

It was from Azusa Street that the movement took on the distinctive characteristics of Pentecostalism: vigorous praise, strong eschatological expectation, evangelistic and missionary drive, popular participation. Here again was a strongly egalitarian movement, proclaiming the availability of Pentecost and the power of the Holy Spirit to every believer, poor and rich, lay and ordained, black, brown and white, uneducated and educated.

One result was that the movement spreading from Azusa Street quickly produced a flood of itinerant preachers, missionaries and witnesses, many of them unconnected with any Church. The movement spread to India in 1906, where it was assisted by an indigenous awakening that had broken out the previous year in the homes run by Pandita Ramabai (1858–1922) at the Mukti Mission

near Poona. It was found in China by 1908, in South
Africa by 1908, in Chile by 1909 and Brazil by 1910. It
reached Europe through Thomas Barratt (1862–1940) of
Oslo early in 1907, and England through Barratt at the
Anglican parish of Alexander Boddy (1854–1930) near
Sunderland later that year.

The rapid diffusion of the Pentecostal stream from
Azusa Street was aided, not only by the high mobility of
many of the first Pentecostals (the early Pentecostal peri-
odicals contain many letters from travelling witnesses on
the move around the world) but also by the expectation
aroused in many evangelical hearts by the Welsh Revival
of 1904–1905. It was also aided by the evangelist Reuben
Archer Torrey's adaptation of the Holiness teaching on
baptism in the Spirit from an emphasis on entire sanctification to one of empowerment for service and mission,
even though Torrey himself was to reject the Pentecostal
manifestations.

A few small Holiness denominations (espousing the
eradicationist teaching on sanctification) were completely
won over to the Pentecostal cause, and these became in
effect the first Pentecostal denominations. These included
the Church of God in Christ (see below), the Church of
God (Cleveland, Tennessee), founded by A. J. Tomlinson
(1865–1943),[2] and the Pentecostal Holiness Church,
founded by J. H. King (1869–1946). All these Holiness
groupings in early Pentecostalism added the baptism
in the Holy Spirit associated with speaking in tongues
to their previous two-stage teaching on conversion and
sanctification.

However, others among the first Pentecostals came
from different doctrinal backgrounds, often Calvinistic and
Baptistic. Many were people impacted by the Keswick-type
Holiness teaching, particularly those in the Christian
and Missionary Alliance. The Alliance was particularly
affected by the Pentecostal outbreak at their Nyack,
New York summer camp in 1907. A. B. Simpson, the
Alliance leader, though not identifying himself with the
Pentecostal message, wrestled with the matter in his
own heart. As a result, the Alliance policy in regard

to the new movement was less thoroughly negative at the outset than some other Holiness denominations that rejected it completely.

The Pentecostals who came out of other denominations tended to form small independent assemblies, mostly meeting in back-street and store-front chapels. Within a decade, the dangers of independence and lack of organization led to a call for the formation of a national body that would set doctrinal standards as a protection against oddities of teaching and that would issue ministerial and missionary accreditation, as a protection against fraud. It was at this point that the inter-racial character of the Azusa Street revival was largely lost. Thus in 1915, the Assemblies of God were formed in the United States; Canada followed suit in 1919, Great Britain and Ireland in 1925. The Assemblies of God represented the Pentecostalization of Reformed theology and Baptist practice. This meant acceptance of the 'finished work of Calvary' (in contrast to Wesleyan-type teaching) and baptism in the Spirit as a second experience imparting empowerment for ministry.

Black Pentecostalism

The black or African-American component in Pentecostal origins has often been ignored or played down in Pentecostal histories. This distortion has been receiving correction through the scholarly research and writings of Professor Walter J. Hollenweger (1927–).[3] Much the largest of the African-American Pentecostal Churches (5.5 million members in 1995) is the Church of God in Christ, founded and then led for over half a century by C. H. Mason (1866–1961).

A division that occurred among Pentecostals in 1914 over baptism in the name of Jesus led to the rise of 'Oneness' Pentecostalism, that has since had a strong appeal to many black believers. The Oneness Pentecostals reject the traditional formulations of Trinitarian doctrine, asserting that Jesus is the proper name for God in the Christian era.[4] In many ways, Oneness Pentecostalism can be seen

as the protest of the poor and the deprived against the
intellectual domination symbolized by the complexity of
much Trinitarian theology. Its appeal to black believers
tends to confirm such an interpretation. Among the black
Oneness denominations is The Pentecostal Assemblies
of the World, led in its early days by G. T. Haywood
(1880–1931). The black Pentecostals have had significant missionary impact in the Caribbean and thence
to the black Churches of Great Britain, both among
the Oneness groups and in two black denominations
that relate to North American Pentecostal Churches,
the New Testament Church of God[5] and the Church of
God of Prophecy.

Black Pentecostalism has its own distinctive patterns
and traditions. It is not simply experiential in the manner
of much white Pentecostalism, but 'heartfelt', expressing,
always vividly and sometimes dramatically, the deepest
aspirations of the soul. This is evident in the style of
preaching (more poetic and even more narrative than
their white peers), in the forms of vocal prayer and of
'interruption' from the congregation, but even more in
the forms of music.

The black Pentecostals also reflect much more strongly
both the corporate experience of God's people and the
experience of suffering and oppression. These are both
related to the biblical paradigms of the people of Israel
(especially in Egypt) and to the suffering of Jesus.

Pentecostals and Evangelicals

The Pentecostals were generally rejected by the evangelicals as dangerously subjective, elevating experience
above doctrine, and given to excess of many kinds. As
a populist movement of the less favoured in society,
Pentecostals were perceived as ignorant and simplistic,
with their use of the Bible lacking the serious study
of the evangelical preacher. In fact, the first generation of Pentecostalism largely corresponded with the
rise of fundamentalism in the conservative evangelical
world. Though Pentecostals are often seen today as

fundamentalists, the latter quickly regarded the former as a grave danger to the purity of fundamentalist faith.

Despite such rejection, most of the Pentecostals, especially the white churches, adopted evangelical categories to explain their own doctrine, which tended to add baptism in the Spirit and the spiritual gifts to evangelical formulations. They also adopted in their formularies the eschatology and the literalism of contemporary conservative evangelicals; so they became pre-millennial dispensationalists in eschatology and upholders of strict biblical inerrancy in the fundamentalist manner. However, Pentecostal investment in fundamentalism and dispensationalism has generally been less than that of conservative evangelicals as these features play a smaller role in their distinctive identity and self-definition.

The Pentecostal stream was strongly egalitarian in its origins. By its very nature, it was preaching the availability of the experience of Spirit-baptism for all believers, and the Holy Spirit's gifting of all the faithful. Even more than the evangelical movement in general with its emphasis on experiential personal conversion for all believers, the Pentecostal stream has stressed not simply the same basic experience as open to all, but also the equipping of all believers for the work and ministry of the Church. Thus Pentecostals have often used the phrase 'every member ministry' to describe the ideal of the local church functioning in the power of the Holy Spirit.

Missionary Impact

Although missionary work has been a major aim in the evangelical stream since its origins, it is the Pentecostal movement that has most dramatically impacted the Third World. Right from Azusa Street, newly-baptized Pentecostals left for missionary work, many with more faith than wisdom. Some died in the swamps of West Africa, the graveyard of missionaries, and others did not persevere. But there were many Pentecostal missionaries

of heroic stature, who brought their faith in a miracle-
working God to remote and unreached peoples.

Among these heroes must be classified the Canadians,
Chawner, father Charles and son Austin (1903–1964),
who went to Mozambique; the American Lillian Trasher
(1887–1961), a missionary to Egypt, who founded an
orphanage at Assiut; the Englishman, William F. P.
('Willie') Burton (1886–1971), field director of the Congo
(now Zaire) Evangelistic Mission for thirty-five years; the
American Victor Plymire (1881–1956), who worked on
the borders of Tibet. Also of great significance was the
itinerant ministry of the uneducated English plumber
from Bradford, Smith Wigglesworth (1865–1947), whose
rugged personality and heroic faith touched large numbers through his preaching and the signs that followed.

The evangelistic impact of Pentecostal faith has been
most evident in Latin America, where at least 75 per
cent to 80 per cent of the continent's burgeoning number
of Protestants are Pentecostals. However, the Pentecostal movement has also seen dramatic growth in Asia,
with one of the largest churches in the world being the
Full Gospel Church in Seoul, Korea, founded by pastor
Yonggi Cho (1936–). The stream influence on Christian
missions will be further examined under the charismatic
movement.

The reasons for the Pentecostal impact in the Third
World are no doubt linked to its orality and its physicality. Whereas evangelicalism has ordinarily majored on
preaching and studying the Word of God, Pentecostalism
is a faith of embodied gestures and rites (in the sociological sense). So Pentecostals typically impose hands
in prayer, raise arms in worship, dance, march, and
shout. Whereas Evangelicalism insisted on literate and
educated preachers of the Word, Pentecostalism insisted
on personal experience of the Holy Spirit and often in its
early days had little time for formal education. David du
Plessis regularly told the story of how his D.D. meant
David the donkey. This highly populist character of the
Pentecostal stream is clearly a major reason for its rapid
expansion in less developed countries. Studies on Latin

American Pentecostalism have brought out that the most rapid growth has been occurring, not among the better educated groups with greater funding from the United States, but among the indigenous Pentecostal groups in the poorest strata of the population, with no links to the First World. The indigenous Pentecostal groups are generally those more open to ecumenical contacts, and a growing number of indigenous Pentecostal churches have been joining CLAI (*Consejo Latino-Americano Iglesias*).

The Challenges within Pentecostalism

More than the preceding streams, the Pentecostal movement soon became a cluster of new denominations. Unlike the evangelical and Holiness streams, the presence of the Pentecostal stream in the mainline Protestant Churches did not survive its first generation. This was not inherent in its character, as the later emergence of the charismatic stream was to demonstrate, but was due to its more violent rejection and ostracism, both by the older Churches and within the existing evangelical and Holiness streams.

The Pentecostals have often found mutual fellowship hard to promote and retain. However, helped no doubt by being ostracized, they have tended to have a strong sense of their common identity as a movement – with the serious qualification of widespread racial segregation in North America. These two factors interacted in the establishment and early history of the World Pentecostal Fellowship (WPF), formed at Zurich, Switzerland in 1947 and in the subsequent Pentecostal Fellowship of North America (PFNA), founded in 1948. The fact that the Pentecostal stream has become a cluster of new denominations has to some degree made the WPF take on the character of a world confessional family. The WPF had very little participation from black Pentecostal churches, and the PFNA none. However, in November 1994, at a moving encounter in Memphis between the white leaders of PFNA and the black Pentecostal leaders, PFNA was abolished and a new inter-racial fellowship

was established to be called the Pentecostal/Charismatic
Churches of North America (PCCNA).

Like all movements born of revivalistic experience,
Pentecostalism has had to face the challenge of how
to maintain the fire and power of the beginnings as
the movement develops its own institutions and traditions. This challenge has perhaps been greater than
with the evangelical and Holiness streams because the
Pentecostal appeal to experience is stronger and because
their stream has become more fully denominationalized,
with all the institutions that separate denominations
tend to generate. The challenge has been evident in
a series of new 'moves' within the Pentecostal world,
for example, the rise of the healing evangelists after
World War II, the Latter Rain revival spreading from
North Battleford, Saskatchewan, Canada from 1948,
and the Faith preachers advocating a 'prosperity gospel'.
All three developments aroused the suspicion and often
opposition of the major white Pentecostal denominations. The Latter Rain current largely stayed within
the Pentecostal orbit though on the fringe, impacting
centres such as the Elim Fellowship in Lima, New York,
while the prosperity preachers have largely opted for the
label 'Charismatic' rather than 'Pentecostal', despite their
common Pentecostal roots.

The adaptation issue also concerns what Pentecostals
understand by maturity. What some see as maturity
others see as declension. Perhaps the wisest Pentecostal
leader has been Donald Gee (1891–1966) of Britain,
the first editor of a worldwide Pentecostal magazine,
Pentecost. Gee was the first Pentecostal writer to address
the weaknesses in Pentecostalism, calling constantly for
a maturity that would not lose touch with the fire and the
power of revival. Characteristic of Gee's emphases was
this heartfelt appeal: 'Before we became so movement-
conscious we thought more often of the Pentecostal
Revival as a means of grace to quicken whomsoever
the Lord our God should call. Denominational loyalties
were a secondary consideration. Let them remain such.
The vital necessity of the Movement is that it shall

continue and grow as a Revival. Nothing less deserves to be called "Pentecostal".'[6] These are the words of a stream-leader par excellence. Another major figure in world Pentecostalism was Lewi Pethrus (1884–1974) of Sweden, who ironically exercised great influence while leading the Scandinavian insistence on congregational autonomy and total opposition to all forms of supra-local authority.

In the last two years, there have been many reverberations from the Memphis event, bringing racial reconciliation more to the fore within North American Pentecostalism. Seeing the link between the impact of Azusa Street and its inter-racial character, these developments could herald a rekindling of the Pentecostal fire. The re-naming of PFNA to include charismatic Churches as well as Pentecostal also indicates another opening, that despite much Pentecostal resistance to a wider Christian ecumenism, could be significant for the future vitality of the Pentecostal stream.

Chapter Five
The Charismatic Stream

In many ways, the closest ressemblance between any of the four streams is between the charismatics and the Pentecostals. This is because both the Pentecostal and the charismatic streams flow from the same experience of baptism in the Holy Spirit associated with the spiritual gifts of 1 Corinthians 12:8–10.

The first awareness that another distinct stream might be emerging came in the late 1950s and the early 1960s when the Pentecostal experience of baptism in the Spirit began to appear on a significant scale among Christians in the historic Protestant Churches. Solid members of respected Churches began to testify to speaking in other tongues, to receiving words from the Lord and to forms of healing, with these novel experiences bringing a new love for the Lord Jesus, new capacities for praise, and a new freedom to witness and share their faith.

Although the Pentecostal stream had an inter-denominational component in its origins, especially in Europe, it had soon in effect become a new stream outside the historic Churches, by whom they were despised or ignored and whom they in turn rejected as dead and beyond resuscitation. Thus by mid-century, the Pentecostal stream had become largely a cluster of Pentecostal denominations, with a smattering of independent Pentecostal assemblies and itinerant preachers. Between this stream and the rest of the Christian world, there was very little contact and even less respect. The greatest tension in fact was between the Pentecostals and the previous streams (evangelical and Holiness), which saw Pentecostalism as a deviation that threatened their own authenticity.

In this context, the reappearance of baptism in the Spirit with spiritual gifts in the historic Protestant Churches represented a profound challenge to the Pentecostals. The great Pentecostal leader, Donald Gee, called it 'Pentecost outside Pentecost'. The assumption of many Pentecostals was that these 'neo-Pentecostals', as they were first called, would soon be rejected by their denominations, and they would then swell the Pentecostal ranks. Others, who were more far-sighted, like Gee, hoped that their Churches would not reject them, and saw this new 'move' as the Lord's way of rekindling the Pentecostal revival.

The public emergence of the charismatic movement as a visible stream happened in the USA through national publicity in 1960 concerning the Episcopal priest Dennis Bennett (1917–1991), then of Van Nuys, California, and soon of St Luke's, Seattle, and in the UK in 1963 through another Anglican priest, Michael Harper (1931–).[1] Other major publicizing factors were David Wilkerson's *The Cross and the Switchblade* (1963), John Sherrill's *They Speak With Other Tongues* (1964) and McCandlish Phillips' article in *The Saturday Evening Post* (May 1964).

By 1963, this new stream was being called 'charismatic', largely out of the ambivalent desire to differentiate themselves from the Pentecostals. In other words, the first charismatics did not see it as an advantage to be thought to have anything to do with Pentecostalism. In this climate of mutual suspicion between Pentecostals and charismatics, the unique ministry of David du Plessis (1905–1987) was of particular importance. Du Plessis' constant message was that the Lord was pouring out his Spirit on all flesh, and that what was now happening across the Churches was the same thing that had happened at Azusa Street at the origins of the Pentecostal movement. It was the risen Lord Jesus exercising his heavenly ministry as baptizer in the Holy Spirit.

The major differences between the Pentecostal stream and the charismatic stream flowed from their different contexts. The first difference was between sectarian-type

groups emerging from humble social backgrounds on one
side and more educated and socially advantaged groups
characteristic of the milieux of the historic Churches on
the other. Secondly, there were the differences between
a stream that was outside the major Church traditions
and had formed its own denominations and an emerging stream that sought to be a leaven within existing
Churches. The latter had necessarily to relate their
experience of the Holy Spirit to long-standing worship
patterns, to received doctrine and theology, and to inherited structures of church government.

The differences between the Pentecostals in their Pentecostal world and charismatics seeking to survive and
grow within existing Church worlds became even clearer
when the charismatic stream spread in 1967 to the
Roman Catholic Church with its strong sense of distinctive church identity. This unexpected bridging of
the Reformation divide was either very exciting or very
threatening or perhaps a mixture of both. Recognizing
the authenticity of charismatic Catholics meant that the
stream heritage coming down from the origins of evangelicalism had penetrated the walls of 'Rome', of what
the stream participants had all regarded as the 'ancient
enemy'. In other words, the transconfessional character
of these modern streams had now in the charismatic
movement reached an unprecedented catholicity in fact,
if not always in spirit.

At about the same time as the charismatic stream
spread to the Roman Catholic Church, the first stirrings
of what has often become known as Messianic Judaism
began to appear. This represented something unknown
in Christian history since the early centuries, namely
the rise of a distinctively Jewish Christianity through
the formation of synagogues celebrating the Jewish feasts
and confessing Jesus or, as they would say Yeshua,
as the Messiah. While not all Messianic or completed
Jews[2] are clearly charismatic in their experience, it is
clear that it was the charismatic impulse that sparked
its genesis and the dynamic power of the Spirit that
created their distinctive worship patterns, that are both

Jewish and charismatic. This can be seen with particular clarity in the music and the dance celebrated among the Messianic Jews.

Its Spread Within the Mainline Churches

While the charismatic movement in the mainline Churches, at least in North America and Western Europe, spread rapidly in the 1970s, it somehow never had the explosive force and missionary drive that came from Azusa Street. Many early charismatic leaders like Larry Christenson (1928–), Michael Harper and Arnold Bittlinger (1928–) were more educated than the first Pentecostals; they were very different in their style and their ethos from the Pentecostal heroes of faith. They were committed, but would rarely be mistaken for fanatics. The 1970s were characterized by conferences and conventions, some of them massive like the Catholic gatherings at Notre Dame and at Atlantic City, and others like the Lutheran conferences in Minneapolis also drawing five-figure crowds. But many of those attending, while entering with exuberance into the songs and worship, seem to have been less deeply touched interiorly than many in the earlier streams. This is suggested by the ease with which many later moved on to other sources of religious attraction.

Through the 1970s, the charismatic stream reached virtually all those countries in the free world that had not been reached in the 1960s. This applies, for example, to most African countries, to the countries of South-East Asia, to the Caribbean, to the Latin countries of Southern Europe. Some Communist countries in Eastern Europe (not East Germany, Hungary and Poland that had earlier origins) only saw the beginnings of the charismatic stream in the 1980s, such as Czechoslovakia, or even after the collapse of Communism at the end of the 1980s, such as Romania and Bulgaria.

In the 1960s and the 1970s there was considerable evangelical resistance to the charismatic stream, which was perceived as dangerously subjective and insufficiently under the authority of the written Word. Its spread to the Roman Catholic Church and other milieux not noted for their evangelical purity increased these fears of an enthusiastic experience without doctrinal content. However, the 1980s saw an increasing penetration of the evangelical world by many features of the charismatic stream: openness to the gifts of the Spirit, especially healing; greater accent on and greater freedom in praise; increased awareness of the role of the Holy Spirit in ministry.

In North America, the charismatic stream in the mainline Churches began to flag by 1980. Some think that this was a consequence of the leaders not heeding prophecies calling for radical repentance at the Kansas City conference of 1977 that drew participants from almost every point on the Christian spectrum. Kansas City provided the extraordinary visual image of Cardinal Leo Joseph Suenens (1904–1996), the Catholic primate of Belgium, Dr Thomas Zimmerman (1912–1991), the general superintendent of the Assemblies of God, and Dr J. O. Patterson (1912–), of the Church of God in Christ, sitting next to each other on the platform.

In the United States, the pattern of charismatic growth or decline has varied from Church to Church, and period to period. The tradition within which charismatic renewal has been making the most impact recently has been the Anabaptist stream (Mennonite and Brethren). Episcopal (Anglican) renewal had held its own until the early 1990s when the continuing liberal drift of the Episcopal Church has led to some charismatic defections; Lutheran renewal seems to have slackened though less than the Catholic; Presbyterian renewal seems to have picked up in recent years after a major slump. In Britain, Anglican renewal has been growing, with a number of flagship parishes exercising a major influence; Catholic renewal, which had never reached the proportions of the United States, has seen a little growth; while renewal in the Free Churches, apart from some Baptist milieux, has been relatively weak. In general, the charismatic stream has had quite a major influence on European Baptists, but much less in the United States, where the Southern

Baptist Convention has been unenthusiastic to put it mildly.[3]

During the last five years, there have been increasing signs of a charismatic revival among the African-American churches, the National Baptist Convention, the African Methodist Episcopal Church and the American Methodist Episcopal Zion Church, sectors largely untouched in the first two decades of the charismatic movement.

Independent Charismatics

From an early stage there were believers within the charismatic stream who did not belong to or identify with any of the historic denominations. Some of these were independent evangelicals, who had been baptized in the Spirit; others, e.g. in Britain and New Zealand, were former adherents of the Plymouth Brethren. Many of the latter, who were almost invariably expelled from the Brethren on acknowledging their charismatic experience, brought with them the characteristic Brethren hostility to denominations and a concern about the nature of the New Testament Church. These former Brethren became the main proponents of a new form of 'Restorationism', that saw this outpouring of the Holy Spirit as for the Restoration of the New Testament Church, where restoration in practice means rebuilding from scratch.

It was only in the early 1970s that the independent charismatic sector really took off and began to become a major phenomenon. In the United States, this was spearheaded by the group known as Christian Growth Ministries based in Fort Lauderdale, Florida (Derek Prince (1915–), Bob Mumford (1930–), Charles Simpson (1937–), Don Basham (1926–1989) and Ern Baxter (1914–1993), though it was also augmented by several pastors like Jamie Buckingham (1932–1992) who had previously been Southern Baptists, a denomination that did not in general take kindly to charismatics. In Britain, the independent charismatics first came into public consciousness as the 'House Church movement', so-called because many of their assemblies first met in homes. Its rapid growth, however, quickly made this designation less appropriate, as new assemblies moved from house venues to larger buildings.

Over the last twenty years, the independent charismatics have made enormous gains in most parts of the world. While charismatic renewal in the mainline denominations in the United States has fluctuated, and in some Churches markedly declined,[4] the independent Churches have been growing virtually everywhere, sometimes steadily, sometimes dramatically. In Britain there are now at least seven major independent charismatic networks, all of which seem to be expanding. Other Western European countries are seeing an upsurge of these assemblies, even countries like France and Germany, where independent Church growth has traditionally been very slow and difficult.[5]

However, it is in Asia and Africa that there is the greatest explosion of new charismatic churches. In South-East Asia, there are major independent Churches involved in church planting in the Philippines, Indonesia and Thailand. The Hope of Bangkok Church in Thailand, led by Kriengsak Chareonwongsak, has had unprecedented evangelistic success in a strongly Buddhist country. In many African countries, there are many new charismatic congregations springing up, like those of the Deeper Life Bible Church in Nigeria led by William Kumuyi (1941–). In South Africa, there are flourishing new charismatic Churches, many enjoying close links with the new Churches in Britain. Among the most influential is the Rhema Bible Church in the Johannesburg area, led by Ray McCauley, who played a significant role in the transition to the post-apartheid era. In Latin America, it is more difficult to distinguish between independent charismatics and independent Pentecostals, both because all are called *Evangelicos*, and because in many places a strong Pentecostal witness has only arisen in the same time-frame as the rise of the independent charismatics. In Africa, the second of these factors is also present, but not the first, as the new

Churches prefer the language of charismatic to that of
Pentecostal.

How Different from the Pentecostals?
Although many charismatics first defined and understood
the charismatic stream as being essentially within the
historic Churches, most now recognize that the independents also belong to this stream. Why is it that this new
wave of independency is aligned with the charismatic
stream rather than with the Pentecostal?

Firstly, the independent charismatics belonged in their
origins to the new wave of the Spirit breaking out beyond
the boundaries of Pentecostalism. Many of their first leaders were baptized in the Spirit through contacts, groups
and meetings that were in some way transconfessional,
like the Full Gospel Business Men's Fellowship, Camps
Farthest Out, the Evangelical Divine Healing Fellowship.

Secondly, the new charismatics were ill at ease with the
narrowness of denominational Pentecostalism. They did
not accept all their doctrine, particularly reacting against
the pessimism of the dispensational pre-millennial eschatology that most of the new Pentecostal denominations
embraced in the first part of this century.

Thirdly, the ethos of the independent charismatics was
very different from that of the Pentecostals. They were
in general better educated, and the new charismatic
Churches have attracted many young professionals. The
cautious narrowness of many Pentecostal Churches was
uncongenial to these new believers. The independent
charismatics are generally marked by a strong confidence
that they are capturing the world for Christ; they often
have close contacts with the media, and the worlds of
business and entertainment. This is in marked contrast
to typical Pentecostal outlooks. Their spirit is perhaps
most visible in the March for Jesus, that has now spread
to most countries in the world.

Fourthly, their patterns of organization are distinctively modern. They have been insistent that the new
non-denominational networks are not new denominations in embryo, even though virtually everyone else

says this is inevitable. They have been able to avoid
such a development, for the most part, by building
relationships between leaders, rather than institutional
links between congregations. The organizational patterns
in which their leaders relate and co-operate show great
similarity to contemporary patterns of business and commercial organization, though with a concern for personal
relations not found in the world.

In the overall charismatic stream, the independent sector is now the fastest-growing; indeed, the independents
are among the foremost advocates and practitioners of
'Church planting'. In fact, the charismatic stream has
probably been the fastest-growing of all the four streams
in the last 250 years, perhaps because of the growth of
the Independents.

Over-all Development

The charismatic stream has been through various phases,
even within its relatively short history. The early years,
perhaps until 1972, were marked, at least in the English-
speaking world, by an emphasis on the charisms, seen
as a distinguishing feature of the movement. There
was great optimism, little organization, and even less
reflection.

The period from 1972–1980 saw the first main efforts
at the organization of charismatic renewal, largely stimulated by the sizeable entry of Roman Catholics on the
charismatic scene. This brought more sense of a mission
to the Churches, at the same time that the independent
churches were attracted to shepherding/discipling concepts. The 1980s saw more effort put into denominational
renewal, which caused a temporary sag in ecumenical
commitment. In the mid 1980s, the signs and wonders
message of John Wimber (1934–), the founder of the
Vineyard churches, attracted much attention, and was a
factor in a much greater charismatic penetration of the
evangelical world than in the 1960s.

The late 1980s and early 1990s have seen a new
attention to inter-church or ecumenical relationships

with a series of major conferences: New Orleans (1987), Indianapolis (1990), Brighton (1991) and Orlando (1995). The proposal that the 1990s should be a Decade of Evangelism fired many charismatics, and has led to a more outward-looking thrust in the charismatic stream as a whole. These years have seen a much greater charismatic involvement in short-term missions, spearheaded by denominational groups like the Anglican SOMA, the Sharing of Ministries Abroad, and PRRMI, Presbyterian-Reformed Renewal Ministries International, as well as by the inter-denominational Youth With A Mission. The evangelistic thrust has also been accompanied by church planting, in which the independent charismatics have become much involved.

In 1994, the so-called 'Toronto blessing', with numerous unusual manifestations, began to attract wide attention, drawing thousands of visitors to the Metro Airport Vineyard Church on a scale not seen since Azusa Street. The message of Toronto has focused on the love of God the Father for all his children that desires to heal them of their wounds and equip them to bear witness in the world. This eruption has since spread to many parts of the world, evoking a wide range of reactions similar to those found at the beginning of the Pentecostal and charismatic streams. Despite the element of controversy, the Toronto blessing has been giving a new lift to the charismatic stream in many countries, most particularly in Britain, but also in Australia, South Africa and Switzerland.

One of the churches most impacted from Toronto has been the Anglican parish of Holy Trinity, Brompton, often known as HTB, in the fashionable South Kensington area of London. This development, which has led to close collaboration between HTB and several independent church leaders, has caused their Alpha course to reach a far wider audience, both across the Churches in Britain and internationally. The Alpha course, which is an imaginative presentation of the basic gospel message aimed primarily at non-churchgoers, is expected to reach 250,000 people in 1996 alone.

Chapter Six

Inter-denominational Agencies

The rise and spread of inter-denominational streams led very naturally to the formation of inter-denominational agencies and institutions. If anything, their emergence was rather slow, for it was over a century from the rise of evangelicalism to the real springtime of evangelical agencies in the second half of the nineteenth century. This slowness or delayed response perhaps reflected not only the strength of long-standing patterns of church life, but also the slow emergence of more democratic ways in largely patrician and aristocratic societies.

One of the first inter-denominational fruits of the streams was the German Christian Fellowship (*Deutsche Christentumsgesellschaft*), founded by Johann August Urlsperger (1728–1806), a pastor in Basel, Switzerland. In the late 1770s, Urlsperger started to gather together Christians concerned for the purity of the gospel and for true holiness of life. The Fellowship spread quite rapidly, especially in Germany, with a membership that included Lutherans, Reformed, Moravians, Mennonites, Anglicans and even some Catholics. It gave rise to several united enterprises: the Basel Mission House, the Basel Missionary Society (1815) and Bible and Tract Societies.

Here in the Basel initiatives, we can see the first signs of a characteristic evangelical enterprise, the formation of missionary societies and mission training institutions to promote what has always been an evangelical priority, that is, missionary work for the proclamation of the gospel to the unsaved. In Britain, the London Missionary Society was formed in 1796 to embrace Congregationalists, Anglicans, Methodists and Presbyterians, though it became more strongly

Congregationalist as the other Churches formed their own missionary agencies. In France, the inter-denominational Paris Missionary Society was formed in 1819.

An inter-denominational agency that was to have a lasting impact was the British and Foreign Bible Society (BFBS), formed in 1804. In its organization, the BFBS was strictly lay and inter-denominational, with a committee of thirty-six made up of fifteen Anglicans, fifteen from other British denominations and six from abroad. This was another initiative close to the heart of every evangelical, the provision of Bibles in as many languages as possible to support the work of evangelism and the basic nurture of converts. Over the near two centuries of its existence, the BFBS has translated the Bible into almost every known language of the world. In North America, Bible propagation was first promoted by several local societies, until the American Bible Society was formed in 1816.

The Rise of Faith Missions

A decisively new phase in the development of inter-denominational missions occurred in 1865 with the formation of the China Inland Mission (CIM) by James Hudson Taylor (1832–1905). Hudson Taylor, a Yorkshire Free Methodist by background with strong Holiness sympathies, became convinced after some initial mission experience in China of the need for a new kind of mission structure. The CIM embodied these convictions:[1] it was inter-denominational,[2] and thus not under the control of any Church authority in Europe (or North America). While there was an evangelical statement of faith, this made no requirements concerning church order; missionaries were members of the Mission not employees; members could be ordained or lay (none of the early CIM missionaries were ordained), male or female; evangelism took precedence over all other ministry; members were paid no salary, but lived by faith; the mission was field-directed, not controlled from a distant head office.[3] Because of the faith-principle regarding financial support, this pattern of inter-denominational missions became known as 'faith missions'.

During the next generation, many faith missions were founded. A married couple, Grattan and Fanny Guinness,[4] much influenced by Hudson Taylor, played a major role in the development of inter-denominational agencies, such as the Livingstone Inland Mission, the North Africa Mission, the Sudan United Mission and the Congo Balolo Mission. Grattan and Fanny Guinness were also encouraged by Hudson Taylor to found an institute for the training of missionaries to serve in the Faith Missions. In 1873, they founded the East London Training Institute, and later influenced A. J. Gordon (1836–1895) to start the Boston Missionary Training Institute (1889) and Emma Dryer to organize the Moody Bible Institute in Chicago. These institutions were the forerunners of the inter-denominational or non-denominational Bible colleges, that are now so numerous in the Christian world and that were to be taken up by the Pentecostals as they overcame their initial suspicion of formal education.

Hudson Taylor's vision was 'inter-denominational' not 'ecumenical'. He was not against the denominations, unlike some who later called themselves 'non-denominational', and he did not urge CIM members to leave their churches of origin. However, he did not have a high view of denominations, and was perhaps more aware of their limitations than of their positive capacity to transmit a faith-inheritance to future generations. Hudson Taylor followed a different pattern when a visit to Norway led to the desire to form a mission linked to the CIM. Instead of advocating a branch of the CIM, as had happened in the USA, he suggested that they form an associated mission; this mission, the *Kinamisjonsforbund*, was then allocated its own area in China within the CIM structure.

One attempt at founding inter-denominational alliances in the United States led rather quickly to the formation of a new denomination, the Christian and Missionary Alliance (CMA). Initially, in 1887, the founder, A. J. Simpson (1843–1919) formed two distinct organizations, the 'Christian Alliance' and the 'Evangelical Missionary

Alliance'. In 1897 these were joined to form the CMA, which gradually took on the form of a new denomination.

By the time of the formation of the missionary training institutes, the Holiness stream was becoming a major force. It quickly developed its own institutions, in particular the annual Keswick convention in England's Lake District each July together with its periodical *The Life of Faith*; and the National Holiness Association in the United States. Other evangelical institutes had a distinct Holiness tinge, such as Moody Bible Institute in Chicago and Nyack Missionary Institute in Nyack, New York, associated with the CMA.

Over the years, the Christian educational institutions that are more stream-related than denominational have increased in number and influence. Some had a church-connection in their origins that was not maintained, e.g. Wheaton College in Wheaton, Illinois. Dating from 1860, and now home to the Billy Graham Center and the Institute for the Study of American Evangelicals, Wheaton College has emerged as a major centre in American evangelicalism. By contrast, Fuller Theological Seminary in Pasadena, California, founded in 1947, represents an evangelical institution established without any direct denominational links.

Youth Evangelism and Recruitment

Besides missionary work and the distribution of Bibles, the modern Christian streams have long given a special place to youth work and the apostolate to students. These concerns first found expression in the YMCA (Young Men's Christian Association) founded in London in 1844 by George Williams (1821–1905). The YMCA was a characteristically lay and inter-denominational association. It sought to win young men and boys for Jesus Christ by uniting them in fellowship through activities aimed at developing their powers of body, mind and spirit, thus preparing them for lives of service to God and neighbour. A parallel association for young women and girls, the YWCA, was formed in 1855.

In the United States, a young student at Princeton, Luther Wishard (1854–1925) helped to launch an inter-collegiate movement within the YMCA (1877), and became its first full-time worker. Desirous of promoting calls to foreign missionary service among college students, Wishard persuaded the famous evangelist, Dwight L. Moody to hold a students' conference at Mount Hermon near Northfield, Massachusetts, in the summer of 1886.

Present at this conference was a young student from Cornell, John R. Mott (1865–1955), who wrote in a letter that there were 225 students present 'all imbued with the YMCA characteristic, work for souls'. The flame of the missionary ideal was kindled at Mount Hermon, and exactly one hundred students committed themselves to serve as foreign missionaries. Thus was realized Wishard's vision for a worldwide student movement for Christ, that took on an organized form two years later as the Student Volunteer Movement for Foreign Missions (SVM), of which Mott would be chairman for thirty-two years.

Twentieth-Century Expansion

In general, the first century of inter-denominational agencies and institutions had a local character. Most were mission-related, taking the form either of missionary societies directed to a particular target area, often one country or one tribe, or of training institutes and colleges in the sending country. Though some mission societies developed their areas of recruitment beyond their countries of origin (e.g. the CIM), many remained products of one country (e.g. the Scandinavian faith missions).

In twentieth century, the non-Church-related faith missions continued to proliferate. In 1917, the faith missions of North American origin founded IFMA, the Inter-denominational Foreign Mission Association of North America, which had 105 member missions in 1991. The period since the end of political colonialism has seen the local churches planted by these missions form new evangelical denominations. What began as an independent mission with various stations next formed a local conference of missionaries. When the prospect of political independence loomed, the participation of native converts was invited. Through a series of steps in which the local Christians acquired greater responsibility, the local churches became part of a new local denomination, aided from outside, instead of a missionary organization.[5]

The twentieth century, particularly its second half, has seen enormous, perhaps spectacular, developments in the growth of Christian institutions not tied to Churches or denominations. This is true in many areas of Christian life: education, evangelism, youth outreach and formation, Bible translation, radio and television, Christian charity and service. Inter-denominational missionary agencies of evangelical convictions have continued to proliferate, augmented by the first Pentecostal bodies. Notable among the evangelical bodies are the Worldwide Evangelization Crusade (WEC), founded by C.T. Studd (1860–1931) in 1913; sacrifice, faith, holiness and fellowship have been described as the four pillars of WEC.[6]

In the sphere of education, the United States has set the pace, with its larger church attendance, greater affluence and scope for Christian initiatives. Most of the colleges founded with a strong denominational link more than a century ago have long since lost that connection or it has become merely nominal without significant influence on the contemporary institution. In this situation, most colleges in the Protestant sphere with a definite Christian identity are either inter-denominational (Wheaton, Gordon-Conwell, Fuller) or belong to a new stream-related denomination (Holiness or most often Pentecostal).

At a global level, the 'non-Church' streams have become a bigger and bigger force in world Christianity; a major element in this has been the rise and rapid spread of the twentieth-century Pentecostal and charismatic streams, allied to the continuing vigour of their evangelical and Holiness forebears. Their rate of expansion has clearly been aided by modern ease of travel and of communication. The information explosion has triggered the rise of global strategies, and favoured the spread of church growth theory.

Multinational Modern Agencies

The second half of the twentieth century has seen the rise of massive organizations, not linked with particular Church traditions, often known as para-church bodies or movements. The biggest have mostly dedicated themselves to evangelism and discipleship-training, as for example, Youth for Christ; the Navigators; Campus Crusade for Christ; Youth With A Mission; Operation Mobilization. Other large-scale international and interdenominational agencies with different goals include Wycliffe Bible Translators and World Vision.

All these para-church agencies reflect a stream inspiration, and represent a channelling of stream energies for practical service on a major scale. Dr James Packer, the well-known evangelical scholar, has spoken of these agencies reaching out 'to tackle churchly tasks for which the organized churches lacked expertise, resources, and sometimes focused motivation'.[7] Motivation reflects the life and thrust of the streams, a burning desire of hearts touched by the Holy Spirit. Whereas these agencies were established precisely to further the concerns characteristic of the streams – evangelism, repentance and conversion, making the Bible known – in the Protestant Churches these issues came under head-office departments for Mission, Education or Youth Work generally lacking the dynamism and focus that the streams produced. In turn, the new para-church agencies have contributed significantly to the continuing dynamism of the streams.

All these agencies are characteristically modern in their style and methods, typifying the post-World War II period.[8] They were all born in the United States and they all represent the impact of American entrepreneurial skills and energy in the sphere of Christian mission. They differ from older missionary organizations in their global vision and in the focus of many on youth discipleship and on short-term missions.

The stories of these major new agencies listed earlier show many important similarities. **Youth for Christ** has been rather untypical of the genre. First of all, its origins are unclear; though formed as an international body in 1945, this formal organization brought together a whole network of evangelistic youth rallies that had been developing in the United States since the early 1930s. In its first official year, the young Billy Graham served as a travelling evangelist. Youth for Christ developed in many countries with full-time directors. From the 1950s, Youth for Christ focused on high school Bible clubs as a form of evangelism.

The roots of **the Navigators** also go back to the 1930s. Dawson Trotman (1906–1956) imbued other young evangelical converts with his zeal for Bible study, Scripture memorization, meditation and evangelism. Perhaps two practical convictions of Trotman's most decisively shaped the ministry of the Navigators. One was the vital importance of follow-up and discipleship formation after initial conversion. Trotman's vision was that these discipled converts would themselves become 'reproducers'. The other was the necessity of 'one-on-one' ministry for the decisive shaping of lives, first in personal evangelism and later in discipleship formation.

Trotman had close links with Billy Graham in the opening years of the evangelist's ministry, and was invited to collaborate with Graham on the follow-up to his crusades. This co-operation joined Billy Graham's gifts for mass evangelism with Dawson Trotman's skills in personal formation. The Navigators' work which had initially spread through the US military during World War II, now expanded into many other countries. Trotman never had a lengthy affiliation with any one denomination, but nor did his work take on any anti-denominational pattern. It was always very American in its strict practicality and the 'no nonsense' directness of its founder. Trotman co-operated generously with other evangelical

agencies, such as the Wycliffe Bible Translators, Youth
for Christ and Campus Crusade for Christ (whose founder, Bill Bright, was powerfully impacted by Trotman).
The Navigators still represent a powerful force for evangelical evangelism, with 3,376 missionaries in at least
fifty-two countries[9] being found in 1986 in sixty-three
countries and having 2,700 full-time staff.

Like Navigators, **Campus Crusade for Christ** (CCC)
was founded in California, though after the war. Its
founder was William R. ('Bill') Bright (1921–), a successful business entrepreneur at a young age, who after
his conversion in 1945 was for some years torn between
evangelism, studies and business. In 1951, Bright sold his
business, left college without graduating, and established
Campus Crusade for Christ. As the title suggests, the
focus of CCC's ministry is the evangelism of college
students on campus. Bright consciously picked up afresh
the slogan coined by John Mott concerning 'the fulfilment
of the Great Commission in our generation'.

In the mid-1950s Bill Bright formulated the Four
Spiritual Laws as evangelistic tools for winning young
people to Christ; these adapted core evangelical doctrines
to knowing and experiencing God's love and God's plan for
each person's life.[10] As a guide to help new converts grow
in their faith, Bright and associates later (1968) produced
a study in 'follow-up evangelism', *The Ten Basic Steps
Toward Christian Maturity* and then a *Teacher's Manual*
to use with the Ten Steps.

More explicitly than the Navigators, CCC sets out to
be the servant of the Church, introducing people to
Christ and helping to train new evangelists. Hence, CCC
emphasizes commitment to Jesus as Lord and Saviour
and expects converts to join churches where they will be
taught the full range of biblical doctrine. CCC was one of
the first para-church evangelistic agencies to take advantage of the media and modern means of communication to
spread the gospel. They have organized some high-profile
evangelistic events, such as Explo 72 (Dallas, Texas:
65,000); Explo 74 (Seoul, Korea: 1.3 million); Explo 85
(600,000 at 100 locations linked by satellite). Currently,

CCC has 16,000 staff and volunteers working in some 150 countries.[11]

Youth With A Mission (YWAM) represents another massive inter-denominational effort to reach and train young people.[12] YWAM has a more Pentecostal-charismatic flavour than Youth for Christ or CCC, coming from its founder, Loren Cunningham (1935–), originally an Assemblies of God pastor. Cunningham had from his youth a vision for reaching young people across the world with the gospel. Formed in the USA in 1960, YWAM had its first recruitment outside the United States in New Zealand, a country that has since supplied many leaders for YWAM. Over the years, YWAM has developed its own programmes, in particular the Discipleship Training School, a four-month course of training and of practical evangelism. It has developed a whole strategy of short-term missions sending teams across the world on three to four-week evangelistic campaigns. It currently has about 9,000 long-term staff worldwide.

Like most of these modern para-church movements, YWAM reflects a high degree of flexibility and adaptation to changing situations. Over the thirty-five years of its experience, YWAM has become much more alert to the need to integrate the newly-evangelized into living church environments, and in the 1990s has become active in church planting. Conscious of the need to remain an inter-denominational service agency, YWAM has been careful not to attach new church plants to itself, but to an existing denomination or network of local churches.

Operation Mobilisation (OM) is, like YWAM, directed toward youth evangelism and short-term missionary involvement.[13] The founder of OM, George Verwer (1938–), converted at a Billy Graham rally in New York, invested all he had in copies of John's Gospel to take to Mexico. Out of this experience, OM was born in 1961 seeking to motivate, develop and equip Christians for world evangelism. OM is more austere in its demands than most para-church organizations, and particularly targets areas resistant to evangelical penetration, e.g. the former Communist countries and the Islamic world.

OM works with existing churches but has now expanded into church planting; their teams are usually a bit larger than YWAM's and they have deliberately sought to have the minimal ongoing organization to facilitate the annual missions, having 2,500 staff members in over seventy nations.

World Vision (WV) was also founded immediately after World War II. Robert ('Bob') Pierce (1915–1978), a young Baptist minister working with Youth for Christ and with a heart for evangelism, experienced the terrible needs of the destitute during two Asian visits in 1948 and 1950. Following the impact of a film Pierce made on Korea, he founded WV in 1950 to promote conjointly evangelistic mission and care for the poor and the outcast. During the 1950s, WV's work expanded throughout Eastern Asia. By the early 1960s, it was extending to other continents, especially Africa and Latin America. During this period, WV's basic objectives were: missionary challenge, evangelistic outreach, Christian leadership development, social welfare services and emergency aid.

WV showed the flexibility and capacity to adapt to changing situations and demands characteristic of modern business enterprise. They realized that their social welfare approach did not address the root causes of poverty, and they began to re-direct energies into local community development. This involvement led to new forms of collaboration with partner agencies, including UNICEF and the World Health Organization. They moved to a more 'holistic' view of Christian ministry, defined as 'a total ministry to the physical, spiritual, mental, economic and social needs of the whole person in the context of community, with the goal of eventual self-reliance'.

In 1967, Pierce resigned as president due to ill-health, being followed by W. Stanley Mooneyham, a former vice-president of the Billy Graham Evangelistic Association, another inter-denominational body.[14] By 1992, WV had more than 6,400 projects in over ninety countries.[15] In 1977–1978, a conflict with the Roman Catholic authorities in the Philippines who accused WV of proselytism

led to a serious study of WV's relationship with the
Churches and the formulation of an agreed policy. While
affirming its evangelical identity, WV said, 'We find no
scriptural mandate for excluding ourselves from any who
name Christ as Lord.'[16]

Wycliffe Bible Translators (WBT) represents an
inter-denominational agency with a more restricted but
important purpose, the provision of Bible translations
in tribal languages. WBT was founded by W. Cameron
Townsend (1896–1982), a missionary to Guatemala,
who had laboured to evangelize tribal peoples who
did not know Spanish and who had himself translated
the New Testament into Cakchiquel, an Indian tongue.
Along with WBT, Townsend established the Summer
Institute of Linguistics, an educational organization
collaborating with governments to teach linguistics to
facilitators and to promote literacy among the tribal
peoples. WBT has more than 5,000 fulltime workers
worldwide, of whom approximately 80 per cent are
North Americans, much higher than the percentage
in other para-church organizations founded by US
citizens. Their collaboration with governments, particularly in Latin America, has led to some criticism, but
over 300 tribes now have the New Testament available
in their language through the work of WBT.

Individual Ministries Incorporated

The last generation has seen a vast increase in the
number of evangelistic associations founded to support
the ministry of a particular preacher, and sometimes of
a married couple. Such associations are almost by defini-
tion inter-denominational or non-denominational, both in
their support and their outreach, even where the minister
concerned holds ministerial credentials in a particular
Church. The Billy Graham Ministerial Association was
one of the pioneering organizations in this category.

The healing evangelists who were generally of Pentecostal background quickly formed such associations, e.g.
the Oral Roberts Evangelistic Association of Oral Roberts

(1918–); the Osborn Foundation of T.L. Osborn (1923–);
Voice of Healing Inc., later (from 1967) Christ for the
Nations Inc., founded by Gordon Lindsay (1906–1973).
The ongoing vigour of the Pentecostal stream and the
rise of the charismatic have led to an avalanche of
new ministerial agencies: some focused on healing, some
on evangelism, some on both. Among the best known
are International World Ministries of Aril Edvardsen
(1938–) from Norway, Christ for All Nations of Reinhard
Bonnke (1940–) from Germany; World Evangelism of
Morris Cerullo (1931–) of the USA; Alberto Mottesi from
Argentina. Some have pioneered a network of ministries,
such as Pat Robertson (1930–) with Regent University
and Christian Television Network, in Virginia Beach,
Virginia.[17] Older evangelical-style ministries include the
Luis Palau Evangelistic Association.

Chapter Seven

The Characteristics of the Streams

The great modern Christian streams (evangelical, Holiness, Pentecostal, charismatic) represent a distinctively new phenomenon in Christian history. This newness lies in the rise of major currents of life that are not limited to or closely tied up with any one Church tradition or confessional family. These streams flow across Church boundaries and have an inter-confessional character. They have characteristically developed within historic Church traditions (Protestant only for the evangelical, Holiness and Pentecostal streams) but also outside them in newly-formed fellowships, networks and ministries.

Streams of New Life

All four streams – evangelical, Holiness, Pentecostal, charismatic – are in their origins and essence currents of new life. They are movements of the Holy Spirit bringing a clarity of message, preaching Jesus Christ as Saviour and Lord, bringing people to conversion, sanctification and empowered witness. Jesus says: 'I came that they may have life, and have it abundantly' (John 10:10). These words could provide the motto for these streams of new life in the Christian world.

All four streams have a distinctive focus in their message that is indicated in their designations. Evangelicals have typically preached the Cross of Jesus and the twin doctrines of substitutionary atonement and justification by faith. Holiness teachers have added to the evangelical creed the quest for Christian perfection, emphasizing the power of the Blood and the Cross of Jesus to cleanse the

heart of the converted. Pentecostals and charismatics
have emphasized the power of the Holy Spirit to equip
the Christian for effective evangelism and service.

All four streams are firmly Christo-centric. For all of
them, Jesus Christ is the God-man, the eternal Word
made flesh. Jesus is personal Saviour and Lord, the Lord
who has come in the Incarnation and who will come again
in glory. For Holiness and Pentecostal believers, Jesus
is also the Baptizer with the Holy Spirit: with many
Holiness people for sanctification, with the Pentecostals
for empowerment. Hence, it is a mistake to assume that
the Pentecostal emphasis on the Holy Spirit necessarily
leads to less attention to the Son. Donald Gee spoke for
Pentecostals in saying: 'There is a Fire of pure love and
devotion to the Person of the Lord Jesus Christ that is
the essence of the Pentecostal Revival.'[1]

These streams typically manifest this accent on new
life by the priority they accord to evangelism and to
missionary work. The deep desire of those touched by
God through these streams is to win souls to Jesus: to
proclaim the message of salvation so that the lost may
repent of their sins and turn to the Saviour who shed
his blood for their redemption. This desire to save souls
was prominent from the start in the evangelical, Holiness
and Pentecostal movements. It was less marked in the
early years of the charismatic movement, but has become
more prominent since the 1980s, particularly in the new
independent charismatic groupings.

Experiential

All the streams with their life-giving focus have had
a strongly experiential character. For evangelicals, it
was vital that all should experience personal conversion to Jesus Christ; for Holiness believers, that they
should experience sanctification and deliverance from
ingrained sin; for Pentecostals and charismatics, that
they should experience the power of the Holy Spirit
both in themselves and in visibly effective ministry to
others.

The fundamentally experiential character of evangelicalism has at times become obscured by the tendencies for what began in revival to become a doctrinal orthodoxy. Thus evangelicals are often perceived as opposing reliance on experience in contrast to Pentecostals and charismatics. In this view, evangelicals would always rely on the objectivity of the Bible, while Pentecostals and charismatics would be liable to surrender that objectivity in favour of the subjectivity of personal experience. It would, I think, be nearer the truth to say that all the streams, at least in their origins and so in their fundamental character, are strongly experiential and resolutely biblical, at least in intention. We need to experience the salvation, the sanctification, the power of which the New Testament speaks.

In this light, the focus of twentieth-century fundamentalism on literal orthodoxy introduces an imbalance not present in classical evangelical convictions, which stressed equally biblical doctrine and experienced salvation. In other words, merely conservative tendencies seeking to fix inherited orthodoxy in set formulae end up by losing the vitality of the Spirit that was in their origins and that made such streams authentically radical channels of new life.

Cumulative Restoration?

Stream participants have regularly sought to decipher God's unfolding purpose in their own history. Pentecostals in particular see a form of progression in the emergence of these life-streams. The emphases of the four streams can be seen to have their own inner order and logic. Thus, evangelicalism as the first stream focused on the basic requirements, both doctrinal and pastoral, for re-birth to new life in Christ. The Holiness stream, arising out of evangelicalism, took this a step further: beyond conversion and regeneration, there is the need for full holiness of life, or what was expressed in phrases widely used in the Holiness movement: entire sanctification, the overcoming life, Christian perfection. The Pentecostal stream, especially in its first generation, and less consistently the charismatic stream, see the empowerment of the Spirit for the Church's mission and service being based upon conversion and sanctification.[2]

Each new stream in some way builds upon its predecessors. This has been expressed by many Pentecostals in terms of a fourfold schema of divine restoration: Justification by Faith recovered by Luther; Sanctification through Wesley; in some schemata, the restoration of Divine Healing through the Blumhardts,[3] Charles Cullis (1833–1892) and others; and the Pentecostal power of the Spirit through the Pentecostals. There is a progression here that reflects something of the divine purpose.

However, this progression is not simply one from the simple to the sublime, or from the lowest to the highest. As in all Christian life, the most basic remains the most important, not just for beginners but always. The later streams are called to build on the previous streams; this was well understood by the first Pentecostals from Holiness backgrounds with their insistence that the Pentecostal baptism with the Holy Spirit had to follow upon experience of conversion and of entire sanctification.[4]

When the later streams stray from the foundation of the earlier streams they quickly find themselves in trouble. Thus, if Pentecostals or charismatics promote an empowering of the Spirit without an adequate emphasis on basic conversion and on holiness of heart, there can be a dreadful trivializing of the Christian life and the danger of serious deception. The key theological issue here is the relationship between the Spirit and the Cross, between Pentecost and Calvary, as Tom Smail (1928–) has frequently insisted.[5] The question is less whether charismatics emphasize the Spirit at the expense of Jesus, an accusation that does not find much confirmation, but whether they think they can be filled with the Spirit without following in the footsteps of Jesus who had to 'suffer these things and enter into his glory' (Luke 24:26).

Common Characteristics of the Streams

I want to single out here and examine in turn some salient characteristics of these four life-streams. These are: Bible; Lay (or Every-Member); Inter-denominational; Modern.

Bible
All four streams strongly emphasize the centrality of the Bible for fruitful Christian life. They all assert the biblical basis for their message. They all insist that the Bible is not only the test of doctrinal orthodoxy, but also the spiritual food for all believers. Thus, all four streams zealously promote Bible-reading and Bible study for all participants.

It is true that there are significant differences in ways of using the Bible within the streams, especially as between evangelicals and Pentecostals. Whereas evangelicals typically prefer teaching passages as the basis for preaching (e.g. the Pauline epistles), Pentecostals often have a penchant for narrative passages (the Gospels, Acts, the books of Samuel, Kings and Chronicles). This represents the more oral post-literary character of Pentecostalism, with its appeal to those with less formal education, but the contrast may also reflect the developments within evangelicalism that have heightened its more cerebral character and moved it further from its revivalistic origins.

To make these claims for Pentecostal and charismatic commitment to the Scriptures is not to deny that there can be within Pentecostal and charismatic circles a casualness about biblical exegesis, abetted at times by an anti-intellectualism, and too great a focus on the subjective that can encourage an eisegesis that reads things into Scripture rather than an exegesis that draws out the real content from the Word. Whatever these deficiencies, it remains true that these streams have a deep attachment to the Bible. This can be seen from the way that even the more bizarre teachings that can be found in some Pentecostal and charismatic groups appeal to the Bible and the manner that such deviations are vigorously attacked by others on biblical grounds.

Lay

All four streams had a strong egalitarian streak in their origins. Each involved the preaching of a clear message and the availability to all hearers of the experienced truth of the message. While sometimes accused of elitism in their attitudes to outsiders, these movements were the opposite of elitist for insiders. All could experience conversion, all could be sanctified, all could be filled with the Holy Spirit.

With this radical egalitarianism at their heart, it was not surprising that these streams quickly gave rise to lay preachers beyond the ranks of the ordained ministry, as in Wesley's Methodist movement long before it separated from its Anglican roots. The early phases of these movements also tended to allow a larger space for women in ministry, particularly the Holiness and Pentecostal movements. This openness often lessened later, especially as new streams gave rise to new denominations.

The Pentecostal and charismatic movements represent a further radicalizing of the egalitarian tendency. For these newest streams preach not only the availability of grace to all participants, but the availability of charisms, specific endowments of the Holy Spirit, to all believers. 'To each is given the manifestation of the Spirit for the common good' (1 Cor 12:7). Endowments of the Spirit such as prophecy and gifts of healing are no longer the preserve of exceptional souls after years of ascetical preparation, as often seemed to be the case in the Catholic and Orthodox traditions – they were generally not even present in mainline Protestantism – but they are now in principle open to any believer who is filled with the Holy Spirit.

Inter-denominational

All four streams were in their origins inter-denominational, not belonging to or being the fruit of any one tradition alone. Some, like the evangelical stream, have largely preserved this inter-denominational character; others, especially the Pentecostal, have largely lost it as a result of the new stream becoming almost entirely a cluster of new denominations or what is often called a confessional family.

Thus within the streams, we can find:

- those who belong to historic Churches and who form a stream movement or current within their Church;
- new denominations that are particular expressions of a stream (e.g. Holiness and Pentecostal denominations);
- independent congregations and networks that are expressions of a stream but are resolved not to become new denominations (e.g. the Fellowship of Independent Evangelical Churches in Britain, and the many new networks of independent charismatic churches).

The independence of the overall streams from church control has made possible the rise of many stream institutions (ministerial, educational, missionary, journalistic) that have a greater flexibility and freedom than their denominational counterparts. Indeed, the desire and efforts of the older Churches to control new initiatives from the streams can encourage the rise of 'non-denominational' structures outside their sphere of control (the story of the difficult relationship between the Full Gospel Business Men's Fellowship and the Assemblies of God in the USA illustrates this point).

Modern

All four streams have a distinctively modern element in their make-up, though their modernity is seen most clearly in the period of their origins and of subsequent mutations. As David Bebbington has shown, evangelicalism in its origins reflected the world and mentalities of the eighteenth century, particularly its scientific bent and its rationalist spirit. Evangelicals brought to bear on Christian faith the very same mentalities that characterized the great thinkers of the Enlightenment: logic,

reason, common sense. They used these weapons of their
age against the secularizing and agnostic tendencies of
the Enlightenment. Thus, there was something in the
origins of the evangelical stream that was at once both
modern and anti-modern, and this combination has been
repeated in the origins of the later streams.

The modern element lies first in the innovative character of each new stream that expresses the creativity of
the Holy Spirit in a particular epoch. The creation of new
forms of dissemination and new patterns of organization
both reflect the adaptation of contemporary models to
Christian life and mission. At the same time, the streams
are committed to basic Christian orthodoxy in doctrine;
this can easily lead them to a strongly conservative
stance in theology and morality, especially when they
see themselves as God's answer to contemporary unbelief
in academia and Church.

The modernity of the Pentecostal stream is reflected in
its oral populist character favouring simple and direct
forms of communication, both vertical to God and horizontal to fellow humans. This has enabled them to take
quick advantage of the modern media, especially visual
means such as television and video. Several scholars
have noted that Pentecostals combine an 'old-fashioned'
doctrine with a facility to make use of modern technology,
contemporary forms of music, etc. The latest expression of
this stream modernity can be seen in the style and ethos
of the independent charismatic networks that have been
springing up in the last twenty years. Tapping a more
educated base, they represent a Christian adaptation of
the methods and know-how of the modern business world
and of management science. This is particularly evident
in the whole concept of networking, that belongs to the
world of faxes and e-mail, of the information highway,
combining maximum input with maximum flexibility of
structure. A recent article gives an accurate sense of this
world, that has influenced the new churches, though their
networks typically represent closer personal bonds than
the author depicts.[6]

The element of modernity in the streams represents

both an advantage and a hazard. The advantage is their greater capacity to communicate with the contemporary world and to disseminate their message more effectively. The hazard is that modernity can slip over into trendiness, so that the contemporary features becomes ends in themselves rather than means to communicate what is eternal. Modernity in the Church always runs the danger of being infected by the spirit of the age, the *Zeitgeist*. Thus, sociologists of religion have remarked that the charismatic movement has tapped into the middle-class ideal of self-advancement to produce upwardly-mobile Christians. This is not simply a negative statement, but indicates this double-edged character of modernity. To desire to be upwardly mobile in the Kingdom of God can indicate a Christianization of a cultural factor; but it may also represent the subversion of the gospel by the contemporary accent on the self that weakens the Christian concepts of self-sacrifice and of the Church as the Body of Christ.

Overall Patterns

Between the four streams there are patterns of similarity, but with significant variations. The evangelical, Holiness and charismatic streams share certain characteristics. First, they all began within the historic Churches. In the evangelical origins, Wesley and Whitefield were Anglicans, Jonathan Edwards a Congregationalist. The Holiness stream began within Methodism in the USA, with a current among the Presbyterians. This was less true of the Pentecostals, who mostly came out of a Holiness background, though there were important leaders like Alexander Boddy, Jonathan Paul (1853–1931) and Thomas Barratt from historic Church backgrounds.

Secondly, these three streams were trans-confessional in their impact from the outset. They did not first belong to a particular Christian tradition, and then branch out from those more restricted beginnings. Thirdly, all subsequently developed a large constituency outside the historic Church confessions. However, the independent

sector of the charismatic stream at this point has taken
the form more of independent congregations and networks than of new denominations. Fourthly, like the
evangelical and the Holiness streams, the charismatic
stream has not ended up as a totally separate stream
outside the older Christian traditions in the manner of
the Pentecostals.

Since the charismatic stream is in many ways the
same spiritual phenomenon as the Pentecostal, but in
a different context and with a different ethos, the similarity with the evangelical and Holiness streams in
contrast with the Pentecostal suggests that with the
charismatic stream the Pentecostal spirituality/blessing
has returned to the more typical pattern, that is of
an inherently inter-denominational or trans-confessional
movement that has significant expression both within
and outside the historic Churches.

Thirdly, the Pentecostal stream had its main impact,
at least in its first two generations, in the poorer social
classes. Although a number of evangelical preachers such
as Wesley and Spurgeon impacted the working-class
people, the evangelical stream with its emphasis on
understanding the preached Word tended to appeal to the
middle class (in Britain divided between the Anglicans
with the more well-to-do and the Free Churches at
the lower end). The charismatic stream represents for
the most part the penetration of the middle class by
the Pentecostal blessing. The levels of commitment in
the charismatic stream seem to be less than among
the Pentecostals, partly perhaps reflecting middle-class
eclecticism, partly the more complex loyalties of mainline
charismatics who accept the grace of baptism in the Spirit
while retaining their Church membership and commitment. The charismatic stream also reflects its largely
middle-class composition in other ways, e.g. its emphasis
on inner healing, where the Pentecostal concern is with
physical healing.

Lastly, all the streams are continuing to grow, at
least at the worldwide level. The most explosive growth
rates appear to be in the Pentecostal and charismatic

streams, though the Holiness stream has maintained an impressive missionary record. The evangelical stream as the oldest of the four has had more ups and downs, but in the Western world has been on the upswing in the last three decades. This continuing vitality and growth reinforces their importance and the necessity for the Churches to come to terms with the challenge they pose. This challenge will be examined in later chapters.

PART III

RENEWAL IN THE MAINLINE CHURCHES

Chapter Eight

Renewal Currents in the Protestant and Orthodox Churches

W hile this book is primarily concerned with the complementarity of the work of the Holy Spirit in the life-streams of the past 250 years and in the Roman Catholic Church, it is necessary to mention other renewal currents in the Protestant and Orthodox Churches during this period. As has been indicated in the chapters treating the major life-streams, these have arisen both within and outside the mainline Protestant Churches. However, the evangelical, Holiness and charismatic streams have not been the only sources of new life within these Churches, and this chapter will therefore treat briefly some of these other renewal currents. The examples chosen focus on the forms of renewal with a more consciously spiritual emphasis, and make no claim to being complete.

The Reappearance of More Catholic Trends

The clearest example of more Catholic trends appearing in the Churches issuing from the Protestant Reformation is the Oxford Movement in the Anglican Communion. For evangelicals, the rise of the Anglo-Catholic wing in the Anglican communion through the Oxford Movement has generally been seen in terms of the inroads of Rome, synonymous with a system alien to the gospel; such an interpretation makes it virtually impossible to see there any authentic work of the Holy Spirit. While it is true that the adherents of the Oxford Movement, or the Tractarians as they were often called, became involved in unrelenting Church battles in urging the Catholic character of the Anglican Church and in restoring Catholic –

not necessarily Roman – practices, it is also the case that there were strong religious and devotional impulses activating the movement.

It is interesting to note that the three great figures of the Oxford Movement in its origins – John Keble (1792–1866), John Henry Newman (1801–1890) and Edward Bouverie Pusey (1800–1882) – all saw the Oxford Movement as the completion of the earlier evangelical revival by which they had each been touched. They were convinced that for evangelical piety to develop into a renewal of the spirit of holiness, it had to be integrated with sound Catholic doctrine and a renewed conception of the Church Catholic. Thus the sermons of the great Tractarians are not simply treatises on church order or polemics against State control of the Church (which did both concern them), but they reflect a profound devotion to the Saviour, a great love for the Word of God and a whole-hearted pursuit of holiness. It was only later that some Anglo-Catholics became more preoccupied with ritual, a tendency that Pusey opposed when he said: 'We had . . . a distinct fear in regard to ritual; and we privately discouraged it, lest the whole movement should become superficial . . . We felt that it was very much easier to change a dress than to change the heart, and that externals might be gained at the cost of the doctrines themselves.'[1]

The Tractarian love for the Scriptures was accompanied by a great love for the biblical interpretations of the Fathers of the Church. While evangelicals had typically concentrated on the Epistles of St Paul and their teaching on the work of Christ, the Tractarians gave increased attention to the Gospels that transmit to us the personality and the life of the Incarnate Son of God. As Dean Church wrote (not wholly fairly): 'The great Name stood no longer for an abstract symbol of doctrine, but for a living Master, who could teach as well as save. And not forgetting whither He had gone and what He was, the readers of Scripture now sought Him eagerly in those sacred records, where we can almost see and hear His going in and out among men.'[2]

Religious Communities

One fruit of the Oxford Movement was the re-entry of forms of religious and monastic life into the Anglican Communion. This impulse was present from an early phase of the movement, and was particularly cultivated and promoted by Pusey. The first religious community of Anglican women was formed in 1845 and fourteen other new communities had been founded by 1860. Another twenty-five followed by 1900. Although the first Anglican sisterhoods were occupied with works of service and charity, they were strongly animated by the desire for holiness of life and a profound life of prayer.

The first religious house of men in the Anglican communion was in fact formed in the United States, when three deacons pledged to celibacy and a common rule founded the Community of Nashotah in 1841 on the western shore of Lake Michigan. The first of the major Anglican men's religious orders dates from 1866, with the foundation of the Society of St John the Evangelist at Cowley, Oxford by Richard Meux Benson (1824–1915). The Cowley Fathers made a foundation in the United States as early as 1870. Other important men's communities followed: the Community of the Resurrection at Mirfield, Yorkshire in 1892 and the Society of the Sacred Mission at Kelham, Nottinghamshire in 1894.

At the same time as the Oxford Movement was arising in Britain, there was a parallel rediscovery of consecrated celibate life in the Evangelical (Lutheran) Churches of Germany and in the Reformed Churches of France and Switzerland. The consecrated women in these new communities were generally called 'deaconesses', a title that emphasized their vocation to forms of service in the Church, while avoiding the impression of simply imitating the Catholic religious orders. The first community of deaconesses was founded in Germany at Kaiserswerth by pastor Theodor Fliedner (1800–1864) in 1836; it grew out of Fliedner's desire as a prison chaplain to provide shelter for discharged women prisoners. Fliedner's vision was not merely charitable, however, as he sought to restore the ancient institution of deaconesses as a true community of service, training them as nurses. Another community, the Bethel-Sarepta deaconesses, inspired by Friedrich von Bodelschwingh (1831–1910), was formed at Bielefeld. In both these instances a commitment to a celibate ideal in community grew within a dedication to the poor and the sick. J. H. Wickern (1808–1881) not only founded a work for delinquent youth in Hamburg, but played a major role in the founding of the *Innere Mission* (literally interior or home mission) whose role he defined as 'The preaching of salvation to a nation which lacks it.' The Community at Neuendettelsau, founded by Wilhelm Löhe (1808–1872), who was a pioneer in Lutheran liturgical renewal restored frequent celebration of the eucharist and the practice of confession.

In France and in Switzerland, the origins of the Protestant deaconesses had a link with the evangelical revival of the early nineteenth century in Switzerland that later impacted the French Reformed Church. On 6 February 1841, a French Reformed pastor, Antoine Vermeil (1799–1864), touched by this revival, wrote to a former parishioner Caroline Malvesin (1806–1889):

> What we Protestants lack, in our poor Church, after faith of course, which includes everything – is the spirit of self-sacrifice. Without this spirit there can be no discipline and no common purpose, no working together and no enduring charities ... We shall never have any schools or hospitals or Rescue Homes or almshouses as long as we do not have some sort of Community like the Sisters of Charity, which do so much good in the Roman Catholic Church.[3]

The very same day, Malvesin wrote to Vermeil, saying that she longed to give up her whole life to God, and that she was ready to accept the humblest work as long as it meant really serving God. Four days later in her reply to Vermeil, Malvesin wrote:

> As for me, I feel that my vocation is to work with God's help to hasten the happy time when there will

be only one flock led by one Shepherd ... Oh, when will that happy time come when no one will remember the words Protestant and Catholic except to give thanks to the Lord for their disappearance, and when the great Christian family will quench its thirst at the fountain of living waters springing up unto eternal life?[4]

Out of this interaction grew the Deaconesses of Reuilly.

The first Swiss community of deaconesses, those of Saint-Loup, was founded in 1842 by Louis Germond, another pastor whose faith had been awakened through the evangelical revival. The Sisters of Bern in Switzerland began in 1844 when a young woman of the aristocracy, Sophie von Wurtemberg (1809–1878) left her family and rented a small house to receive the sick and to form helpers. Other communities of deaconesses were formed in Holland (1844), in Sweden (1851) and in Denmark (1863). Although the initial emphasis in these Protestant communities was on the care of the needy, there was also a vision of deeper consecration: as Pastor Vermeil wrote: 'There must be souls totally consecrated to their Lord, detached from their own wills, and available; souls whose sole aim would be to live the Gospel fully and to put it into practice; and who would preach more by their example and actions even than by their word.'[5]

The twentieth century has witnessed a further resurgence in community formation within the Protestant world, including a number of communities of a more monastic and contemplative type. These include the well-known Community of Taizé in France, founded by Roger Schutz, and the Sisters of Grandchamp in Switzerland and of Pomeyrol in France. Lutheran Germany has also seen the foundation of several new communities, for example Casteller Ring at Schloss Schwanberg near Wurzburg (women only), that has a strong liturgical emphasis, permeated by the Benedictine spirit, and the Christus Bruderschaft (the Brotherhood of Christ) at Selbitz in Bavaria (both women and men), with an emphasis on worship, evangelism and service. A recent

German community that developed associations with the charismatic movement is the Evangelical Sisterhood of Mary at Darmstadt, led with prophetic vigour by Mother Basilea Schlink (1904–).

A major centre of Christian renewal in Scotland has been the Iona Community founded by George MacLeod (1895–1991) in 1938. The vision for restoring the ruined monastery on the island of Iona off the west coast of Scotland had come to George MacLeod as he grappled with the challenge to the Church of the economic depression of the late 1930s in his parish of Govan, where the shipyards were short of business and 80 per cent of the men were unemployed. Iona Community represents what now would be called a holistic vision: a desire to bring together the personal and the social, a desire to bridge the gap between the Church and the contemporary world; a desire for an evangelism that would flow out from corporate worship to the market-place and the factory. Unlike the other communities mentioned, Iona is a dispersed community, with a small staff living on the island in the abbey buildings, and its full and associate members scattered throughout the parishes, chaplaincies and educational institutions of the Commonwealth countries, but especially in Scotland. Close links are maintained by retreats, conferences, and local meetings, as well as a regular news-sheet.

Movements of Revival and Renewal in the Orthodox Church

Little is known in the Western world about movements of the Spirit of God within the Orthodox Churches of the East. However, it is important if we are considering the relationship between the new life-streams and the renewing work of the Holy Spirit within the ancient Churches neither to ignore the Orthodox Churches in general nor the identifiable currents of new life within them. The Eastern Church has always preserved the ideal of radical holiness of life, associated particularly with the monastic tradition. We can get some sense of the spiritual depth mediated by Russian Orthodoxy in their modern saints, such as Seraphim of Sarov (1759–1833) who said that 'the goal of the Christian life consists in the acquisition of the Holy Spirit', and John of Kronstadt (1829–1909), who wrote that 'In the Holy Scriptures we see God face to face, and ourselves as we are', urging that the Bible be translated into Russian: 'Otherwise, how many millions are deprived of its riches by reason of its being written in the old Slavonic language, not understood by many.'[6]

Currents that Western Christians would recognize as having a definite evangelical component in terms of emphasis upon conversion, personal knowledge of Christ and the importance of explicit evangelism can be found within the Orthodox world, both those who uphold the Council of Chalcedon (451), often called the Eastern Orthodox, and those who dissented from it, often called the Oriental Orthodox. Among the latter is the Coptic Church of Egypt, that has seen a marked revival in recent decades, centred upon the monasteries. The outreach of spiritual renewal has given rise to a vigorous Sunday School movement, that now has 30,000 teachers in Cairo alone. This movement was directed, before he became the Pope of Alexandria, by Mgr Shenouda, who continues to attract large crowds to weekly Bible lectures in his cathedral.

In Greece, the Zoe movement, founded in 1911 is predominantly a movement of lay theologians, dedicated to the teaching of the gospel of Christ in the Orthodox Church of Greece. They have given a priority to publication of the Scriptures in low-priced editions, and run Sunday schools as well as a school to train Sunday school teachers. The members of Zoe live in a monastic community, but without monastic vows. Their members have agreed not to accept high office in the Church, and to retain a spirit of anonymous service that rejects any focus on outstanding personalities. There have also been a number of evangelical initiatives that included efforts to help Greek Orthodox people to a living faith in Christ within their Church, though such outside help is often suspect to the Church authorities.[7]

In Romania, a movement that has had considerable impact but not without arousing controversy is
the *Oastea Domnului* (the Army of the Lord). Founded
by Iosef Trifa (–1938), a Romanian Orthodox priest,
the Army of the Lord clearly preaches Christ crucified;
Father Trifa wrote: 'The Army of the Lord seeks to bring
sinners to the source of righteousness and power . . . to
Jesus the Saviour.' They place a strong emphasis on
moral transformation through the cross, and had from
its start a commitment to promoting temperance with
alcohol: 'We preach a renewal of the soul, we preach
a change of life's foundation, we preach a new life.'
It is a voluntary lay movement that emphasizes the
responsibilities of lay people in preaching, evangelism
and the leading of local fellowships. Lastly, the Army of
the Lord is totally committed to the Scriptures: Fr Trifa
wrote that 'a soldier of the Lord without the Bible is like
a soldier without his gun'. Fr Trifa defined the Army of
the Lord as a grassroots, Bible-based force for revitalizing
the Romanian Orthodox Church. This movement grew
to embrace hundreds of thousands of believers. Not long
before he died, Fr Trifa was excommunicated – the
bishops judged that he did not pay sufficient attention
to the liturgy, the Church and the role of icons – and
the movement split, with part following a bishop and
part Fr Trifa. Under Communist persecution after World
War II, the section under the bishop died out, and that
faithful to the principles of the founder flourished. Since
the fall of Ceaucescu in 1989, the Orthodox hierarchy has
rehabilitated Fr Trifa's memory and has given official
recognition to the Army of the Lord. But many tensions remain, as the movement has been determined to
maintain a certain autonomy of Church control, while
remaining firmly within the Orthodox tradition.

In Russia, there has been a long tradition of prophetic
currents despite (or perhaps because of) Church entan-
glement with the State. During the years of severe
Communist repression, there were countless and largely
unknown heroes of faith who suffered and died in the
Gulags and the prisons of the Soviet Union. One example

known in the West is the witness of the priest-scientist Fr Pavel Florensky (1885–1937); spared in the early years of persecution because of his scientific contribution, Florensky spent the last four years of his life before his execution, in prison camps, first in Siberia and then in North-Western Russia near Archangel. Florensky refused the possibility of emigration, making his own the words of St Paul: 'I have learned, in whatever state I am, to be content. I know how to be abased, and I know how to abound; in any and all circumstances I have learned the secret of facing plenty and hunger, abundance and want. I can do all things in him who strengthens me' (Phil 4:11–13).

Initiatives for the renewal of faith among the Orthodox in Russia have often been quite local. One notable example was the pastoral ministry of Fr Aleksandr Men (1935–1990), parish priest of the Church of the Circumcision in Novaya Derevnya, a small village just north of Moscow. Aleksandr Men came from a Jewish family that had recently accepted Christianity. When he was baptized secretly in the catacomb church at the age of seven months, the priest, a starets with spiritual gifts, foretold an important future for this baby. An avid reader, the young Aleksandr devoured the Scriptures, the Fathers of the Church and the Russian religious philosophers. By his teens, he could read fluently Hebrew, Greek and Latin, as well as many modern European languages. Ordained a priest at the age of twenty-five, Fr Men wrote a book on Christ, *The Son of Man*, a series on the world religions and a nine-volume dictionary of the Bible. People came from far away to seek his counsel, especially educated people who responded to his gift of presenting Christianity in an intellectually convincing way. The famous writer Aleksandr Solzhenitsyn was baptized by Fr Men. Even during the oppression of the early 1980s, he continued to organize groups for Bible study, prayer and catechesis. Since he was mysteriously murdered in September 1990, his parish has remained a centre for the renewal of living Christian faith.

Though Western movements of renewal have generally

produced few ripples in Russia, there have been some
signs of liturgical renewal in some Russian Orthodox
milieux. One has been the parish of Our Lady of Vladimir
in Moscow, where Fr Georgi Kochetkov introduced modern Russian into the liturgy, and sought to promote
greater popular participation in the liturgy in ways
akin to the directives of Vatican Two in the Catholic
Church. Fr Georgi had also, even in the Communist
years, formed a catechetical centre and a theological
college, and cultivated an evangelistic missionary spirit
among his people. Like Fr Men, Fr Georgi Kochetkov
took a strongly ecumenical stance, which earned him the
hatred of the more rabid nationalist clergy and people.
As a result, he was removed from his parish early in
1994, and was transferred to a small parish with poor
facilities: at his new church, Fr Georgi told the people:
'The only sacred language is the language of the Church,
and the language of the Church is the language of love,
the language of mercy, the language of repentance. There
is and there will be no other sacred language.'

Dozens of Orthodox brotherhoods and sisterhoods have
sprung up in Russia since perestroika and the end of
Communist persecution of Christianity. Many have primarily charitable aims, though others like the Orthodox
Charitable Brotherhood in St Tikhon's parish in Klin
county near Moscow have wider aims; formed in 1991
for missionary, catechetical and charitable work, it is
animated by a desire to bear an Orthodox witness to
Christ in a culture in which few people have anything
but the sketchiest idea of Christian faith.[8]

In Armenia, the end of Communism has seen the resurrection of an ancient movement within the Armenian
Orthodox Church, known as the 'Brotherhood'. The
Brotherhood, found in all the major cities in Armenia,
gathers up to 700 people a week to pray and preach.
Its emphases are more evangelical, but its framework
is Orthodox. A charitable arm also publishes Christian
materials, and is supported by some Protestant agencies
as an effective way of spreading the gospel in a country
with a strong Orthodox tradition.

Chapter Nine
Preparations for Catholic Renewal

It is not my purpose to attempt even a potted version of currents of revival and renewal in the history of the Roman Catholic Church. The more restricted aim is to examine the renewing work of the Spirit of God among Catholics during the same period as the rise of the revival streams in the Protestant world.

There have always been currents of renewal and of reform within the Catholic Church. These currents have been most evident in the lives of those men and women, later canonized as saints, and in the orders, congregations and works that they often founded. Clearly some centuries have seen stronger forces of renewal and reform than others, e.g. the thirteenth century was a high point with the whole Franciscan movement and the founding of the Dominican order; the late sixteenth and early seventeenth centuries were also in the more restricted sphere of post-Reformation Catholic Europe times of significant spiritual stirring, with the Carmelite reform of St John of the Cross and St Teresa of Avila, with the French spiritual schools of Cardinal de Bérulle (1575–1629), Monsieur Olier (1608–1657), and the start of the wide-ranging apostolate of St Vincent de Paul (c 1580–1660).

What stirrings of the Holy Spirit were there among the Catholic contemporaries of George Whitefield and Jonathan Edwards? The most striking parallel is in the rise of two preaching orders or congregations, whose message centred, as their names indicate, on the Passion of Jesus and the redemption that Jesus won on Calvary: these are (1) the Congregation of the Passion, known as the Passionists, founded by St Paul of the Cross

(1694–1775); and (2) the Congregation of the Most Holy Redeemer, known as the Redemptorists, founded by St Alphonsus Liguori (1696–1787).

While the context and culture of the missions preached by these new orders of Italian origin were very different from the ethos of the Evangelical Awakenings, it is noteworthy that these were orders dedicated to preaching salvation to sinners through the proclamation of the Crucified Saviour. Jay Dolan in his history of Catholic America in the nineteenth century noted a parallel between the revivalistic preaching of men like Charles Finney in the Protestant world and the Catholic parish missions preached especially by the Passionists, the Redemptorists and the new American congregation of the Paulists. These missions introduced into Catholic preaching a distinctive content focused on the cross, redemption, repentance and confession of sins. Until this kind of preaching fell into some disfavour after Vatican Two, Catholic practice generally retained a sharp contrast between regular Sunday preaching in the parishes which were more didactic and moralistic and the mission sermons that were more 'evangelical' and conversionist.

The renewing and reforming currents in post-Reformation Catholicism largely occurred within a defensive framework concerned to prevent the further spread of Protestantism, to correct the most glaring abuses that had provoked such protest and to protect the faithful from contagion by non-Catholic sources. Post-Reformation Catholicism, often called Post-Tridentine because of the decisive influence of the Council of Trent (1545–1563), strongly affirmed Roman Catholic distinctives in doctrine and devotion, and emphasized the importance of authority and the virtue of obedience. During this period, devotional life became increasingly separated from an immobile liturgy and from a theology that was both polemical and rigidly codified. The Church also came increasingly to the fore in Catholic teaching in a way that it had never been in the Middle Ages, but with a strong emphasis on the Church as a hierarchical institution with its God-given powers and inalienable rights.

The seventeenth and eighteenth centuries saw several other saintly figures within the Catholic world, who served to deepen devotion and promote moral reform, without challenging the overall framework. Another Italian saint from this period whose preaching had a major impact was St Leonard of Port Maurice (1676–1751), to whom were attributed what charismatic Christians today would call words of knowledge; on one occasion, St Leonard interrupted a sermon to say, 'My heart tells me there is here present an obstinate sinner. Unless he repents at once, he is doomed. This very night God's punishment will overtake him.'[1] It was a period of development in popular devotions, particular to the Sacred Heart of Jesus, the eucharistic presence of the Lord Jesus, and to Mary, the mother of the Lord. In this self-enclosed Catholic world, anything that smacked of Protestantism (or of secularism and anti-clericalism) was suspect; so lay initiatives and Bible reading were far from prominent.[2]

However, by the early nineteenth century, there were initial signs of a Catholic desire to return to a pastoral and theological life rooted in the Scriptures and in the Fathers of the Church. Important figures here were two German scholars, J. M. Sailer (1751–1832), later bishop of Regensburg, and Johann Adam Möhler (1796–1838). Both Sailer and Möhler had a deep sense of the Church, which went beyond the institutional emphases of the day to the richness of patristic teaching. Both represented the retrieval of a living concept of tradition in contrast to mere conservative attachment to recent observance.

In the same period, a Roman priest, later canonized, Vincenzo Pallotti (1795–1850) made a serious attempt to invigorate and mobilize the Catholic laity, another trend that prefigured Catholic developments of the twentieth century. Pallotti founded the Society for the Catholic Apostolate, often known as the Pallottine Fathers. Similar goals though in a more educated setting were pursued by Antonio Rosmini (1797–1855), founder of the Institute of Charity, and author of the remarkable reforming work with the English title of *The Five Wounds of the Holy*

Church. Rosmini, apparently on the point of being made a Cardinal, fell out of favour with this book, which was placed by Rome on the Index of Forbidden Books, though his new congregation was not threatened. In this bold and prophetic message, Rosmini likened the state of the Church to the wounded body of Christ on the cross; he identified the five wounds of the Church as: the division between people and clergy at public worship; the insufficient education of the clergy; disunion among the bishops; the nomination of bishops by civil governments; and restrictions on the free use by the Church of her own temporalities.

Rosmini's diagnosis of the ills of the Catholic Church was remarkable in many ways. He identified the scourge of clericalism, and anticipated the call of Vatican Two for an active participation of all in the Church's worship: 'He [God] cannot permit the people upon whom the light of the Word has shone, and who have been reborn for the worship of the Word, to be present at the great acts of worship as though they were statues or pillars in the Lord's temple.'[3] His account of the low level of seminary studies in the nineteenth century[4] reveals the desperate need for a Catholic return to the sources, of which the Scriptures form the heart. Rosmini has a wonderful passage about the Bible:

> In it eternal truth speaks in every way known to human language. Truth narrates, teaches, judges, sings. Memory is nourished with history; imagination attracted by poetry; intellect enlightened with wisdom; feeling moved in all these ways together. The teaching is so simple that the uneducated believe it written for themselves; so sublime that the learned despair of grasping it. The text is human in form, but the vehicle of God's own word.[5]

Thus Rosmini looks for an education that will be rooted in the Word of God, that will nourish the whole person, imagination and memory, mind and sensitivity. These ideals he inculcated in the Institute of Charity, often

known as the Rosminians, and in the educational institutions they conduct.

Perhaps the towering figure of this pre-renaissance was
John Henry Newman (1801–1890), who most fully anticipated the thrust of twentieth-century Catholic renewal.
First a leader of the Oxford movement within the Church
of England, Newman was not only a defender of Catholic
church order, but also an energetic opponent of State
encroachment on Christian territory and an advocate
of practical holiness rooted in the Scriptures and the
Fathers of the Church. Newman was both a profound
thinker and a zealous pastor-preacher. He brought both
these characteristics with him into the Roman Catholic
Church in 1845. Much of his doctrinal teaching is found
in collections of sermons, and his framework of thought in
The Idea of the University and *The Grammar of Assent.*

Part of Newman's greatness was that he sensed profoundly and saw the evil inherent in the spirit of the
dawning age, the belief in inevitable progress and the
accompanying self-confidence in human knowledge and
skills. He was thus a profound critic of the liberal suspicion of authoritative divine revelation. But at the same
time, Newman's mind was strongly historical, and he was
no defender of the timeless schemata often favoured by
conservative church people. This side of his theology is
particularly evident in the *Essay on the Development
of Christian Doctrine* (1845). Thus, part of Newman's
greatness and relevance is his refusal to fit into the
stereotypical moulds of conservative-liberal opposition.

Coming from a very different ecclesial and theological background to post-Tridentine Catholic theology,
Newman re-introduced into Catholic scholarship a more
biblical and patristic method as an alternative to the pre-
vailing scholasticism. He also insisted on the importance
of an active and trained laity, more philosophically in *The
Idea of the University* (1852) and more historically and
perhaps polemically, in his small work, *On Consulting
the Faithful in Matters of Doctrine* (1859). Newman here
examined the role of the *sensus fidelium* (the sense of the
faithful) in the profession and the transmission of the

Catholic faith, laying a foundation for a new Catholic respect for the laity as an integral part of the Church. This work ends with a well-known passage:

> I think certainly that the *Ecclesia docens* [teaching Church] is more happy when she has such enthusiastic partisans about her as are here represented, than when she cuts off the faithful from the study of her divine doctrines and the sympathy of her divine contemplations, and requires from them a *fides implicita* [implicit faith] in her word, which in the educated classes will terminate in indifference, and in the poorer in superstition.[6]

A greater emphasis on the Scriptures and a higher valuation of the Catholic laity were to be fundamental elements in the renewal currents of the next century. Another important ingredient that linked both these concerns was the desire for a liturgical renewal that would make the Church's public worship a vital expression and a nourishing source for the Christian life of the faithful. An important pioneering figure here was the French Benedictine abbot Prosper Guéranger of Solesmes (1805–1875). Abbot Guéranger's multi-volume book, *L'Année Liturgique*, translated into many languages, played a major role well beyond his lifetime in preparing the reading Catholic public for the liturgical renewal of the twentieth century.

Until the last quarter of the nineteenth century, these first seeds of renewal did not receive much encouragement from Rome. This situation changed significantly with the pontificate of Leo XIII (1878–1903). Following the longest-ever and increasingly conservative reign of Pius IX (1846–1878), Pope Leo, already sixty-eight years old at his election, took several steps that opened the door to Catholic renewal. Besides making Newman a Cardinal in 1879, remarkable after Newman's position as an 'inopportunist' at the time of Vatican One (1869–1870), Leo XIII was the initiator of official Catholic social teaching, especially with his encyclical letter *Rerum Novarum*

(1891). He was also the pope who opened the door to the renewal of biblical studies in the Catholic Church with his encyclical letter on the Scriptures in 1893 and in 1897, he lifted the restrictions on Catholics buying and reading approved translations of the Bible. Leo XIII also took steps to promote the study of the works of St Thomas Aquinas, and thereby initiated the jettisoning of a debased scholasticism that paid lip service to Aquinas but lacked his probing mind and theological creativity.

Of particular importance for our purposes was Pope Leo XIII's accent on the Holy Spirit. This owed much to the vision and courage of a remarkable woman of faith, Elena Guerra (1835–1914) from Lucca in Italy.[7] It was in 1882, the year that she founded a new order of nuns, that Guerra had her first intuition of her call to recall the Catholic Church to the role of the Holy Spirit. In 1893, a kitchen worker at the convent told Mother Elena that the Lord wanted her to write to the Pope urging him to institute a regular prayer to the Holy Spirit; Elena took well over a year before she acted on this word, and then told the Pope that all Christians should turn to the Holy Spirit as the Holy Spirit was turning to them. Pope Leo responded within three weeks by instituting a solemn time of prayer to the Holy Spirit throughout the Catholic Church between the feasts of Ascension and Pentecost. Mother Elena continued to write to the Pope about the Holy Spirit, and in 1897 he issued his encyclical letter on this subject, *Divinum Illud Munus*. As the new century approached, she begged the Pope to begin the first day of the century by singing the hymn *Veni, Sancte Spiritus* (Come, Holy Spirit) in the name of the whole Church, which he did.

The last decade of the nineteenth century saw a significant new step that was to prepare the ground for a changed Catholic attitude towards other Christians and their Churches. This was the friendship between a French Catholic priest, Fernand Portal (1855–1926), and the Anglican, in fact strongly Anglo-Catholic layman, Lord Halifax (1839–1934). They met on the island of Madeira at the end of 1889, Portal convalescing from illness, the

Halifaxes seeking a better climate for the health of a sickly son. Although their efforts for rapprochement and the Roman recognition of Anglican orders were repulsed, and their immediate hopes dashed, this friendship was to endure and sow a seed that was to bear fruit much later in the coming century.

Chapter Ten

The Beginnings of Catholic Renewal

T he effective beginnings of thoroughgoing renewal in
the Roman Catholic Church really belong to the
twentieth century. The eighteenth and nineteenth-century
saints, theologians and church leaders mentioned in the
last chapter were really the precursors rather than the
architects of renewal. From early in the twentieth century,
identifiable movements for renewal with their own publications and centres began to develop, so that there arose
a cumulative thrust for Church renewal that had not been
present before. Along with the rise of coherent currents
of renewal, we find an interaction with Church authority
that led increasingly, though not always without tensions,
to official endorsement of the renewing trends.

The thrust towards Church renewal found expression
at both the scholarly and the pastoral level. This chapter
will look particularly at the scholarly developments. In
general, the renewal currents were strongly pastoral
in motivation, and sought to revitalize parochial life
through a deeper understanding of the gospel and the
Church. However, renewal thinking had the greatest
practical impact in the organized movements for spiritual
and pastoral renewal that have proliferated among the
Catholic faithful since the 1920s. These movements will
however form the subject matter of the following chapter,
due both to the number and variety of such movements
and to their significance for Catholic renewal.

Liturgical Renewal

The first of the Catholic renewal currents to take clear
shape was the liturgical movement. In retrospect, we

can see a providential character to the pre-eminence of
liturgical renewal, from the ways in which it correlated
biblical and patristic renewal with an interest in the
Christian East and thus implicitly with ecumenism.

The interaction of the scholarly and the pastoral in the
movement for liturgical renewal can be seen clearly in the
life of the priest generally credited with being its founder, Dom Lambert Beauduin of Belgium (1878–1960).
Beauduin, first for a short time a diocesan priest and
then a Benedictine monk, was a selected speaker at a
major Belgian Catholic conference in 1909. His subject
was 'La vraie prière de l'Eglise' [the authentic prayer
of the Church]. His learning was put at the service of
pastoral renewal. His plea was for the official worship of
the Church – the daily office and the sacramental rites,
especially the eucharist – to become truly the prayer of
the whole body of Christ, ordained and lay. This address
is regarded as the launching of the liturgical movement,
because it gave rise to a number of initiatives for the
renewal of Catholic worship that mushroomed throughout the world right up to the full official endorsement
of this vision in Vatican Two's Decree on the Liturgy
(1963).

It is hard even for many Catholics today, probably
even harder for Protestants, to imagine what Catholic worship and piety was like in 1900. It is very
difficult to be objective and fair in its description, for
many conservative Catholics look back to the pre-Vatican
Two liturgy as a golden age ruined by liturgical reform
and 'modernistic' theology, while reformist Catholics too
easily disparage the genuine piety and devotion of pre-
conciliar Catholics.

Beauduin saw that the liturgy was not truly the prayer
of the people. They were present at the liturgy, but their
prayer was often independent of the liturgical action.
They had no active role, they did not sing, they did not
respond, they were silent spectators of what the priest
did at the altar. One result of the people's distancing from
the liturgy was that the prayer of their hearts found other
outlets, especially in the numerous patterns of public

devotion that surrounded the sacramental presence of the Lord, and that invoked the Blessed Virgin Mary and other saints. It was at these exercises of piety, mostly held in the evenings (evening Mass was only authorized in 1954) that the people used their own language, that they sang hymns and responded vocally.

The progress of the liturgical movement, which occurred mainly in France, Germany and the Low Countries, was closely allied to the renewal of biblical and patristic scholarship in the Catholic Church. The reasons for this connection are not hard to see. The patristic period, especially the first five centuries of the Christian era, saw the formation of the major liturgies of East and West, the origins and rise of monasticism and the development of a theological reflection that was much closer to the thought-patterns and the imagery of the Scriptures than were the theological patterns of the second millennium. These three elements were closely connected. Most of the great patristic teachers were bishops, and so their teaching always retained a strong pastoral character. These bishop-teachers were monks, and it was in the monasteries that the biblical manuscripts were copied, studied and pondered.

Thus, the growing study of the Fathers of the Church was closely linked to the study of liturgical origins. There was growing realization of the strong influence of Jewish patterns of synagogue worship on the worship of the early Christians. There was a clearer recognition of the importance of the Word of God in the Christian liturgy, as in the Jewish synagogue, and a realization that each liturgical celebration properly begins with a liturgy of the Word that is neither a preliminary to the 'real thing' nor mere instruction prior to worship. It is the living Word actualized afresh in the midst of God's people.

One obvious fruit of the study of liturgical origins concerns the institution of the catechumenate in the early Church for the formation of candidates for baptism. It was realized that the Catholic rite of baptism as it had come down to us in this century had in fact telescoped into one ceremony, generally for infants, what had been spread out, for adults, over a period of weeks and months. The distinctive parts in the baptismal liturgy had originally been essential elements in a process of spiritual and pastoral formation involving the whole community of believers. These studies have led to the official restoration of the catechumenate in what is called the Rite of Christian Initiation of Adults (RCIA).

The close links between biblical, patristic and liturgical renewal are exemplified in a book, Jean Daniélou's *The Bible and the Liturgy*.[1] Daniélou (1905–1974) presents a depth of scholarly knowledge in a relatively simple way, treating the transition from the great Jewish feasts to the Christian liturgical year and the biblical typology in which New Testament symbols were prefigured in the Old.[2]

Theological Renewal

The renewal of Catholic theological studies had a strong historical component, involving a detailed examination of the whole tradition and how it developed. The Jerusalem Bible and the patristic series, *Sources Chrétiennes*, were among the many fruits of this renaissance. A co-founder of *Sources Chrétiennes* with Fr Daniélou was a fellow Jesuit, Henri de Lubac (1896–1991). De Lubac was the author of an important study on the ways the Bible was interpreted and used in the Middle Ages.[3]

The renewal of Catholic theology through a return to the sources and the utilization of modern resources focused especially on the mystery of the Church. The way indicated by Möhler and Newman away from an apologetic theology defending the legitimacy of the Church institution, the legacy of post-Reformation polemics, led to a more organic vision of the Church as one visible body of believers formed by the Holy Spirit's action in Word and sacrament. In this development, seminal works included *The Whole Christ*[4] by Emil Mersch (1890–1940), a study of the doctrine of the Church as the body of Christ throughout the centuries, and *The Spirit of Catholicism*[5] by Karl Adam (1876–1966). De Lubac's important books on the Church, *Catholicism* and *The Splendour of the Church*, that only appeared in English (in 1950 and 1956) some years after the French originals, did much to spread this more biblical and patristic vision of the Church. These developments were further encouraged by the encyclical letter *Mystici Corporis Christi* (1947) of Pius XII (1939–1958), all of which prepared the ground for the key document of Vatican Two, the Dogmatic Constitution on the Church (*Lumen Gentium*) of 1964.

Other elements also played an important role in the renewal of Catholic ecclesiology. These included ecumenism and a new focus on the laity.

Ecumenism

As with liturgy and ecclesiology, there were a few nineteenth-century forerunners of a Catholic ecumenism, but the emergence of a visible movement awaited the twentieth century. Among the Catholic pioneers, Fernand Portal was one who suffered much and saw little fruit in his own lifetime, though his long friendship with Lord Halifax made possible the Anglican–Catholic Malines Conversations (1921–1925) under the powerful patronage of the Belgian Primate, Cardinal Mercier (1851–1926). Mercier, a figure of great moral stature enhanced by his role during the German occupation in World War I, was the man who had earlier encouraged Beauduin's liturgical initiatives. In the meantime, Beauduin had become involved in a project encouraged by the newly-elected Pope, Pius XI (1922–1939) for some Benedictine houses to specialize in relations between the Catholic West and the Orthodox East. This led to Beauduin becoming the founder of a Benedictine monastery established to work for Christian unity, first at Amay and then at Chevetogne, both in Belgium. In 1925, Mercier invited Beauduin to contribute an anonymous paper to the Malines Conversations entitled 'The Anglican Church, united not absorbed'. When Mercier died in 1926, also the year of Portal's death, the Catholic opponents of all dialogue with Anglicans prevailed and Beauduin was exiled from his newly-founded monastery for more than twenty years.

The seed sown bore fruit, despite the frigid climate following Pius XI's negative encyclical on ecumenism of 1928 (*Mortalium Animos*). In the early 1930s, a French priest from Lyon, who had been pained by the tragedy of Christian division through his work with Orthodox refugees from the Soviet revolution of 1917, came to visit the unity monastery at Amay. The Abbé Paul Couturier (1881–1953) felt a deep interior call to pray for Christian unity. He was not content with the Catholic form of prayer for unity, known as the Church Unity Octave, founded in the United States in 1909, that prayed explicitly for the return of separated Churches to the Roman obedience. Couturier was convinced that all Christians should pray the same prayer for unity, and that there must be a way to do this together. The answer he arrived at was surely the wisdom of the Holy Spirit: that all could and should pray for unity according to the prayer of Jesus in John 17. For the rest of his life, Couturier promoted this prayer that all may be one as the Father and the Son are one, in the way that the Lord desires.

The genius of Couturier was his recognition that Christian division is above all a spiritual issue to which repentance is the necessary response. From the mid-1930s he composed litanies of repentance, and promoted public as well as private intercession and repentance for Christian unity. This development, seemingly small, was of immense significance, for it represented a move away from the idea that it was impossible for the Roman Church to admit fault and to accept the Church's behaviour as sinful.

Meanwhile another current for Catholic–Protestant rapprochement had arisen in the German-speaking world. A German priest, Max Josef Metzger (1887–1944), had been inspired during World War I to work for peace and against all war. He saw the incongruity of a divided Church with centuries of polemics, opposing all war. Thus, Metzger was led to work increasingly for Christian unity, founding in 1938 an association, *Una Sancta*, to promote prayer for unity. Not surprisingly, a priest firmly opposed to war fell foul of the Nazis and Metzger was imprisoned first in 1939 and finally in 1943 until his execution for 'high treason' in April, 1944.

During his first spell in prison, Fr Metzger wrote a remarkable letter to the new Pope, Pius XII.[6] I give some extracts from this moving appeal to convey something of the spirit of this modern martyr:

> Holy Father! The need of our day – and through it God is speaking to us – imperatively demands the utmost effort to heal the dismemberment of the Christian Church, to make Christ's kingdom of peace effectual throughout the world ... I hope Your Holiness will not take it amiss if I state – in all humility but in true frankness – what, in my opinion, has hitherto hindered the reunion of Christendom, and what must happen if the final desire of our Lord is to be brought nearer realization? ... The opinion of the best kinds among non-Catholic Christians is that a certain proud self-righteousness on our side prevents our acknowledging the faults and failings within our own Church, the sins and errors through which we share in the guilt of these divisions; it prevents that readiness to repent which, they say, we always exact from others. . . . Of course I do not agree with these criticisms . . . and yet it seems to me, from my wide experience, that this denial is not due to enmity, but to a deep inward mistrust. This can only be overcome when Church leaders, in all humility, examine themselves to see whether in the practice and defence of the rights of Church authorities, there may be sometimes an element of self-assertion which springs merely from the 'natural man' ...
>
> Anyone who is familiar with the inner development of the Churches separated from us will admit the truth of the following statement, that dogmatic differences – however serious and important – are not today the main element which hinders reunion. Much more important is the spiritual attitude on both sides. This cannot be settled merely by speaking

of 'truth' on the one side and 'error' on the other, for
it has often to do with tensions which are soluble
only in the universality of the one Church such as:
God or Man? Christ or the Church? Written Word
or Tradition? Grace or Works? Law or Liberty?
Justice or Love? Letter or Spirit? Law or Gospel? A
Sacramental or a Spiritual Religion? Popular Piety
or Higher Mysticism? A National Church or a World
Church?[7]

The first major call for an ecumenical stance by a Catholic
theologian came from a young French Dominican, Yves
Congar (1904–1995), named a Cardinal by Pope John
Paul II in the last year of his long life. Congar had
been brought up in Sedan close to the Belgian border,
where there was a strong Protestant presence and where
his closest friend was the son of a Reformed pastor.
These seeds were to bear fruit throughout his long life.
Congar's first book, *Chrétiens Desunis* (1937), provided
a theological background to the pastoral and spiritual
apostolate of Couturier. The positions of Metzger and
Congar in the 1930s and 1940s may not seem very
radical to post-Vatican Two Catholics, but in the post-
Tridentine Church they sounded an unfamiliar note.
Their biggest departure from received attitudes was
in their rejection of the view that the only way forward was through individual 'conversions' and in their
calling for steps towards the reconciliation of separated Churches. For the first time since the Reformation, Catholic theologians were treating the Protestant
Church communities as Christian entities communicat-
ing, albeit imperfectly, the life of grace. In another seminal book *Vraie et Fausse Réforme dans l'Eglise* (1950),[8]
Congar addressed the touchy subject in pre-Vatican Two
Catholicism of the constant need of the Catholic Church
for reform.

The Lay Apostolate
Also important in the decades preceding Vatican Two
was the growing importance attached to the laity in

the Catholic Church. This development received impetus
from Pius XI, who is often called the Pope of Catholic
Action, for he saw the mobilization of the laity as an
essential counter-move to the advance of secularism. It is
from the time of Pius XI that movements like the Legion
of Mary and the Young Christian Workers took their rise.
It was also Pius XI who canonized St Thérèse of Lisieux
(1873–1897) and held up her 'Little Way' of perfect love
as a model for holy living to all Catholics. The impact of
St Thérèse on Catholic life represented both a form of
popular spirituality touching all levels of the Catholic
laity and a piety focused on the love of Jesus.

The forty years from the accession of Pius XI in 1922
to the opening of Vatican Two were the years of the 'lay
apostolate'. This was envisaged as the enlistment of lay
people to help with the ministry of the hierarchy. Fr
Congar also contributed significantly to the promotion
of the laity through his major work *Lay People in the
Church* (1957).[9] One important aspect of Congar's work
was that it set the role of the ordained hierarchy in
relation to Christ as the way (and the means) and the
role of all the members of the body in relation to Christ
as the life, with the means being at the service of the
life. This was a step away from a pyramidical view of
the Church, and a stronger assertion of a servant view
of Christian ministry.

The pontificate of Pius XII (1939–1958) saw important
advances in official Church endorsement of these currents of renewal. Several encyclical letters of great weight
and richness affirmed and forwarded this renewing work
of the Lord: *Mystici Corporis Christi* (1943) treated the
Church, *Divino Afflante Spiritu* (1943) addressed the
Scriptures and *Mediator Dei* (1947) took up the liturgy
as the worship of the Church. All three letters prepared
in significant ways for the teaching and reforms of
Vatican Two.

In some other areas, Pius XII authorized smaller
advances, that nonetheless contributed to the long-term
growth of renewing groups: for instance, the Roman
Instruction of 1950 on the ecumenical movement, while

not exactly opening the door to full Catholic participation, did recognize the ecumenical movement as responding to a moving of the Spirit of God. Likewise, the Pope's address to the 1957 congress on the Lay Apostolate sought to promote greater lay involvement in the mission of the Church, but its perspective remained one of lay people being authorized to assist in the apostolate of the hierarchy; the area seen as proper to the laity was that of the transformation or consecration of society. A more theological understanding of the laity in the Church would await the work of Vatican Two. In the 1950s, Pius XII also initiated the worldwide reform of the Latin liturgy: in reforming the worship of Holy Week restoring the ancient Easter Vigil celebration of the Resurrection on Holy Saturday night; in reducing the eucharistic fast and in permitting the celebration of Mass in the evenings. These too were harbingers of things to come.

Chapter Eleven

Vatican Two and After

Pope John XXIII and the Council

Only three months after his election, the 77-year-old Pope John XXIII (1958–1963) announced the summoning of a General Council of the Bishops of the Catholic Church. The first for almost a century, and only the second since the Reformation, this event was described by the Pope as a 'sudden inspiration'. The expectations aroused by the Council were strongly influenced by the personality and personal impact of Pope John. He revealed a heart open to all; he spoke warmly of other Christians; he was clearly not afraid of change. He made it clear that the Council was to be pastoral in purpose, seeking a renewal of the Church that would increase its impact on the world. It was to be a **renewal** Council. The Pope himself prepared a prayer for Catholics to recite for the Council which began 'Renew, O Lord, Thy wonders in our day as at a new Pentecost'.

While the writing of documents, however good and inspiring, does not guarantee changed hearts and lives, the importance of the work of Vatican Two for Catholic renewal can hardly be exaggerated. First of all, the four-year process was a work of re-education and renewal for the bishops themselves. It was literally an eye-opener for many, especially from the English-speaking world, that had not played as large a role in the preparatory currents as the continental Europeans. Secondly, the resulting documents had official authority for the entire Catholic Church, and would thus serve as practical markers for many decades to come.

The key document that situates almost all the other

documents (there were 17 in all) is the Dogmatic Constitution on the Church, named like encyclical letters after
its opening Latin words, *Lumen Gentium*. The bishops
rejected a first draft that simply placed the hierarchy
before the laity to have a preliminary chapter on the
People of God, including both clergy and laity, before
treating in turn the hierarchy, the laity, the call of
all to holiness, and the place of religious. Other more
practical decrees on the lives of bishops, of priests, of
the laity, of religious had their doctrinal foundation
in *Lumen Gentium*. Here too was a recognition that
Christian believers in other Churches are within, though
imperfectly within, the one mystery of the Church. This
was further developed in the Decree on Ecumenism,
Unitatis Redintegratio, in which for the first time the
Catholic Church recognized the role of other Churches
in the salvation of their members.[1] This decree explicitly
committed the Catholic Church in communion with Rome
to the ecumenical movement. From this point, ecumenism
becomes a constituent element of Catholic faith, though
the full implications of this revolutionary change would
take many years to work out.

Another element in *Lumen Gentium* that was of great
significance for Catholic–Protestant rapprochement was
the rediscovery in Catholic teaching of the local church.
For many centuries, Catholic teaching on the Church
was almost wholly restricted to the universal Church,
the Church Catholic, and not much attention was paid
to the fact that in the New Testament, *ekklesia* also
refers to the local body of believers. Vatican Two helped
to restore a balance between the universal Church and
the local church, seeing the local church (the diocese),
not as a branch of a universal organization, but as a
manifestation locally of the one Church of Christ that
is universal and cosmic.

The Council sought to restore the Scriptures to the
centre of Catholic life. The role of the Bible was spelled
out in the Constitution on Divine Revelation, *Dei Verbum*,
which abandoned the widespread formulation of Scripture and Tradition being two (separate) sources of Divine

Revelation, for a much more nuanced view that sees Scripture and Tradition as inseparably intertwined. In this conciliar sense, Tradition means the whole life of the Church founded on the Word of God. All the Council documents began with a biblical foundation; *Dei Verbum* called for all theology to be fed by the Word, for 'the study of the sacred page is the soul of theology' (para 24). Further, 'easy access to sacred Scripture should be provided for all the Christian faithful' (para 22). Here particularly, the Council was opening up the well-springs of spiritual renewal, an initiative that has transformed the practice of countless Catholics across the world and awakened a new hunger for the Word of God.

While the subject of the Church in terms of Trinitarian communion formed the doctrinal focus of the Council, that of the liturgy provided the entrance point and the first sphere of practical application. It was in the reform of the liturgy[2] that the Conciliar Church found practical expression: in the opening up to vernacular languages so that the liturgy could be understood by all; in the revision of the lectionary to allow for readings from a wider selection of the Scriptures;[3] in the revision of the prayers and actions so that they would be simple and not require long explanations;[4] in the promotion of the active participation of the people in the diversification of liturgical ministries so that not everything is done by the priest; in the encouragement of corporate celebration over individual piety.

The Pastoral Constitution (a new designation) on the Church in the Modern World, *Gaudium et Spes*, took up the understanding of the Church as a pilgrim people in history on their way to the City of God and sought to understand the contemporary world, its societies, cultures and institutions in the light of Christian faith. 'At all times the Church carries the responsibility of reading the signs of the time and of interpreting them in the light of the Gospel' (para 4). This injunction was to inspire many Catholics of the immediately post-conciliar generation to bring a Christian motivation and framework to the work for justice and peace in the world.

Another important ingredient in the conciliar renewal found expression in the Declaration on Religious Liberty, that was the distinctively American contribution to the Council. The theologian who had made this development possible was Fr John Courtney Murray (1904–1967). This document removed the last planks beneath the old Catholic argument for the state suppression of heretical groups; the view that 'error has no rights' was replaced by the teaching that each person has rights, including the right to choose their religious faith and to exercise it.

The Post-Conciliar Period

The thirty years since the end of the Second Vatican Council have proved much more turbulent than anyone expected. Many factors have contributed to this turbulence: the growing uncertainties of the modern world; the shock for many Catholics of such radical changes after centuries of apparent stability; the heady excitement of a new freedom in the Catholic Church and the vigour of a thorough re-thinking and re-assessment of the entire Catholic tradition.

To many it appears that the 'progressive' victories won at the Council have been clawed back by Rome. To others the pontificate of John Paul II seems like a return to sanity after a spell of lawless indiscipline and experimentation. In fact, these thirty years have seen creative ferment as well as turbulence. Besides the new movements in the Catholic Church (to be described in the next chapter), there has been a marked heightening of lay consciousness. This has included a remarkable explosion of lay theological education, especially in the United States. Linked to this has been the rise of many lay ministries, both within the liturgy and outside in the spheres of catechesis and social concern.

The need to scrutinize 'the signs of the time' affirmed in *Gaudium et Spes* has encouraged Catholic reflection on significant trends in secular society and the bringing to bear upon them Christian convictions and values. One of the most important of these developments has

been liberation theology, which was the first indigenous
Latin American contribution to Christian teaching and
practice. Another has been the women's movement, particularly strong in North America, issuing in various
forms of feminism, raising the voice and asserting the
rights of women in a largely man-shaped world. Both
these currents within the Church represent Catholic
responses to secular movements, seeking to develop a
Christian and Catholic expression of the movement's
vision and ideals. This makes their development and
reception by the Church distinctively different from currents of exclusively Christian inspiration and vision.

In both cases, the reaction of the Church authorities
has been somewhat suspicious and cautious. While recognizing that there is a foundation in both the Scriptures
and the Church's tradition for social liberation and for
the affirmation of women's dignity, there is a concern
that these currents are deeply permeated by ideas that
are alien to the gospel: in the case of liberation theology
of a Marxist view of class conflict that encourages violent
revolution and of a materialist philosophy with a totally
this-worldly 'eschatology'; in the case of feminism of
asserting women's rights not simply in the face of men
but also in an autonomy from God in relation to the fruit of
her own body. Nonetheless, these are important currents
in the contemporary Church that cannot be excluded
from a consideration of renewal, for the Church cannot
legitimately refuse to recognize the truth that is in these
currents.[5]

Devotion to the Blessed Virgin that has long been a
distinctive mark in Catholic piety went through a period
of lessened intensity in the wake of the Council. The
bishops had narrowly voted to include the treatment
of Mary within the constitution on the Church, rather
than make this a separate document. The ecumenical
and liturgical progress made at the Council implied
the need for a reform in Marian piety that would not
abolish it (*Lumen Gentium* called for it to become more
biblical), and it was clear that there was a considerable
gap between the world of much Marian devotion and that

of liturgical and biblical renewal. During the pontificate
of John Paul II, with a more vigorous assertion of Catholic
distinctives and identity, there has been a marked resurgence in Marian piety; this upsurge also owes much to the
events in Medjugorje in Bosnia, where it is said that the
Blessed Virgin has been appearing regularly since 1981.
Marian apparitions have also been reported in several
other countries, including the Ukraine, Rwanda, Ecuador
and the United States. These milieux manifest both
elements of spiritual renewal (the messages associated
with these apparitions generally have a strong emphasis
on repentance) and of patterns of piety still often needing
biblical renewal.

The thirty years since Vatican Two demonstrate that
authentic renewal requires more than theological discussion and the issuance of decrees. The increasingly-
discussed question of 'reception' must mean more than
acceptance of ideas and more than outward obedience to
decrees. Renewal involves a whole interior reception of
the Word of God, a yielding to the Holy Spirit calling us
to holiness of life and deeper communion with one another
within the body of Christ.

What is becoming more evident in the 1990s is that (1)
much of the Catholic Church has experienced an epoch of
major change, but has not yet experienced any depth of
renewal (this is an accurate perception of those Catholics
who decry the loss of the older devotional patterns); and
(2) nonetheless many currents of spiritual life and energy
have been released in the Catholic Church through the
conciliar reforms. In other words, there are real grounds
for great hope, and yet no reasons for complacency or
self-congratulation.

What are the signs of this release of new spiritual
energy and vitality in the Catholic world? First, the
Scriptures have been let loose in the Catholic Church –
through liturgical reading of the Scriptures in vernacular
languages, through the encouragement of Bible reading
and translations, through the gradual dissolution of the
widespread attitude that love of the Bible was somehow
Protestant. The result has been a new thirst for the

Scriptures among large numbers of Catholics and a corresponding surge of new life in the Church.

Secondly, despite an element of trivialization and banality in liturgical adaptations, there are an increasing number of places where a living liturgy is overcoming the gap that Rosmini and Beauduin deplored between official worship and authentic piety. Interestingly, this process of liturgical renewal is being matched on the Protestant and stream side by an increasing sense of a need for a corporate, embodied and sign-filled worship that goes beyond what has been called the 'hymn sandwich' and beyond the pattern in which the climax of worship is the sermon.

Thirdly, despite an undeniable element of increased centralization in the pontificate of Pope John Paul II (1978–), there has been a marked renewal in the style and the methodology of official Catholic teaching. John Paul II has issued many encyclical letters, all of which bear the imprint of his own thought, the combination of a Christian personalist philosophy and a profoundly meditative and more biblical–theological mind. One has only to compare for example the encyclicals on the Holy Spirit of Leo XIII (*Divinum Illud*, 1897) and John Paul II (*Dominum et Vivificantem*, 1986) or the documents on the laity of Pius XII (1957) and John Paul II (*Christifideles Laici*, 1988) to see the change and deepening that have taken place in Catholic teaching through this century of renewal.

Of particular significance, as John Paul II has recognized, has been the extraordinary explosion of new movements and new communities of faith in the Catholic world. This development, which in fact antedates the Council but which received a great boost from it, is of great importance for our topic, and will be the subject of the next chapter.

Chapter Twelve
New Movements in the Catholic Church

The determination of Pius XI (1922–1939) to mobilize the Catholic laity in order to combat the growing irreligion and atheism of secularist society, in effect European society, led to new Catholic efforts to educate and train lay people for what was commonly called 'the lay apostolate'. The laity were to be mobilized in what the traditionally Catholic nations called 'Catholic Action'. Catholic Action was always run by priests under the close supervision of the bishops.

Nonetheless, significant new movements began to emerge between the two World Wars that foreshadowed the later rise of more authentically-lay movements. The pre-World War II movements generally belonged, at least in their origins, to an established Catholic world that did not see the need for a profound renewal of the Catholic Church. They represented rather a harnessing of lay skills and energies for the defence and the spread of the Church and her values. This was the case with the Legion of Mary, founded in 1921 by an Irish layman, Frank Duff (1889–1980), who mobilized ordinary Catholic lay people for works of mercy, and the reclaiming of the lost. Governed by a handbook that prescribed every detail of the weekly meetings, the Legion of Mary appealed primarily to the less educated, for whom it provided an approved and effective tool for active service in the Church. Opus Dei, founded in Spain around 1928 by a priest, Josémaria Escriva (1902–1975), though having a priestly section, has a strong lay component among (mostly educated) Catholics seeking to lead a life of holiness in the world. The Opus Dei vision has been one of penetration of the world, especially the professions, with a spiritual message and motivation, though its spirit has been fairly hierarchical and somewhat secretive. Also dating from the pre-World War II period is the Schönstatt movement, founded in 1914 by a German priest, Fr Joseph Kentenich (1885–1968), with a strong Marian accent and the mark of much suffering (Kentenich exercised a remarkable ministry in the concentration camp at Dachau and was later in his old age exiled by church authorities to the United States for thirteen years).

One of the first Catholic movements to bear a more distinctively modern imprint was that of the Young Christian Workers (YCW), the 'Jocistes', founded by a Belgian priest, Joseph Cardijn, later Cardinal (1882–1967). Cardijn was deeply impressed from his seminary days by the need to bridge the gap between the Catholic Church and the working-class population. The movement really developed in the aftermath of the World War I. He insisted that religion not be separated from life, and sought to make young Catholics apostles to their world. Adopting a methodology of 'See, Judge, Act' applied to both the Scriptures and to their life-situations at home and at work, the YCW engaged in evangelism and formation in a way that encouraged initiative and a Christian penetration of working milieux.

The new Catholic movements that were more distinctively renewal-orientated, bringing the Scriptures and a vital Christ-centredness back to the Catholic people, began to appear after the World War II. One of the first was the **Focolari** movement, begun in war-torn Italy at Trent in 1943 by a young woman, Chiara Lubich (1920–), who heard a call to life-long celibacy for the sake of the kingdom. Chiara Lubich wrote of that time: 'We were very young, yet at any moment we could have lost our lives. The shelters we fled to were not safe from the bombs . . . Whenever we went into the shelters (up to twelve times a day) we took with us the Gospel.'[1] Chiara was led first to 'Not every one who says to me, "Lord, Lord" shall enter the kingdom of heaven, but he who does the will of my Father who is in heaven' (Matt 7:21), and then to 'A new commandment I give to you, that you love one another;

even as I have loved you, that you also love one another'
(John 13:34).

As the first Focolarini grew in love for one another,
they grew in love for the Lord Jesus. 'By practicing
among ourselves mutual and constant charity, we had
God to help us understand better the words of revelation.' The Focolarini emphasize love for the crucified and
abandoned Jesus. Another Scripture verse that spoke to
Chiara Lubich was the prayer of Jesus to his Father 'that
they may all be one; even as thou, Father, art in me, and
I in thee' (John 17:21). The Focolari movement quickly
spread to other European countries, and later to other
continents. Until 1960, it was an exclusively Catholic
movement, but then they met some German Lutherans
and shared something of their vision and experience. As
a result, the Focolari movement began to spread among
Lutherans, and has since spread to many other Churches,
including the Orthodox. As Chiara Lubich has written:
'We want to have together with them, Jesus in our midst.
If we are baptized, Jesus can be in the midst of us. And
one thing is certain: the greatest theologian is Jesus. If he
is in our midst, he is there not only as love, but as truth.'
By 1987, over 30,000 other Christians across the world,
including 13,000 Lutherans and nearly 8,000 Anglicans
were living the spirituality of the Focolari movement.

A Catholic movement that had an element of papal
inspiration in its origins was the **Movement for a Better
World** (*Movimento per un Mondo Migliore*), founded by
an Italian Jesuit, Fr Riccardo Lombardi. In the years
after the devastation of World War II, Pope Pius XII
returned time and time again to the theme of spiritual,
moral and social reconstruction. In February 1952, the
Pope said: 'It is an entire world we must remake, from
its foundations – that we must transform from savage to
human, from human to divine; that is to say, according
to the heart of God.'[2] Fr Lombardi heard this message as
a call from the Lord, and in 1953 he held two meetings
each with a hundred priests, from which a course 'for a
better world' was formed that became the major training
instrument of the new movement. This course, which was

based on the doctrine of the Church as the Mystical Body of Christ, had three main parts: I: General; II: Individual renewal; III: Reform of collective action.[3] The Movement for a Better World never involved membership, but represented rather a vision and an inspiration communicated by retreats and courses and promoted at their major centre just outside Rome.

Several modern Catholic movements were founded with a clear vision for the evangelization of nominal Catholics, those who in the words of Cardinal Suenens had been 'sacramentalized' but not 'evangelized'. One of the first and most effective was the **Cursillo** movement, begun in Majorca, Spain in 1949 by a retired bishop, Mgr Juan Hervas y Benet (1905–1982). The Cursillo, literally 'short course,' was a three-day residential gathering, generally for thirty to thirty-five people at a time, to present them with the foundational truths of Christianity (the full title for the movement was 'Cursillos of Christianity').[4] The initial aim was that participants would have a living experience of basic Christian faith, that was both personal and corporate. The first day focused on the message, the second on the faith-response of conversion, and the third on the faith lived out in the world.

The Cursillo movement spread beyond Spain in 1953 and first reached the United States in 1962 (their *Leaders' Manual* was first translated into English in 1964). Since then, it has spread rapidly in the English-speaking world, and been welcomed into some other Churches, particularly the Anglican communion. Cursillo has never aimed at forming permanent separate Cursillo communities distinct from the local parishes, but offers ongoing courses ('Ultreya') to deepen conversion and promote a Christian animation of society.

Another Catholic movement aimed at evangelization of the nominal Catholic arose also in Spain. This was the **Neo-Catechumenate,** founded by a layman, Francisco ('Kiko') Arguello, in a shanty town near Madrid in 1964. Kiko Arguello went to the poor armed solely with a Bible, a crucifix and a guitar, planning to live among them in the spirit of the French Sahara hermit, Charles de

Foucauld (1858–1916). Neo-Catechumenate grew out of this experience of sharing the gospel with the poor.

Unlike Cursillo, Neo-Catechumenate does seek to establish permanent renewed communities of its members, an aspect that has proved controversial in some Catholic circles. Their message focuses on the proclamation of the resurrection of Jesus, as the offer of new life in the New Adam; on the way of faith and conversion; and on the community as the realization of the Church. Conversion is seen, not as a single and decisive experience, but as an increasing turning to God and a growing aversion from sin. The catechesis from the Word of God aims to bring a knowledge of the one God, an awareness of sin, and the discovery of the glorious cross as the destruction of death.

A Catholic movement that has had a profound influence in Poland is known as **Light-Life** (LL). Its founder was Fr Franciszek Blachnicki (1921–1987), who experienced a conversion while under sentence of death in a Nazi camp during World War II. Ordained a priest in 1951, Fr Blachnicki was put in charge of organizing retreats for boys who served at Mass. He worked out a new form of two-week retreat to present a way of following Jesus in their daily lives. In 1957, Fr Blachnicki began a national crusade for abstinence from alcohol, the success of which earned him a year's rest in prison. He continued to work on Oasis retreats for renewal of faith, finding support for a biblically-based renewal in the documents of Vatican Two. The developed movement was named Light-Life in 1976: it sought first to lead people to Christ, so that they could receive him and accept him as Lord of their lives. Secondly, LL led converts to a new maturity in love of Christ and service of others. Thirdly, it sought to create a new environment animated by Christian love. The renewed community of faith would give rise to a new faith-based culture. He saw that Catholics could learn about effective evangelization from evangelical Protestants, and in 1975 embarked on a close collaboration with Campus Crusade for Christ. After accusations of 'Protestant penetration of the Catholic

Church' made against LL had been dismissed by an official Church commission, among whose members was the Cardinal Archbishop of Krakow, now Pope John Paul II, Fr Blachnicki defended this co-operation, arguing that the ecumenical movement was in an impasse because 'attempts at Christian unity had become separated from the process of renewal of the Church and evangelism'. Blacknicki's grasp of this link between ecumenism and evangelism affirms one of the threads running through this book.

Fr Blachnicki fought a running battle with the Communist authorities for many years. During the severe winter of 1977, he was not allowed to buy coal for heating the LL centre in southern Poland; so he sent out an appeal to all members and thousands of small parcels each containing a piece of coal began to arrive at the village post office. In fact, LL thinking came to provide the spiritual basis for much of the Solidarity movement, that played so great a role in the resistance to Communism and paved the way for a non-violent revolution in 1989.

A spiritual renewal movement that began quite slowly was the **Foyers de Charité** (FC), literally Homes of Love, begun in 1936 at Chateauneuf-de-Galaure in the Drôme department in South-Eastern France. FC represents the dissemination of the spiritual teachings and life of a remarkable mystic, Marthe Robin (1902–1981), who ate nothing except the eucharist after 1928 and who in 1930 received the stigmata of Jesus's wounds in her body, in a mysterious way re-living the passion, death and resurrection of Jesus each week for fifty-one years.[5] Marthe Robin was convinced that the Lord would send her a priest to lead the work that became FC. This priest, Fr Georges Finet (1898–1990), came in February 1936, when Marthe prophesied to him that the Lord would send upon the Church 'a new Pentecost of love', preceded by a renewal and a purification of the Church that would launch a great missionary thrust in which many lay people would be involved.[6]

The FC movement, established by Fr Finet under Marthe Robin's inspiration and guidance, consists of a network of homes, in which lay men and women consecrated to the celibate state live a life of love, service and unity under the leadership of a priest. FC emphasizes both union with the crucified Jesus and acceptance of the spiritual motherhood of Mary. Marthe Robin heard the Lord tell her: 'I want all the members of this work to be saints, who will through the example of a deeply supernatural life and the constant exercise of love radiate their dedication in every trial through the gift of self to each one and to all in a total self-giving to God.' The FC spread first in France and in the French-speaking countries in Africa, and have now spread to many other lands; they place a big emphasis on evangelization, on teaching retreats open to the public and on hospitality.

Another significant movement in contemporary Catholicism is called **Communion and Liberation** (CL). CL grew out of a youth movement among students begun in Milan in 1954 by a young priest, Luigi Giussani (1922–). The transition to CL occurred with the student unrest of 1968 when the students involved had moved from secondary school to university. Unlike other Catholic organizations in Italy, CL was not divided into male and female sectors. Giussani grappled with the essence of Christianity and how to communicate it to the student world. He focused on Christ as the centre of the cosmos and of history and on the community of the Church as the locus of Christ's presence in history. Unlike Cursillo and the Focolari, the thrust of CL has been more on the public than on the private. Jesus Christ is placed at the centre, and the Christian has to know Christ as the centre; but CL has refused to accept the privatization of Christian faith, so that each Christian is encouraged to take hold of Christ as life for the whole person understood as essentially person in society. So Giussani and CL have built up a vision for the creation of a new Christian culture through evangelization understood as the proclamation of Christ to the whole person and a whole society. The title indicates liberation through and for communion.

Unlike many other Catholic movements, CL does not have formal membership. Participation is by personal involvement in meetings and groups animated by the ideals, priorities and vision of CL. This leads to a shared experience of Christ in the Church, and this regular shared experience and resulting personal bonds are what really constitute CL as a coherent movement.

CL was largely restricted to Italy until the mid-1980s, when it began to spread to other European countries and to the New World. It is not the largest Catholic movement in Italy, but it is almost certainly the most influential and probably the most controversial. Because of its emphasis on the transformation of public life, many members of CL have become involved in Italian politics, and CL is seen in some quarters as yet another instance of Church interference in the political arena. However, the primacy of the spiritual is very clear in the teachings of Giussani, who has sought to embody in CL the theology of the Swiss scholar Hans Urs von Balthasar (1905–1988), perhaps the most important and spiritually creative of modern Catholic theologians. At the heart of CL, there is a group of celibates, called **Memores Domini,** people who live the memory of the Lord, sharing all things in common, living together in small communities and working in the world, while being committed to chastity, poverty and obedience, but without wearing religious habits or taking any explicit vows.

A quite different Italian movement is the **Community of Sant' Egidio,** that dates back to a meeting of Roman high school students during the disturbances of 1968. About a dozen young men and women sensed that they could no longer live their lives for themselves. They discovered life in the Scriptures, and felt they were to live out the gospel in solidarity with the poor. The community now numbering over 15,000 members is named after the convent chapel in Trastevere where its members have gathered each evening for more than twenty years. Cardinal Martini of Milan has said of them: 'What impresses about Sant' Egidio is its unique integration of a profound sense of prayer and Scripture with an intelligent commitment to the poor and to difficult issues of social justice.' Like the other modern Catholic movements described here, Sant' Egidio has rediscovered the primacy of God's Word and the necessity for explicit evangelization. As a Catholic movement, Sant' Egidio has sought to express their rekindled faith in a revitalized liturgy that restores and deepens their sense of the Church that is to be a light to the world. Perhaps more explicitly than any of the other new Catholic movements, Sant' Egidio reflects the implementation in pastoral practice of the Vatican Two documents on divine revelation, the liturgy, the Church, and the Church in the modern world.

Their commitment to the poor and to social justice attracted world media attention when a peace accord was signed in Mozambique between the official government and the rebels as a result of lengthy and patient mediation by members of the Sant' Egidio Community. This diplomatic activity did not represent a departure from their vision or the adoption of a political stance. Their work for peace in Mozambique arose out of their service to the poor in that country. They grieved over the disastrous effects of the war. They began to meet with the leaders of each side, listening, taking each person seriously; in this they discovered the power of the peace that resides in each committed Christian and specifically in the Christian community. They have since been actively involved in trying to bring an end to social strife in Algeria, through a similar seeking first to meet and then to bring together all the parties in conflict. To date, the Algerian government have been reluctant to enter such negotiations.

This survey of the rise of lay movements in the Catholic world of the twentieth century manifests first an accelerating tempo; more and more initiatives for the spiritual renewal and the mobilization of the laity have been springing up as the century has progressed. Secondly, it is clear that the Second Vatican Council has been a major catalyst in this regard; it has provided both the inspiration and the theology for lay engagement rooted in the baptism common to all rather than in any delegation from Church authority. Thirdly, it is clear that a large number of these movements have a vision for spiritual renewal to lead to the transformation of society and culture.

PART IV
LOOKING AT BOTH TOGETHER

Chapter Thirteen

Similarities and Differences

It is a mark of the virtually total opposition of the world of the life-streams, the Evangelical world we might call it, and the Roman Catholic Church, that the history of currents of spiritual revival in the one has been almost totally unknown in the other. The self-understanding of each 'side' has, at least until recently, precluded the possibility of recognizing authentic reviving and renewing works of the Holy Spirit on the other side. This should be a salutary and shocking reminder of the extent to which blinding prejudice can affect even the most godly and zealous of believers in Christ.

In fact, each side has nourished and been inspired by remarkable men and women of deep faith in Jesus Christ. Think of those who were almost exact contemporaries, but who are hardly ever considered let alone admired by the same people:

Alphonsus Liguori (1696–1787) and John Wesley (1703–1791)
Jean Vianney (1786–1859) and Charles Finney (1792–1875)
Cornelia Connelly (1809–1879) and Phoebe Palmer (1807–1874)
John Bosco (1815–1888) and Charles Haddon Spurgeon (1834–1892)

Similarities

After reading the outlines of revivalist streams in the Protestant world and of renewal currents in the Roman Catholic Church over the past 250 or more years, it will

be evident that there are not only differences between the
two sides, but there are significant and perhaps remarkable similarities. No doubt, some of these similarities are
simply signs of modernity, with both sides adapting to
and using the patterns and skills of the modern world.
Yet it should be clear that the similarities cannot credibly
be reduced simply to parallel forms of modernization.
Rather, the most important similarities lie in the con-
stellation: Christ–Gospel–Bible–Laity/all believers.

The Centrality of Christ and the Gospel
Both sides, the life-streams in the Protestant world and
the renewal currents in the Roman Catholic Church,
have emphasized the centrality of Jesus Christ and
his atoning work on the cross. A sharp focus on Jesus,
cross and atonement leading to repentance and personal
experience of conversion has always been one of the
major characteristics of evangelicalism. However, the
great Catholic preachers, epitomized by St Alphonus
and St Paul of the Cross, preached constantly on the
great love of Jesus the Saviour for all sinners. The same
message was conveyed by preachers of devotion to the
Sacred Heart of Jesus.

There was of course a great difference in style and context between the evangelical and the Catholic expressions
of devotion to the Saviour and the ways in which the
grace of the cross was received. On the Catholic side, the
closest parallel to the evangelical preachers is found in
the religious orders involved in the preaching of parish
missions. Preaching during parish missions was significantly different from and generally of higher quality than
the regular preaching of the parochial clergy.

Catholic mission preachers held up the crucifix before
a congregation that would not have been avid readers of
the Bible; the evangelical preachers held up the Word in
a church before a bare cross that received little attention.
Catholics focused their message of the love of the Saviour
for sinners and the message of atonement on the symbol
of the Sacred Heart of Jesus. Protestant preachers would
have eschewed all symbols and 'special devotions'.

Nonetheless, both sides had a great horror of sin and preachers both Protestant and Catholic graphically depicted the horrors awaiting the unrepentant sinner (Whitefield and Liguori were both renowned for this). Both were concerned that the repentant sinner stay repentant and not fall back into sin. This was consistently so, despite each side having a prejudicial view of the other on this point: Protestants denounced Catholic confessional practice as being indulgent to the sinner, as if frequent confession were a substitute for a change of heart; Catholics often interpreted Protestant teaching on justification by faith as condoning sin as long as you believed, with an occasional appeal to the famous saying of Luther 'pecca fortiter' (sin more strongly). The truth is that both sides knew so little about the real practice and convictions of the other that prejudice dominated and vitiated any interaction between them.

Catholic preaching was no doubt less concerned to produce a particular pattern of subjective experience, and more directed to eliciting a particular pattern of practice (sacramental confession and reform of life). But perusal of mission-type sermons shows clearly that preachers did look for and encourage an experiential piety.

Despite the almost total mutual exclusion and isolation, the points of commonality were such that occasionally something passed from one side to the other, generally from the Catholic to the Protestant, without any real lowering of the barriers. This can be seen from both hymns and books. One Catholic preacher in England, Frederick W. Faber (1814–1863), was as prolific with hymns as with devotional books: and some of the former found their way into evangelical hymnals. The French Catholic writers, Archbishop François Fénelon (1651–1715) and Madame Jeanne Guyon (1648–1717), who were both suspected by the Catholic authorities of Quietistic tendencies, both found a following in Holiness circles, as did *The Spiritual Combat* of the Italian, Fr Lorenzo Scupoli (1529–1610).

The Bible
Whereas the Protestant revivalist streams have always

upheld the Bible, and promoted Bible reading for all converts, regular reading and study of the Scriptures among
Catholics has largely been a twentieth-century development, the fruit of movements of renewal. The more scholarly currents of theological and liturgical renewal have all
advocated a shift from a more scholastic and metaphysi-
cal method to one that is more biblical and historical. But
the same has been true at the practical level of the popular Catholic movements such as the Focolari, Cursillo,
Light-Life, Neo-Catechumenate and Sant' Egidio. These
movements have typically introduced Bible reading and
study into their formation programmes.

The dogmatic constitution on Divine Revelation at
Vatican Two, *Dei Verbum*, encouraged for the first time
easy access of all the Catholic faithful to the Holy Scriptures, and encouraged co-operation with other Christians in the provision of translations (para 22). This
abandonment of old Catholic cautions about an 'Open
Bible' has launched what is in effect a revolution in
Catholic piety. There is a whole new thirst among Catholics for the Scriptures, aided perhaps by the vernacular liturgy and a wider range of biblical readings at
Mass. Popular Catholic publications such as *The Word
Among Us, God's Word Today, The Bible Today* and *Bible
Alive* (from the English-speaking world) that offer aids
to Bible reading and study, have proliferated and found
a huge market. This revolution has removed one great
barrier at the level of popular piety, and has made
possible new forms of sharing between Catholic and
Protestant in house–neighbourhood groups and Bible
studies.

The Laity

One of the most striking features of these currents of
spiritual revival and renewal among both Protestants
and Catholics is their predominantly lay character. It
is true that here the Catholic pattern lagged behind the
Protestant: the lay character was marked from the origins
of Evangelicalism, but intensified in the nineteenth century (Bible societies, youth movements, faith missions).

Within Catholicism, however, this lay thrust is largely a twentieth-century development.

By 'lay character' is meant first, the enlivening and empowering of ordinary Christian believers; secondly, that both the streams and many of the new lay Catholic movements have a mass dimension, as they are touching large numbers of people. In this, they are different from smaller church groups that form a kind of spiritual élite.

The egalitarian and mass character of the four streams is clearest in their origins and their earliest development. All four streams have also experienced later currents of reinvigoration of the stream's life: later waves in evangelical revival; new thrusts towards Holiness living and teaching; new waves of Pentecostal power (like the New Order of the Latter Rain) and new thrusts in the charismatic stream (now evident with the 'Toronto blessing' and associated currents). These spurts of revitalization all manifest the egalitarian aspect of touching all kinds and states of Christian believer.

The new Catholic movements of the past half-century vary in their ethos, their emphases and their style. Some have a more pronounced lay character than others: this is obviously true of those founded by lay Catholics, e.g. the Focolari, Sant' Egidio and Neo-Catechumenate; but some movements founded by priests have a firmly lay character, often because they envisage a strong element of insertion in the contemporary world, e.g. the Young Christian Workers, Comunione e Liberazione, the Movement for a Better World.

Clearly, one major difference between the streams in the Protestant world and the new movements in the Catholic Church concerns ecclesial insertion. The Catholic movements are only such as they find their place within wider Catholic life; full insertion in the historical–institutional Church is an integral part of their vision. By contrast, many stream organizations, e.g. the Lausanne conferences, Keswick, the International Charismatic Consultation on World Evangelization, have at the most a goal of serving the Churches, but are not 'inserted' in the Church. They belong more to a particular stream (evangelical, Holiness or charismatic) than to any particular Church.

The most interesting similarity between streams and the Catholic Church may lie in the international agencies that have sprung up in the global village of the last generation. Both the major stream agencies (mentioned in chapter six) and the largest Catholic organizations (mentioned in chapter twelve) are international movements with a regular flow of personnel and resources across national and continental boundaries. Most of the stream agencies have their origins in the United States, while a majority of the Catholic organizations have their roots in Europe. Both tend to have an orientation towards youth and devote energy to Christian formation, often called discipleship training in the stream side. Being international and multi-cultural, they exist on a scale that is not easily rivalled by mainline Protestant church agencies that are typically limited to their nations of origin.

It is surely significant that the major break-throughs in Catholic–evangelical co-operation came through the modern international lay organizations, Campus Crusade and YWAM and that in one major instance it was the Catholic movement Light-Life in Poland, with which they both co-operated. Not only do these international agencies manifest greater organizational flexibility than denominationally-controlled bodies, being able to deploy resources wherever the need and the openness are, but they are freer of theological restraints coming from the doctrinal battles of past centuries.

It would seem then that the inter-denominational agencies like Campus Crusade and YWAM accurately reflect the character and giftedness of the streams, which are themselves inter-denominational. Maybe there is some parallel here on the Roman Catholic side, in that the new Catholic lay movements are perhaps the groupings that represent most fully the renewing gift of the Lord through the Second Vatican Council. Some prominent Catholics would dispute this, being concerned that many

of the new Catholic movements are insufficiently rooted
in the local church, are too exclusive and have exaggerated views of their own importance and centrality.
However, there is no doubt that Vatican Two called for
a participatory active and committed laity; and that
the movements provide this in a way that the constant
efforts at parish renewal find very difficult to achieve.
It is in this sense that the lay movements may be
most characteristic of the post-Vatican Two Catholic
Church.

Ecumenical or Inter-Denominational

The streams have typically begun as movements of new
life that spanned many denominations. The evangelical
stream has clearly retained that multi-denominational
character within the Protestant world. Some streams
have spawned new denominations, often because of
Church resistance to their message. In the case of the
Holiness stream, this happened to a considerable degree;
but with the Pentecostals the rejection was more total.
If a new life-stream becomes largely denominationalized,
then it loses much of its ecumenical potential and it
also tends to lose its lay character, as denominations
are typically led by ordained officials.

On the Roman Catholic side, the currents of renewal
have had an ecumenical dimension from an early stage,
as can be seen in the remarkable pioneering work of
Dom Lambert Beauduin in both the liturgical and the
ecumenical movements. However, given the practical
isolation of the Roman Catholic Church in the early twentieth century, the ecumenical dimension was expressed
more in contacts, writings and friendships than in public
inter-Church collaboration and discussion. The story of
the Catholic–Anglican Malines Conversations in the
1920s illustrates the limits of what was then possible
and the hostile climate that had to be overcome before
regular and public dialogue could begin.

However, with the ecumenical break-through at the
Second Vatican Council, the door was open for renewal
circles in the Catholic Church to move beyond initial

theological sympathy to take on a genuinely ecumenical component. This can be seen in the Focolari movement, which since the 1960s has developed Orthodox, Anglican and Lutheran sections; and in the Cursillo movement, which has found a welcome in the Anglican (Episcopal) Church. Other Catholic movements, like Light-Life, have welcomed training input and expertise on evangelism from evangelical sources. This inter-action is of course particularly marked in sections of the Catholic Charismatic Renewal.

The Differences

Ecclesiology
One of the most obvious differences between the Protestant and the Catholic developments is that the stream patterns among Protestants tended to be inter-denominational (or non-denominational), while the Catholic initiatives were founded within the Catholic Church as Catholic organizations or movements. This is not simply an organizational variation but reflects a fundamental difference concerning the centrality and the understanding of Church.

The Catholic (and Orthodox) understanding of the Church is strongly liturgical and sacramental, so that the Church on earth, which is both visible and invisible, is most fully present and manifest in the liturgical assembly gathered in Christ to worship the Father and to be fed by Word and sacrament.[1] The Church is an organic reality in which the members are included and bonded by enacted rites that express the faith and creed of the Church. The Catholic conception of Church is then truly earthed and anchored in the social reality of an identifiable people with an unbroken history. While the theologically essential elements of the Church are the liturgical-sacramental structures of ministry, teaching and worship, including the relations between the bishops and the Pope as bishop of Rome, the institutional dimension is ensured and regulated by a detailed system of canon law and official jurisdiction. Church renewal in the Catholic context always involves subordinating the legal-jurisdictional to the theological-liturgical, and the theological-liturgical to the Word of God coming from Scripture through the Tradition.

In the Catholic understanding, the Church on earth (the Church militant) is in communion with the Church that has gone before, the saved who are in a process of purification (the Church suffering) and the saints in glory (the Church triumphant). Thus, Catholic preaching and devotional life, that inculcates devotion to Mary and the Saints, is an expression of communion in the one body of Christ; one of the most sensitive areas in Protestant–Catholic relations. In view of the extreme sensitivity of this topic, especially Marian devotions, in the Catholic–evangelical encounter, it is directly addressed in chapter twenty-four.

While it is not fair to claim, as some Catholics have done, that the revivalist streams have no concept of Church, it is true that it is not as central and all-pervasive as the Catholic conception. Where the revivalist streams have been more Church-conscious, Church has often been seen primarily as the fruit of evangelism more than as its agent.

In fact, it is one of the fruits of renewal that the world of the streams is learning to pay more attention to Church, just as renewal currents in the Catholic world have been transforming the understanding of Church from an institutional-administrative emphasis to one that is more biblical, organic and spiritual. However, more spiritual does not here mean opposing outward and inward, institutional and spiritual, but making the former the expression of the latter.

The differences over the role and the centrality of the Church can be illustrated from the contrast between the typically Protestant language of **revival** and the characteristically Catholic language of **renewal**. Both these terms are key terms in the self-understanding of the life-streams on the one hand, and of the modern Roman Catholic Church on the other hand. However, it should be noted that the language of renewal is also used in various mainline Protestant church circles. For, as we shall see, renewal is an inherently more Church-related term than revival. So some Protestant Churches with a solid evangelical constituency in their midst are familiar with both terms.

It remains true, however, that revival is a term characteristic of evangelicalism and the subsequent streams in a way that renewal is not. For revival has been a constituent element in evangelical, Holiness and Pentecostal identity, and these streams have always overflowed church boundaries, for the mainline Protestant Churches have not been able to contain them.

The language of revival emphasizes the sovereign activity of God. It belongs to a world with a Protestant accent on discontinuity, in which what really matters are the spasmodic and unpredictable interventions of a sovereign God. Renewal by contrast points to a world of continuity, in which the organic body of Christ is built up and purified through the march of history.[2] Something of the flavour of this view of God's work through the ages appears in Pope John Paul's Apostolic Letter on the third millennium:

> Seen in this light, the whole of Christian history appears to us as a single river, into which many tributaries pour their waters. The Year 2000 invites us to gather with renewed fidelity and ever deeper communion along the banks of this great river: the river of Revelation, of Christianity and of the Church, a river which flows through human history starting from the event which took place at Nazareth and then at Bethlehem two thousand years ago. (para 25)

In the evangelical Protestant world, so much shaped by revival and the longing for revival, there is a tendency to focus on the latest or the next move of God. This is exemplified in the language of **waves**, that implies that each new wave breaks after the one before has washed up on the shore. In this perspective, there may not always be much concern to relate each revival to the whole plan of God.

Individualist versus corporate

Stream thinking has tended to be strongly influenced by the individualist ethos of modern Western society. Indeed, the streams in their distinctive character since the 1730s have both reflected and capitalized on both the rationalism and the individualism of the Enlightenment and its aftermath. By contrast, the Catholic Church has preserved much more sense of the corporate character of the Judaeo-Christian tradition; as a result, Catholics shaped by this inheritance will see each person and grace in an historical framework of God's ongoing dealings with his people.

We can however overdo this contrast. It is not true for example that evangelical Protestantism has no sense of the corporate and is totally individualistic. There is a whole heritage from the Puritans of the centrality of the covenant and of the Church being a covenanted people, a sense that was stronger in this respect than in the Catholic public of that period. Nor is it the case that the Catholic Church has preserved untarnished a shining witness to the biblical vision of the body of Christ in which each member plays a vital part. As has been noted, the renewal of the Catholic tradition has involved a recovery of a more biblical vision of the Church that is both spiritual and visible, historical and meta-historical. In fact, Pope John Paul II has played an important role in bringing to the fore the concept of the human person who is essentially a social being related to other persons; in his teaching Jesus is the fulfilment of God's plan for the human person, and the Church the revelation of God's purpose for the human family. But this vision has yet to be brought alive in the minds and hearts of many Catholics, especially in the New World, where the forces of individualism and consumerism have made the deepest inroads.

Eschatology

Here too there are important differences between the
streams and the Catholic Church. The streams have
been the main seedbed for a rediscovery of hope in
the Second Coming of Jesus, though this is truer of the
nineteenth and twentieth centuries than of the eighteenth. By contrast, the renewing currents in the Roman
Catholic Church have to this point not paid much attention to eschatology, though more apocalyptic scenarios
have arisen in some milieux impacted by some Marian
apparitions.

The recovery of eschatological hope was particularly
associated with currents of the 1820s and 1830s that
initially had some mutual contact but subsequently
became antipathetic: the circle that gathered at Albury in
Surrey that led to the formation of the Catholic Apostolic
Church and the group that met at Powerscourt, near
Dublin in Ireland, that gathered most of the men who
spearheaded the rise of the (Plymouth) Brethren. Both
circles held several meetings centred around the theme
of prophecy. Edward Irving (1792–1834), the precursor
rather than the founder of the Catholic Apostolics, was a
remarkable theologian, who translated from the Spanish
a work on eschatology by a Jesuit priest, Fr Juan Lacunza
entitled *The Coming of the Messiah in Glory and Majesty*.
Here Irving rediscovered the millennialism of some of the
early Fathers of the Church free of the dispensationalism
and the rapture of the Church that came out of the other
circle formed by the Plymouth Brethren. The Brethren, influenced particularly by John Nelson Darby, were
more exegetical both in a more literal and in a more
figurative way, and were given to the erection of systems. From Darby came the system of pre-millennial
dispensationalism, with belief in the sudden rapture
of the saints prior to the thousand-year rule of Christ
on the earth. While the Brethren never became a big
movement within evangelicalism, their dispensational
teaching eventually won over most evangelicals, Holiness people and Pentecostals. Dispensationalism was
accompanied by a pessimism about the present world

and the possibility of societal change and improvement; the duty of the Christian was to keep oneself pure and await the deliverance of the rapture.

The world of the mainline Protestant Churches was never comfortable with the biblical exegesis, the system-building or the pessimism of the dispensationalists. Similar attitudes prevailed among Roman Catholics, although they were generally unaware of dispensationalism. Although the twentieth century has seen a number of important studies on eschatology by biblical scholars, these have had little impact on most church-goers. Outside evangelical, Holiness and Pentecostal circles, sermons on the Second Coming have been few and far between, despite this theme's prominence in all historic liturgies. Eschatology was largely abandoned to those dismissed as fundamentalist fanatics. It is interesting that there is more reference to eschatology in Pope John Paul II's letter on the Eastern Churches (*Orientale Lumen* of May 1995) than in his letter on preparation for the third millennium; this may reflect a deliberate concern not to encourage wilder speculation about the end of the world.

There have however been pockets outside the dispensationalist world where the Holy Spirit has been restoring a living hope for the second coming and the resurrection of the dead. We find this in the German Catholic writer Romano Guardini (1885–1968). Many have a connection with the Pentecostal and Charismatic streams: in France, Louis Dallière (1897–1976) and the Union de Prière;[3] in Germany, Mother Basilea Schlink (1904–) and the Mary Sisters of Darmstadt. In the Catholic Charismatic Renewal, Frère Ephrem and the Beatitudes Community (originally named Lion of Judah), who were influenced by the Union de Prière.

In general, it can be said that a living eschatological hope has largely been enkindled and preserved within the revivalist streams, though there it has been handicapped by an overly rationalist systematizing mentality that too easily shifts the attention from the core of the hope to the mechanics and timetable of its realization.

By contrast, the currents of renewal in the mainline Churches, Protestant and Catholic, have mostly been weak on eschatology, and have been unable to translate any scholarly perceptions into a living hope. The major exception is the charismatic stream, although here the eschatological hope intrinsic, I believe, to baptism in the Spirit has greater difficulty thriving in an unreceptive atmosphere than in the evangelical and Pentecostal worlds.

Chapter Fourteen

The Contribution of the Charismatic Movement

I t is the appearance and spread of the latest lifestream, the charismatic movement, that has dramatically altered the Christian landscape. This is important to recognize, as the significance of the charismatic movement often escapes Christian leaders and scholars, whether those who are not sympathetic to revivalist streams in general or those open to the earlier streams who can dismiss it as the least clearly-defined and the most ambiguous of the four streams. The radically new situation created by the rise and spread of the charismatic movement is manifest in the new milieux reached beyond those touched by the previous streams, in the distinctiveness of the new churches to which it has given rise and in its greater unitive potential.

The Same Gift in Different Contexts

The spread of Pentecostal-type blessing to the main-line Churches in the charismatic stream represents the transmission and eruption of the same blessing as the Pentecostals had known (and had called Baptism in the Holy Spirit) within the historic Churches that had previously ignored or rejected the Pentecostal movement. Anglicans and Lutherans, Presbyterians and Methodists, Baptists and Roman Catholics were now receiving the same gift, experiencing the same fruit, and exercising the same gifts common to the charismatic stream.

The testimonies concerning personal experience of the Spirit's work and the manner of reception together point to the identity of the gift conferred. While the terminology used naturally reflects the church background of the recipients, the witnesses to the work of the Holy Spirit in their lives are remarkably consistent. Those baptized in the Holy Spirit regularly report a new directness of relationship to God, including a new knowledge and love of Jesus as Saviour and Lord, new capacities to praise and to evangelize, the experience of spiritual gifts, a new hope for the second coming of the Lord. Thus, in the wake of the new charismatic stream, there arose spontaneously many forms of common worship, centred on praise; forms of shared ministry and witness; forms of common service; even new forms of inter-denominational community.

When Pentecostals or evangelical charismatics questioned the doctrinal orthodoxy and reliability of non-evangelical Christians baptized in the Spirit, the decisive argument was not doctrine but the evidence of the work of the Spirit. Several pointed out the relevance of the words of Peter in Acts 11:17: 'If then God gave the same gift to them as he gave to us when we believed in the Lord Jesus Christ, who was I that I could withstand God?' The coming of the Spirit should not lead to an indifference to doctrine, but to a sifting and deepening of the ways in which we have articulated Christian orthodoxy.

The Spread to New Pastures

Roman Catholics

When the charismatic movement spread to the Roman Catholic Church, in early 1967,[1] something explosive was taking place. For the first time in history, a spiritual movement that had begun outside the Roman Catholic communion was appearing within it and being accepted by Church authority. Such a remarkable development had been made possible by the Vatican Two Decree on ecumenism that had recognized the presence and work of the Holy Spirit in other Christian communions. Now less than three years after the close of the Council, Roman Catholics were being baptized in the Holy Spirit, often through the ministry of Protestant charismatics and of Pentecostals. What was immediately clear to the participants was that there was not a Catholic baptism in the Spirit different from that of Protestants and Pentecostals. These Catholics were being given a new directness of relationship with the risen Lord Jesus, a new love for him and his Word, a new ability to praise God and to bear witness with power, a heightened sense of the world to come, the experience of hearing the Lord and knowing his guidance, as well as shared experience of the spiritual gifts of 1 Corinthians 12:8–10. Not only did Catholics baptized in the Spirit know and do these things, as well as their Protestant brothers and sisters, but they found that they could do them together.

The challenge of these developments among Catholics was first felt by Pentecostals and Protestant charismatics. How could such things happen in Rome? Often the first reaction was that, if authentic, these Catholics would soon see the incompatibility of such biblical gospel life with Catholic dogma; they would then leave and join them in their world of pure biblical doctrine. But it was soon evident that the majority of renewed Catholics were not about to leave, and indeed, often to Protestant puzzlement, they manifested a heightened sense of commitment to their Church and to distinctive features of its tradition.

In general, the majority of Protestant charismatics welcomed the developments among Catholics, but this lead was only followed by a minority of the Pentecostals. Not only was baptism in the Holy Spirit 'their thing', but Pentecostals who were very missionary-minded were aware of having been harassed and persecuted by the Catholic Church in countries such as Colombia and Italy. Among the Pentecostals who courageously accepted and welcomed the charismatic renewal in the Catholic Church were Vinson Synan (1934–), the Pentecostal historian, now Dean of the theology department at Regent University in Virginia Beach, Virginia; the late Jerry Sandidge (1939–1992), a missionary to Belgium, who lost his missionary credentials for his commitment to Pentecostal dialogue with the Catholic Church; Cecil

M. Robeck (1945–), a professor at Fuller Theological
Seminary in Pasadena, California and now co-chair of
the Catholic–Pentecostal dialogue. I recall in particular
a moving moment at the European Charismatic Leaders
conference in Paris in 1982 when Alfred Missen (1916–),
former general superintendent of the Assemblies of God
in Britain, repented publicly for his anti-Catholic attitudes in the past and his walking out of the Fountain
Trust conference at Guildford in 1971 because of the
Catholic charismatic presence.

The Anabaptists

The charismatic stream has also brought a bridging of
another gap, between the life-streams and the Anabaptist
traditions of the Radical Reformation. There has been
extensive charismatic renewal among the Mennonites
and in the Church of the Brethren.[2] In fact, these
Churches in the United States have taken the charismatic renewal more seriously than other Protestant
Church leaders.[3]

The Anabaptist groupings, though sympathizing with
aspects of the evangelical and Holiness streams, had
never felt wholly comfortable with them. The reasons
for this discomfort were complex, but maybe were rooted
in their unease with the individualistic spirit of the
streams. The Anabaptist Churches have always maintained a stronger corporate witness, and a commitment
to an alternative lifestyle based on the ethos of the
Sermon on the Mount (non-violence, pacifism, refusal
of oaths, etc.). As the Mennonite C. Norman Kraus
has written: 'A . . . difference in orientation between
anabaptism and evangelicalism is denoted by the words
prophetic and *evangelistic*. American evangelicalism has
put great stress on evangelism, but very little emphasis
on prophetic witness.'[4]

Perhaps because the Anabaptist Churches are not very
large numerically – and they certainly do not receive
much publicity – the importance of the full entry of Anabaptist Christians and congregations into the charismatic
stream has not received much attention. It does however

contain the potential of a significant reconciliation and rapprochement between the Radical Reformation and the mainline Reformation Churches, that mostly persecuted the Anabaptists with as ruthless a vigour as the Roman Catholics.

Messianic Judaism

Of even greater significance is the rise of Messianic Judaism, which is also a fruit of the charismatic outpouring. This too has not been sufficiently noticed, perhaps because Messianic Judaism may have appeared at first to many Gentile Christians as simply a more successful new phase in evangelical Protestant missions to the Jews, for evangelicals have had for many decades a strong concern for Israel and her conversion.

In fact, Messianic Judaism, with the restoration of synagogues of Jews confessing and honouring Jesus as the Messiah within a framework of Jewish liturgical observance, represents a stunning new development that restores for the first time since the first Christian centuries a distinctively Jewish form of faith in Jesus the Christ. It represents a creative work of the Holy Spirit that is fundamentally corporate, not just leading individual Jews to faith in Jesus as Messiah, but establishing assemblies that observe the Jewish liturgical year and retain a Jewish identity.

The rise of Messianic Judaism is of enormous significance for Christian unity, first of all because the nature of the Christian Church according to Ephesians 3 is the union of Jew and Gentile in the one body. The Messianic Jews have in principle a potential to be a powerful catalyst in the overcoming of historic differences between Catholic and Protestant. For Messianic Jews are or ought to be at home with Catholic concepts of historical continuity, for it is part of Jewish identity to be a son or daughter of Abraham and to be part of a long genealogy; the Christian principle of liturgical commemoration, of Spirit-led memorial (*anamnesis*) of the acts of God in salvation history is rooted in Jewish tradition. On the other hand, Messianic Jews mostly come from evangelical

Protestant backgrounds that emphasize the centrality of personal conversion and of sovereign interventions of God for the history of the Church; their own existence is for them a new instance of divine intervention.

The New Churches

As mentioned in chapter five on the charismatic stream, the period since 1980 has seen an astonishing explosion of new charismatic churches in almost every part of the world. Most of these see themselves as in some way part of the charismatic stream. They contribute most to the newness of the charismatic stream by the ways in which they are different from independent evangelical churches and from the Pentecostals. These would generally include a greater sense of the corporate life of the Church, of the need to escape from the limitations of one-person pastorates to develop corporate leadership patterns utilizing a fuller range of gifts and ministries.

The Implications and Challenges of this Expansion

As noted above, through this fourth stream of divine life God has begun to bridge the divide between the life-streams and the Roman Catholic Church. It is the charismatic movement that has brought these two distinct worlds, the evangelical–Holiness–Pentecostal streams and the Roman Catholic Church, into a degree of inter-action. This bridging has such immense implications because these two worlds had been so far apart and so suspicious of each other that any rapprochement or positive exchange had been considered impossible. The implications of such a breakthrough, that are so deeply challenging to both sides, will inevitably take time and experience to grasp and later evaluate. Through this charismatic stream of new life appearing in both camps, the Lord is challenging both to rethink their mutual hostility and is calling them to mutual repentance. The challenges posed and the repentance required will be explored in subsequent chapters.

The appearance of the charismatic stream in the Catholic Church has not simply brought a new emphasis on the power and the gifts of the Holy Spirit. It has also given a distinctively evangelical thrust to the Catholic Chrismatic Renewal, particularly in those places where there are regular ecumenical expressions of renewal. This point underlines the connectedness of the four streams in the Protestant world, and the importance of the later streams not losing their grounding in their predecessors. Thus, the opening of the Catholic Church to the charismatic stream also includes an openness to receive the fruit of the earlier streams.

This bridging involves a coming together – necessarily tentative and provisional at first – of the complementary concerns of renewal and revival; of a valuing of historical continuity and the affirmation of sovereign interventions of a God of power; of Word and sacrament (or enacted Word); of charism and institution; of church authority and spiritual freedom; of liturgy and of free prayer; of gathered church and intentional community.

The Possibility of a Richer Theology of the Streams

The spread of the Charismatic stream to milieux not penetrated by the evangelical, Holiness and Pentecostal streams has opened up the possibility of a richer theology of movements within the Church. The earlier streams did not really develop an adequate understanding of their relationship to the Church and the Churches. Their theological self-understanding was largely limited to the terminology of **revivals**, and focused largely on the nature of revivals and whether or not they could be prepared or hastened.

Since evangelical and stream teaching has always had a strict insistence on a firm biblical basis, its theological understanding of contemporary works of the Holy Spirit has suffered from insufficient study of the modern data for fear of attributing more importance to them than to the Word of God. Thus significant elements in the Pentecostal stream such as its retrieval of physical expressions of the Spirit, its oral post-modern character, its playfulness and its spiritual rehabilitation of the masses have not received the same attention as more obviously biblical topics such as the relationship of baptism in the Spirit to conversion-regeneration and the spiritual gifts.[5]

The spread of the life-streams beyond the revivalist world makes possible a more challenging and exciting theology of the irruptive-invasive work of the Holy Spirit within and without the historic Churches. The theological traditions and tools of the new milieux reached can do three things that are very important for God's work through the streams: first, they can deflate the naive and exaggerated claims sometimes made for any new stream by those who do not recognize any authentic or significant work of the Holy Spirit anywhere else; secondly, they can point to the real originality and creativity of the new streams by a more accurate and careful study and reflection on their distinctive characteristics; and thirdly, they can bring wider historical perspectives that can enrich the revivalistic categories within which the streams are normally understood and commended.

The charismatic stream thus has a greater potential to demonstrate both to the revivalist traditions and to the wider Church that these streams in fact contain a deeper and richer reality than their proponents and defenders have often conveyed. This truth – that every work of God is deeper and richer than our human minds are immediately able to grasp – has been overshadowed by the rationalist and over-confident mood of much of the evangelical world.

Ecumenism and Renewal

The spread of the charismatic movement to the Roman Catholic Church also injected a strong new ecumenical thrust. Pentecostals as well as many Protestant charismatics had been deeply suspicious of the ecumenical movement, seeing it as a man-made attempt, deeply marked by liberal exegesis and theology, to patch together dying and emasculated churches. Catholic charismatics by contrast instinctively experienced their new fellowship in the Spirit with Protestants and Pentecostals as part of the ecumenical opening made possible by Vatican Two.

However, the charismatic movement has not up to this point had much influence on leadership within the ecumenical movement. Despite occasional efforts to get the World Council of Churches and some national Councils of Churches to take the charismatic movement seriously, not much progress has been made. Nonetheless some ecumenical progress has clearly been a fruit of the charismatic movement. The possibility of positive relations of any kind between Roman Catholics on the one hand and evangelicals and/or Pentecostals on the other hand is largely due to the spiritual fruit in Catholic charismatics, who manifest the signs of being converted and filled with the Spirit. It may be in turn that the growth of evangelical–Catholic relationships will help the theologians and church leaders who control the official ecumenical agenda to pay more attention to the newest and most dynamic of the life-streams and their ecumenical potential.

One of the Catholic contributions to this needed rapprochement is the tight link between ecumenism and Church renewal. This link was the hallmark of the ecumenical apostolate of the Abbé Paul Couturier and the heart of what he termed 'spiritual ecumenism'. Couturier's teaching was later endorsed by the Catholic bishops at Vatican Two and incorporated into the Decree on Ecumenism (paras 6–8). This accent on spiritual ecumenism, despite its endorsement by the Council, seems to have been lost in the ecumenical movement over the past twenty years. It has strongly reasserted in the recent encyclical of Pope John II on ecumenism (*Ut Unum Sint*, 1995). Indeed, it seems unlikely that it can be fully recovered without integrating within an ecumenical vision the contributions of the four life-streams that are so directly concerned with the revival and renewal of spiritual life.

For the charismatic movement to bear its full ecumenical fruit, it is necessary for the Catholic charismatics to affirm the movement's inherent ecumenical character and for the Protestant charismatics to accept fully their Catholic brothers and sisters in their Catholic identity. This is a battle that is still far from won. The temptations remain strong for the Catholics to develop a self-enclosed Catholic Charismatic Renewal that is only incidentally related to the movement in other Churches, and for the Protestants to welcome Catholic charismatics, but not to accept fully their Catholic identity. However, it is clear from many initiatives that a sense of the Spirit's move on all Christian flesh is deeply rooted in the charismatic stream, and that this impulse keeps resurfacing despite all discouragement.

Chapter Fifteen

The Differences between Church and Streams

I t will have been evident from the beginning of this study that there are major differences between on the one hand what I have called the life-streams in the Protestant world (evangelical, Holiness, Pentecostal and charismatic) and the ancient Churches on the other hand (especially the Catholic and the Orthodox). If there is to be positive interaction and effective collaboration between the two, it will be necessary to become more aware of these differences.

In effect, all the differences flow from the basic contrast between Churches, that are organic bodies organizing and expressing the total life of historic faith-communities, grounded in Word and sacrament, and streams as currents of life whose identity depends on common affirmation of basic principles and priorities, but which neither represent total faith-communities nor possess clear-cut boundaries.

All the differences between Churches and life-streams flow from this fundamental contrast between total faith-communities and movements characterized by a common vision and/or common emphases. These differences affect forms of participation, doctrine, worship, education and formation, ministry and missionary work.

Forms of Participation
All Churches have **members,** who have joined through specific forms of initiation. These forms of initiation, particularly in the historic Churches with liturgical traditions, are understood to mean much more than signing up in an association; they involve being marked or sealed

with the sign of Jesus' death and resurrection and being
granted a share in the heavenly inheritance of God's
people. By contrast, the streams as movements do not
have members or forms of initiation. The streams have
participants, who are the people who identify with the
basic characteristics of the movement. There are of course
many stream-type organizations, in which membership
may be by denomination or by congregations, such as the
National Association of Evangelicals (USA) or the Evangelical Alliance (UK), or in which membership may be on
an individual basis, such as the Evangelical Theological
Society and the Society for Pentecostal Studies. But it is
not membership of a body that makes one an evangelical.
People join because they are evangelical, not to become
evangelical. Thus Churches have procedures for becoming
members, that streams do not.

It should be noted that the streams as a characteristically modern phenomenon reflect in attitudes to
membership and participation features that typify much
of contemporary society, especially in the West: a much
greater mobility of population, a wider range of available
choices in almost every area of life, a greater reluctance
to make absolute and exclusive commitments. Thus, the
concept of participation is often vaguer and less clearly
defined for the charismatic movement than it was in the
early stages of the previous streams.

Doctrine
It is part of the character of a Church that it has a
belief-system, a set of doctrines that the Church confesses
and teaches. These doctrines are normally set forth in a
Creed or a Declaration of Faith, listing the beliefs characteristic of that Church. Membership normally depends on
acceptance and profession of the doctrines contained in
the Creed or Declaration. Life-streams by contrast have
something more limited; they will normally have some
doctrinal convictions that characterize the movement.
But these are generally a core of central convictions rather
than a complete Creed. The streams then have some
central doctrines that they emphasize, but they typically

allow a freedom over other issues perceived as less central. Thus, while evangelicals are typically strong supporters of the atonement understood in substitutionary terms, they do not have a particular position on matters like infant baptism or ministerial ordination, or a particular view of ministry, as a denomination is virtually forced to do. However, when streams spawn new denominations, as in the Holiness and Pentecostal movements for example, the new denominations have to adopt positions on the initiation of believers, the training and commissioning of ministers, etc. In this process, it is possible for a stream to become less movement-conscious and to lose some of its stream-characteristics in becoming more like other confessional families representing a communion of sister-denominations or Churches.

Worship
Similarly, Churches have particular patterns of worship, expressing their understanding of the stance of the believing community before the triune God. The historic Churches understand their liturgies to be expressions of the mystery of the Church, in which the Church on earth is united with the chorus of angels and saints before the heavenly throne. In the liturgical traditions, the forms of worship have been shaped over the centuries, while denominations with freer forms often have unwritten customs that strongly influence their order of worship. The streams on the other hand will have **distinctive emphases** in their worship, that reflect their stream-focus: thus evangelicals have always made the preaching of the Word central in their worship, and have developed forms of call to conversion and repentance, in altar-calls and decisions for Christ; Pentecostals and charismatics give prominence to expressive praise, and allow space for the exercise of spiritual gifts. Stream-participation is therefore quite compatible in itself with Church worship traditions, when the stream-focus is brought into the full pattern of a particular Church or denomination.

Education and Formation
The life-streams have typically given rise to new institutions for education and formation. It is not hard to see why this is so. The streams have been born out of revivals and reviving–renewing movements of the Spirit of God. Leaders in the streams want to pass on their emphases and convictions to coming generations. Colleges and seminaries may then be founded that are stream rather than Church or denomination-based. Such institutions are committed to the basic convictions and emphases of the stream (or a sub-section of a stream). In a society like the United States where many Christians are more committed to a stream emphasis than to a particular Church or confession, such stream institutions may be more attractive and offer more than those tied to a particular denomination.

Missionary Work
Churches form their own missionary work, seeking to plant their own Church tradition in new places. The greater the identification in its doctrine of the particular Church with the one Church of Jesus Christ, the greater will be the insistence on having its own missionary patterns and societies. There are also important differences between the Roman Catholic Church, that forms one Church organizationally at the world level, and historic Protestant Churches organized at the national level. With the latter, missionary work is obviously aimed at the eventual formation of new national Churches within their confessional tradition.

The streams, on the other hand, that have virtually all had a strong evangelistic and missionary thrust, have readily formed missionary societies. This is seen especially in the phenomenon of Faith Missions. However, such stream (non-Church) missions inevitably face the dilemma of what to do with the new congregations being formed as the fruit of their labours. The choice is generally either between on-going control from afar by the non-Church missionary agency, or the formation of a new denomination by the congregations formed by the mission in a particular country or region.

Authority

A difference that underlines all those listed above is the presence of structures of authority within the Churches and the absence of any authority within the streams. Each Church necessarily has some authority structure, whether it be episcopal, presbyterian-synodal or congregational in pattern. The streams as such cannot have any supervisory or organizing authority over a whole stream. At the most, they can have service bodies, such as the Evangelical Alliance, that seek to serve the evangelical stream in their territory; while such bodies can determine their criteria for association, the relationship of their officials to their stream public is one of service and is different from that of a Church leader, even in denominations with a federal or associational pattern at national level.

The Advantages and the Disadvantages of the Churches and the Streams

The Churches as total life-communities of faith have a definite physiognomy that is not present to the same degree in the less structured world of the life-streams. The Churches are thus more embodied; they have clearer structures. They are organized on a local level in parishes and/or congregations, at regional or intermediate levels in dioceses or districts and at national level in bishops' conferences (Catholic) and denominational structures (Protestant).[1] By contrast, the streams are fluid, existing both within the Churches and outside them.

The more clear-cut character and definite physiognomy of the Churches is both an advantage and a disadvantage. It is an advantage to have a more specific heritage and testimony: there is something very definite to communicate and to transmit to future generations. There is a richness in the ancient traditions that cannot be reduced to mere systems of conduct and spiritual know-how. On the other hand, the richness can become mere complexity. The highly detailed belief-system may hide more than it reveals the central life-giving truths of Christian faith.

By contrast, the streams have the advantage of a clear
focus on what is central and life-giving. They often convey
a sense of vitality compared to the fustiness and the dull
routine of much in the Churches.

The streams and stream-organizations generally have
a flexibility that the Churches rarely manifest. This can
be seen in Britain in the role played by the Evangelical
Alliance in the highly-successful Spring Harvest meetings that have gathered larger numbers of Christians
than any other regular events in the United Kingdom.
It can be seen in the imaginativeness and rapid diffusion
across the world of the March for Jesus. More recently the
immense appeal of Promise Keepers to men across North
America shows the drawing power of a movement for men
not limited to any particular Church tradition and based
on core gospel values upheld by the life-streams.

The New Churches

The new charismatic churches that have been springing
up in so many countries have arisen within the charismatic stream, and reflect the vitality and flexibility of
streams in full flow. But they are also more conscious
than many previous stream-groupings of the need to
build new and renewed believers into communities of
living faith and effective witness. They are thus in the
vanguard of 'church planting'. They are much concerned
with the question of Church. However, they are determined not to become new denominations, and so they
have been experimenting with forms of association and
fellowship that reflect a sense of Church beyond the
merely local level.

Thus, the new churches seek to have the flexibility of
the streams with the full lifestyle of Church. They want
to have the corporate life of the body of Christ, that the
streams can serve but in themselves are not. And they
want to avoid the bureaucratization and the routinization
of the denominations. Their leaders want to be apostles,
prophets, evangelists, pastors and teachers, not denominational officials, presidents of boards, chairpersons of

committees. In other words, the new churches are born
from the streams, in particular from the charismatic
stream, but have a clear desire to become more than
a stream, without losing the characteristic vitality and
freedom of the streams.

The Complementarity of Church and Streams

The fact that Church and streams are really quite different kinds of entity could paradoxically make it easier for
them to relate and to collaborate. For streams that do not
pretend to be Church are not claiming to be rivals. The
examination of the differences reveals not their inherent
opposition, but their need for each other. This mutual
need is shown by the renewing role that the streams
continue to play in the life of the historic Churches, as
well as by the longing of the new churches to be Church,
not established Church but Church as an organic body
that grows and moves.

The mutual need of Church and streams will be made
clearer through the challenges that they pose to each
other. These challenges of streams to Church and of
Church to streams will be examined in chapters eighteen
and nineteen. What is important to note here is that
the Church and the streams need each other, precisely
because they are not the same kind of entity. They are not
rivals seeking to defeat each other, but complementary
works of God that need each other in order to be fully
what God has called each to be.

Chapter Sixteen

The Two Divine Missions

T he relationship between Church and streams is perhaps one that we find difficult to approach theologically. The first half of this book has been largely devoted
to an historical summary to demonstrate the rapid spread
and increasing significance of the life-streams in world
Christianity at the same time as there has been inten-
sifying renewal in the mainline Churches, especially in
the Roman Catholic Church. Catholic theologians have
long attached great importance to the theology of the
Church, or ecclesiology, but few have examined the place
of currents of revival and renewal and their relevance
for ecclesiology.[1] Evangelical scholars have frequently
debated the theology of revivals, but these writings have
rarely been integrated into a theology of the Church.

It seems to the author that a promising line of approach
lies in the theology of the two divine missions, the mission
of the Holy Spirit and the mission of the Son. These two
missions are distinct, because the Holy Spirit and the
Son are distinct persons within the Trinity. But they are
integrally related, for the three persons that form the
divine Trinity constitute one God. Both these missions
exist eternally in the Trinity, but both have operated *ad
extra*, that is 'beyond' and 'outside' the Trinity in creation
and redemption. The nature of the two missions is not
changed by their extra-Trinitarian operations, for the
Spirit and the Son act in the created sphere in accordance
with their eternal inter-relationship and their eternal
relationship to the Father.

It is the Incarnation that reveals most clearly the
distinctiveness of the two missions of the Spirit and
of the Son, for it is through the Incarnation that the

Trinity is revealed. In the Incarnation, it is only by the
mission of the Spirit that the Son takes on human flesh,
and is conceived of the Virgin Mary, as the Apostles'
Creed states. It is only by the Spirit that the Son can fulfil
his earthly ministry that commences with his baptism in
the Jordan. It is only by the Spirit that Jesus is raised
from the dead. At no point in Jesus' life and ministry is the
Holy Spirit not present and active, though the presence
of the Holy Spirit in Jesus intensifies and is made more
visible with his baptism (Luke 3:22; 4:1) and even further
with his resurrection from the dead (Acts 2:33).

Yet, it is only the Son that takes on human flesh and
enters human history. The Holy Spirit is active at every
point in this process, but the Spirit does not enter and
belong to human history in the same way as the Son who
acquires a human nature. The Holy Spirit is always sent
from heaven; in Acts 2:33 we are told that the glorified
Jesus, exalted to the right hand of God 'has poured out
this which you see and hear'. Earlier 'a sound came from
heaven like the rush of a mighty wind' (Acts 2:2).

One consequence of the Son, but not the Spirit, becoming incarnate, though the Spirit is the instrument of
incarnation, is that there is an **immediacy** about the
work of the Holy Spirit, whereas the Son who has become
man through the Spirit becomes the **mediator**. It is the
presence and activity of the Holy Spirit that rightly
grounds the conviction of revivalistic stream Christians
that they are experiencing an immediacy of the Spirit: in
hearing the Lord, in worship, in reading the Scriptures,
in guidance, in ministry to others. But the life of the
Spirit is always entering human history and human
lives, so that the fruit of the Spirit's sending is within
history, acquires a history and forms a tradition. Thus
the Catholic conviction that the Incarnation involves the
embodiment of divine grace in the Church of history is
solidly grounded in the biblical witness to God's dealings
with sinful humanity. The grace of God is truly mediated across the centuries through the historic Church
that dates back to Jesus Christ and the apostles whom
he chose.

The Complementarity Character of the Divine Missions

This brief sketch suggests that we are to see in the complementarity of the two divine missions the role both of an immediacy of the Holy Spirit and of historical mediation through the Church. It is here that we can begin to sense the relevance of the theology of the divine missions for the relationship between the Church and the streams. Perhaps this can be helpfully illustrated by outlining the kind of distortion that occurs when there is any tendency to oppose Spirit-immediacy and Church-mediation as though one has to be chosen to the exclusion of the other.

What we may call the Catholic imbalance occurs when the distinctive mission of the Holy Spirit is not fully grasped, and everything Christian is explained in horizontal terms. That is to say of the historical foundation of the Church and its transmission from generation to generation through the apostolic succession of Pope and bishops. In an extreme version of this view, nothing would come from heaven now, but everything would come down through 2,000 years of history. Any tendency of this type weakens the sense that each Christian in every generation has direct access to the Father, and direct access to the Scriptures. Everything would come through the Church, understood in a one-sidedly institutional manner, so that the official Church, its ministry, its liturgy and its magisterium in effect replace the exalted Christ, though officially acting in his name.

What we may call the charismatic imbalance occurs when the immediacy of the Spirit is exalted in a way that is suspicious of any historical mediation. In this tendency, all the emphasis is placed on the direct illumination of each believer by the Holy Spirit; any appeal to history and to the decisions of Church leaders and councils is perceived as a threat to the freedom of the Spirit and the authenticity of Christian life. Everything comes straight from heaven now, and everything created and historical is at best only the target of the Holy Spirit and is never a mediating instrument of God's grace apart from immediate illumination and inspiration.

In practice, of course, hardly any Catholic and hardly any charismatic adopt these positions in such extreme forms. The Catholic who believes in the God-given guidance of the magisterium of the Pope and bishops will recognize in various ways that the Holy Spirit is active and needed, and is more recognizable at some points in history than others. Likewise, the most enthusiastic charismatic is likely to recognize the need for some independent test of direct inspiration, especially submission to the Bible as the Word of God. No doubt because the dangers of uncritical and unchecked charismatic illuminism are more obvious and more immediate in the damage they cause, what I have called the Catholic imbalance is often more difficult to recognize and correct.

There is in fact an evangelical imbalance different from the charismatic that is often as plausible to Protestant minds as the Catholic imbalance can be to Catholics. This is making the Bible the sole yardstick of Christian life, without any recognition of the constant need for the Holy Spirit and the need for the Church of history. In fact, both the Catholic and the evangelical Protestant imbalances ignore the role of the Holy Spirit ever sent afresh direct from heaven and they also ignore what the other represents: the written Word of God and the Church of history. Both of these rely one-sidedly on a mediated and mediating reality: the body of Christ and the Word of God.[2] Both are expressions of the mission of the Son: the Church as the body of Christ the Son, and the Scriptures as the written Word that conveys and bears witness to the personal Word of God, the Logos through whom and for whom all things were made.

For these reasons, it is important to assert the complementarity of Church, Bible and the light of the Holy Spirit. The life of Christ does come to us through the historic Church, it does come to us through the Word of God, and both receive their vitality directly from the light and the power of the Holy Spirit.

There is thus a necessary complementarity of the

two divine missions of the Spirit and of the Son. They correspond to the vertical and the horizontal dimensions of Christian faith. The Spirit comes from heaven, and the Son is made flesh in space and time. The Spirit continues to be poured out from heaven, and the Son forms the Church at Pentecost. The Spirit continues to be showered down from heaven, and the Church records her witness in the New Testament itself created from the encounter of the Old Testament with the Holy Spirit that effects the Incarnation. The Church does hand on faith from generation to generation (creed and Bible, liturgy and decalogue) but this faith is constantly enlivened by the Holy Spirit sent direct from heaven. The Church constantly celebrates the eucharist in obedience to the command, 'Do this in memory of me', and each eucharist becomes the pasch of the Lord through the invocation (*epiclesis*) of the Holy Spirit. There are ordained ministries handed on from age to age, but there are also charisms of the Spirit that are simply given from heaven, and are not transmitted in the manner of the ordained ministries.

The Relevance for Church and Streams

It will be clear from the absolute mutual relationship of the Son and the Spirit that the relevance of the two divine missions to our subject of Church and streams cannot be to suggest that the historic Church is simply the work of the Son and the streams are simply the work of the Holy Spirit. Nonetheless, it remains true to say that the life-streams represent a form of direct witness to the contemporary outpouring of the Holy Spirit of God. Likewise, the historic Churches bear continuous witness to the Word made flesh in the Church as the body shaped by Word and sacrament through the action of the Spirit.

The rootedness of the life-giving streams and of the historic Churches in the two divine missions can encourage us to see that it is the nature of the Holy Spirit to engender the Son, to bear witness to the Son and so give glory to the Father. Similarly, it is the nature of the Son to receive the Holy Spirit and to pass on the Spirit, eternally to the Father and in time to us and to the Father. The Spirit's engendering of the Son continues in the Son being brought to birth in Christians by regeneration ('the Spirit gives birth to spirit' John 3:6 NIV) and so the Church is born. And the Son's ministry in space and time requires the Spirit both to begin and to continue.

The doctrine of the procession of the Holy Spirit has been a point of dispute between the Orthodox, who say that the Spirit proceeds from the Father, and the Catholics, who say that the Spirit proceeds from the Father and the Son (*Filioque*). More ecumenical and less polemical theological approaches have led many scholars to affirm that the Spirit proceeds from the Father through the Son.[3] This formula brings out more clearly the point just made that the eternal sending of the Spirit is not logically subsequent to the generation of the Son, but that the eternal breathing or spiration of the Holy Spirit both effects the generation of the Son and flows from the generated Son back to the Father in the bond of infinite love.

This formulation also accounts more readily for the activity of the Holy Spirit in history that prepares for the Incarnation. Here though it is wrong to imagine that the Spirit is active for thousands of years before the Son appears. The unity of the missions of the Spirit and of the Son is such that the preparatory work of the Holy Spirit results in advance signs and manifestations of the Son. This unity is explained in this way in the new *Catechism of the Catholic Church*:

> From the beginning until 'the fullness of time' the joint mission of the Father's Word and Spirit remains hidden, but it is at work. God's Spirit prepares for the time of the Messiah. Neither is fully revealed but both are already promised, to be watched for and welcomed at their manifestation. So, for this reason, when the Church reads the Old Testament, she searches there for what the Spirit 'who has spoken through the prophets', wants to tell us about Christ.[4]

Then, when the Son is made man, and enters his glory, he sends forth the Spirit from the Father (see John 15:26) and forms the body of Christ that is at once hidden and manifest, visible and invisible.

In our modern situation, this understanding of the two missions that are one would seem to have application to the work of the Holy Spirit outside the visible structures of the historic Churches. Because it is the Holy Spirit that makes possible every presence of Christ, limits cannot be placed in advance on where and when the Holy Spirit may work; this divine activity cannot then be restricted to the official and public sphere of the visible Church of history. But because of the unity of the two divine missions, every activity of the Spirit is directed towards the presence and manifestation of Jesus and to the formation of the one body of Christ. Then the Spirit operates through the Church that is formed by the Spirit.

This understanding of the divine missions suggests that the work of the Spirit within and through the historic Churches is necessarily related to the work of the same Spirit in the manifestations of the streams that are outside these Churches. Once we admit that the Holy Spirit is truly present among groups of believers on the 'other side', Church or stream, we cannot theologically say that the Spirit of God is present, but the body of Christ is not. Hence there is more of the Holy Spirit in the historic Churches than most stream Christians, especially the Pentecostals and the new charismatics are likely to admit, and there is more of the visible Church being formed through the life-streams than the Catholics and the Orthodox are likely to recognize.

Ministries and Charisms

The theology of the two divine missions may provide a way of understanding the complementarity of the ministries of the historic Churches legitimated by apostolic succession and the ministries arising within the streams, particularly in the new Pentecostal and charismatic churches, many of which believe in the availability today of the 'fivefold' ministry of Ephesians 4:11 (apostles, prophets, evangelists, pastors, teachers). The former clearly come down through history as an expression of the mission of the Son, that nonetheless still require the coming of the Spirit, invoked in all ordination rites. The latter are clearly forms of ministry that arise **from below** (among the Christian people) and **from on high** (by the gifting of the Spirit), and belong more to the area that recent Catholic theology has been recognizing as that of the charisms of the Holy Spirit.

The possible importance of seeing historic and new ministries in this way is that recent Catholic teaching has been recognizing – though basically within the framework of the communion of the Catholic Church – the complementarity of the historic ordained ministries and of freely given charisms of the Holy Spirit. To invoke this model is not to exempt the historic ordained ministries from searching analysis and profound renewal, but it is to recognize that there is a greater fixity about these ministries handed down from age to age, and that there is a great freedom in the power of the Holy Spirit to distribute charisms as, when and how the divine giver determines. Such a theology may in fact correspond better to the great variety and flexibility of ministries in the new charismatic churches than their own occasional attempts to build a 'system' of ministries on their selection of New Testament texts.

The most important points about the relevance of the theology of the two divine missions for our subject are then that it grounds the essential relationship between the person and work of Christ and the activity of the Holy Spirit, and that it potentially provides the strongest theological basis for the necessity of seeing the work of God in the historic Churches and the work of God in the life-streams as complementary.

PART V

THE ISSUES AND THE CHALLENGES

Chapter Seventeen

The Challenge of the Spirit to All

We have looked at the history of currents of revival and renewal in the past 250 years, both in the streams that began with the evangelical revivals of the 1730s and 1740s and within the Roman Catholic Church. We have seen that there has been a noticeable intensification in the tempo of revival and renewal over this modern period. We have also seen that the charismatic movement has been the first stream to touch equally the Protestant world impacted by the earlier streams and the Roman Catholic world that had been totally apart.

Notwithstanding the wonderful grace of the charismatic renewal, and the unprecedented coming together in worship and ministry of evangelical Protestants and Roman Catholics, it is clear that huge differences remain between these two worlds, differences in doctrine, in worship, in church government, and differences concerning the role and authority of the Bible. The outpouring of the Holy Spirit on Protestant and Catholic alike has not simply abolished these differences, though it has opened doors, changed hearts and made possible fellowship and communication previously deemed impossible.

It is God's loving mercy that has made possible this bridging of the abyss resulting from the religious wars of the Reformation, both spiritual and military. The new fellowship between revivalist Protestants and renewed Catholics is very precious but it is still somewhat fragile; those graced to have experienced reconciliation and fellowship have a responsibility not to allow these young buds to die through the rekindling of old suspicions and animosities. How can we ensure that the new fellowship in the Spirit survives and grows?

One attempted way is to assume that the differences will just wither in the wind as ice melts in the warmth of spring. In practice, this attitude generally assumes that the other side will come round to 'our way of seeing things'! It often involves patronizing assumptions that this must already be happening for the present fellowship to be possible. Thus, an evangelical or Pentecostal, who is delighted to find Roman Catholics proclaiming salvation through the Blood of Jesus and witnessing to a personal conversion, may then be shocked to find these same Catholics still praying the Hail Mary, accepting the authority of the Pope and believing in the sacrifice of the Mass. In a rather different way, but perhaps a similar spirit, Catholics may assume that any Protestant who begins to appreciate any aspect of the Catholic tradition, such as the Lord's real presence in the eucharist or the call to celibacy for the sake of the Kingdom of God, is on the point of becoming a Catholic, and will be disappointed or judgmental when this does not happen.

The Challenge is Equally Great to Both Sides

It is important to realize that any authentic coming of the Holy Spirit has to be deeply challenging to the recipients. When the **Holy** Spirit of God comes, all that is not holy is confronted and contested. 'When he [the Spirit] comes, he will convince the world of sin and of righteousness and of judgment' (John 16:8). This challenge applies at the corporate level of church life every bit as much as at the individual level. If the Spirit of God dwells in the Church and not just in the individual Christian, and the Spirit of God is invoked upon the Church and not just upon the individual believer, then the Spirit's coming upon the Church will profoundly challenge the Church and confront all that is not of God and is not holy within the Church.

The coming of the Holy Spirit to each Christian tradition, whether ecclesial or stream, will be equally challenging. This statement will probably appear shocking at first to both sides. The loyal Catholic may be outraged

at the idea that the 'one true Church', coming down
through the centuries from Christ and the apostles, could
need as much change as other Christian bodies of lesser
vintage and deficient heritage. The zealous evangelical
or Pentecostal may regard as ridiculous the idea that
evangelicals and Pentecostals need to change as much as
a Church that they have typically regarded as apostate.

First of all, let it be said that the equality of challenge
is not a statement that all Churches and Christian bodies
are on a par. I do not believe that all the Churches and
denominations are equal in significance; indeed they are
not even the same kind of entity, a fact often disguised
by the common use of the term 'church' and our more
democratic instincts. So the equality of the challenge is
not because the bodies being challenged are equal, but
because before God we are all equally sinners in need of
God's grace, and because all that each tradition has from
the Holy Spirit is equally sheer undeserved grace.

This equality of gracedness and fickleness is touched on
by St Paul in the context of his teaching on Israel and the
nations in Romans 11. He tells the Gentiles not to boast
because they, the wild olive branches, have been grafted
into the natural olive of Israel: 'They were broken off
because of their unbelief, but you stand fast only through
faith' (Rom 11:20). And he concludes this passage with the
statement: 'For God has consigned all men to disobedience, that he may have mercy upon all' (Rom 11:32).

The Dangers in Our Traditional Strengths

Once we leave behind aggressive triumphalist attitudes
that look down on other Church traditions, it is easy
enough to recognize that we have both strengths and
weaknesses in our Church heritage. What is less easy
to see is that what we consider to be our strengths may
be as dangerous as our most obvious weaknesses.

It may be in our areas of greatest perceived strength
that we as Churches will be most severely tempted. We
can easily develop mentalities that say: this is central to
authentic Christianity and we have it; this is what they,

the other side, lack. These points then become areas in which our genuine faith witness becomes mixed up with very human forms of loyalty and pride, leading to very unchristian forms of arrogance. That leads directly to the conclusion that we have nothing to learn from the others in what really matters.

It is the Lord's reproach to Jerusalem that 'you trusted in your beauty, and played the harlot because of your renown' (Ezek 16:15). When our strong points become a matter of confessional pride, and we forget that all we have is the sheer grace of God, then we are trusting in the beauty of our tradition: its liturgy, its theology, its doctrinal purity, its martyrs, etc.

We can approach this point by looking at what we see as our particular strengths: how Catholics see the Church, and how evangelical Protestants see the Bible. Church and Bible are symbolic of the two worlds of the Churches and the streams.

Church

Catholics typically see themselves as those who understand Church, who are the Church. 'We are the one true Church', a sentiment somewhat mitigated at the level of the better-informed by the conciliar recognition of the ecclesial character of other Christian bodies with whom the Roman Catholic Church is in 'imperfect communion'. Strong Catholics are proud of their apostolic heritage, of possessing the right pedigree.

From this background, the Protestants are not really Church. They do not understand Church. The Catholic stereotype of Protestantism, especially perhaps its evangelical segment, sees 'private judgment' as the supreme Protestant principle, associated with an individualism that allows no real place for Church. It is generally ignorant of those milieux within the Protestant life-streams for which the subject of the Church has become important. Thus Catholics have nothing to learn from Protestants about Church.

While these are not official positions, they are widespread mentalities. They also survive behind the more

recent ecumenical frontage (façade would be too dispar-
aging a word), for the newer attitudes take time and
openness to displace the deeply ingrained suspicions and
exclusivism of four centuries.

Bible

Something similar is true of evangelical Protestant attitudes towards the Bible. We are the people of the Book.
We know the Bible. It is our glory. Our Protestant doctrines are biblical, our worship is biblical, our practice
is biblical. The other side, the Catholics, do not know
the Book.

From this standpoint, the Catholic Church, its doctrines, its worship and its patterns of piety, are a priori
unbiblical. The stereotype does not recognize the strands
of biblical thinking and imagery that are powerfully
present in the Catholic and Orthodox worlds. And so to
the inexorable conclusion that evangelicals do not have
anything to learn from Catholics about the Bible.

These two mentalities confront each other with equal
self-confidence and with equal disdain for the other. Protestant convictions about Church and Catholic convictions
about the Bible are dismissed as irrelevant and as forms
of distortion of what we the true believers possess.
Or, if there has been some progress beyond traditional
stereotypes, people may think that the 'other side' may
have some inkling of 'Church' or 'Bible', but it remains
something so inferior to our knowledge that there is
no idea of learning from the others or of needing their
witness.

In fact, Catholics can and must learn about Church
from the Protestants, and Protestants can and must learn
from Catholics about the Scriptures. There is a mutual
need for each other. The teaching of 1 Corinthians 12
about the limbs and organs of the body that need each
other applies here. We all need every testimony that is
of the Holy Spirit of God. Catholics need the witness of
the Spirit among Protestants concerning the reality of
Church. Protestants need the witness of the Spirit among
Catholics concerning the Scriptures. This learning will

make the Catholic Church more fully Church, and will
make evangelical Protestants more biblical.

Catholics can learn from assemblies with a congregationalist ecclesiology something about the rightful
autonomy of the local Church, though this will correct
their unbiblical forms of excessive independence that
deny the need for organic communion of the local
churches; they can learn more of the practical implications of faith in the priesthood of all believers. Catholics
can learn from the Plymouth Brethren further implications of the Church's belonging to Christ. Catholics can
learn from the new independent charismatic churches
about the inter-relationship of local assemblies, about
forms of corporate leadership, about *episcope* in the
Spirit. That is to say that the new patterns of relationship
developing between leaders in the new churches may have
something to teach the historic Churches about episcopal
authority and episcopal fellowship, even though and
perhaps because these relationships find expression in
non-sacramental forms in the new churches.

Similarly, evangelicals and Pentecostals can learn
much about the Bible from Catholics. They can learn
about older forms of biblical exegesis that pre-date
post-Enlightenment rationalism, forms that are nearer
to the way the New Testament authors interpreted the
Old (as in 1 Corinthians 10:1–13 and Hebrews 8–10). They
can learn about biblical symbols and their enactment in
the liturgical worship of the Church. Catholics can help
them to discover things in the Bible that have not featured
prominently in the streams: the importance of the body
and of the material creation, the relationship between
the body and community, the role of the angels, the place
of vows, the calling of celibacy in the New Testament,
the understanding of poverty. All of these elements
not only bring understanding of further dimensions of
Christian life, but they also enrich our understanding
of what we already treasure, because of the organic
interconnectedness of Christian faith as a whole.

Chapter Eighteen

The Stream Challenge to the Church

In this chapter, I want to look at the challenge of the streams to the Church. I will do this by examining the challenge to the Roman Catholic Church in particular, because both the opposition or tension between Church and streams and the potential benefits from positive interaction are here much greater. But most of the points of challenge from the streams apply to a considerable degree to the mainline Protestant Churches, and Protestant readers are invited to make a parallel application.

Many of the ways in which the streams challenge the Church(es) are very similar from one stream to another, and so much of what is developed in the next two chapters applies to all four streams. However, there are some challenges that are more particular to one stream than to another, and I will indicate where this is the case.

The Sovereignty of God

Before coming to the more obvious challenges of the streams to the historic Churches (e.g. the relationship of structures to life, of rigidity versus flexibility), I want to address the way in which the streams confront the Churches with the free and overriding sovereignty of God. The four life-streams (evangelical, Holiness, Pentecostal, charismatic) all arose out of revivalistic impulses. They all sprang up in an environment of intensified faith in outpourings of the Holy Spirit, sudden irruptions of the Spirit of God in the Church and in human history. They can all be described in the words of Acts 3:19 as 'times of refreshing'.

The Freedom of God

The streams manifest to the Church the sovereign power
and absolute freedom of God to pour out the Holy Spirit
wherever, whenever and in whatever way God pleases.
Jesus knew the impossibility of programming the Spirit
of God. So he told Nicodemus: 'The wind [*pneuma*] blows
where it wills, and you hear the sound of it, but you do
not know whence it comes or whither it goes; so it is
with every one who is born of the Spirit [*Pneuma*]' (John
3:8). We will look later at how such words challenge
every spirit of control in the Church, whereby church
leaders, theologians and others limit what God is 'per-
mitted' to do.

The streams manifest to an unbelieving world and to
a half-believing Church that the God Christians confess
is not just an abstract theological concept or a detached
heavenly observer, but the Lord who acts in history, the
Lord who manifests his power at specific moments in
specific places through specific people. They remind us
of what is virtually a refrain throughout Isaiah's Book of
Consolation: 'I am the Lord, and there is no other' (Is
45:5, 6; see also 43:11; 44:6, 8; 45:14, 21–22; 46:9). This
sole God is the one who says: 'I declared and saved and
proclaimed' (Is 43:12). The streams then challenge the
Churches to faith in a real acting Lord who acts with
divine power and wisdom to change the hearts of sinners
and to renew the face of the earth. 'I am God, and also
henceforth I am He; there is none who can deliver from
my hand; I work and who can hinder it?' (Is 43:13).

The salvific works of God cannot be reduced to a mere
co-ordination of 'natural causes' with no divine 'surplus'.
When God acts to save and to sanctify, the results are
fruit that can only be produced by the Holy Spirit.
Certainly God can and does work through the created
order, but in the work of salvation and sanctification,
there is always the divine surplus, that is the specific
work of the Holy Spirit, that can never be reduced to
sociological or psychological causes.

In times of spiritual revival, there is a heightened level
of faith in the living Lordship of Jesus. There will be a

greater expectation that God will act in identifiable and challenging ways. What people popularly call miracles are really the cases in which what I have called the divine surplus not attributable to merely human or created causes is both substantial and visible. The life-streams thus challenge the Church to faith in a God who acts; to faith in a God who acts with power; to faith in a God whose power is shown in signs and wonders that visibly transcend the natural order of creation.

Every living encounter with the Lord involves this challenge to let God be God. 'Who has directed the Spirit of the LORD, or as his counsellor has instructed him? Whom did he consult for his enlightenment, and who taught him the path of justice, and taught him knowledge, and showed him the way of understanding? (Is 40:13–14). This verse is cited by St Paul at the end of Romans 11, when he is marvelling at the plan of God concerning Israel and the nations (11:34).

In this light, the radical question each stream poses to the Church is: 'Is this of the Holy Spirit?' The streams as irruptions of life make discernment a central issue. Whether what is happening is unexpected, whether it is appearing in an improbable place, whether it squares with our received theologies, whether it contains unusual and puzzling elements, all these are irrelevant as objections if a proper discernment grounded in biblical principles shows that what is happening is truly the fruit of the Holy Spirit.

The Lord of History
The streams also challenge the Church to rediscover the hand of the Lord in guiding history towards its fulfilment. In general, this is not the way the Churches operate, particularly at the local level. Church synods, councils, assemblies certainly scrutinize the signs of modernity, but they often have difficulty in proclaiming with a firm faith that God is the Lord of history, who is actually directing the human story towards its fulfilment and who is working out his saving purpose through all the vicissitudes of human sin and ambiguity.[1]

The four life-streams confront the Churches with new initiatives of the Holy Spirit. This is not to say that only these streams are initiatives of the Spirit of God, but it is to say that they are striking and visible signs of such an initiative. They force us to ask: What is the Lord doing? What does this mean at this point in the history of God's people? Why is God doing this now?

This means that in God's providence, there are new phases that are inaugurated not by the secular revolutions of human history, but by divine initiative. Certainly, God may use events such as the French Revolution of 1789 or the collapse of Communism in 1989 to stir the Church. But new phases in the outworking of God's plan are never simply **reactions** to events in the world.

It is certainly true that no subsequent events can rival the Incarnation, the Resurrection of Christ and the outpouring of the Holy Spirit at Pentecost; the attempts to create further dispensations between the Pentecost-event and the second coming of Christ lead to exaggeration of the element of newness in the history of the Church. This would be true both of the teaching of Joachim of Flora (c 1132–1202) on the coming of a new age of the Spirit, and of elements in the dispensational teaching of John Nelson Darby.

Nonetheless, there are decisively new acts of the Holy Spirit in the course of Christian history. Catholics could see instances in the origins of monasticism (in the third and fourth centuries) and in the call of St Francis of Assisi (1182–1226) and the rise of the mendicant friars. The origins of the evangelical stream in the 1730s provide another example. Many Christians see that the impulse towards Christian unity has been a specific work of God in the twentieth century.

'You have heard; now see all this; and will you not declare it? From this time forth I make you hear new things, hidden things which you have not known. They are created now, not long ago; before today you have never heard of them, lest you should say, "Behold, I knew them"' (Is 48:6–7). Thus, the newness in God's acts is a reproach to our unbelief and to our arrogance. God delights to do what we in our self-confidence could not have imagined. Who before Vatican Two could have predicted the meeting of Pope Paul VI and Patriarch Athenagoras in Jerusalem in 1965? Who in 1890 at the time of the death of Cardinal Newman could have foreseen the centenary celebration in St Paul's Cathedral in London in 1990 at which most of the Anglican and Roman Catholic bishops of England thanked the Lord together for Newman's life that was recalled by a Methodist preacher? Who could have predicted the rise of the charismatic stream that would penetrate the Roman Catholic as well as the Protestant world? Who could have foretold the amazing impact of the Pentecostal stream in Latin America?

A Revived Eschatology

The life-streams all present the Church with a rekindled faith in the second coming of Jesus, and with a renewed longing for this consummation. In this light, the sense of new phases in the history of the Church means new developments that move the Church towards its fulfilment in the second coming and the resurrection of the dead.

This eschatological challenge calls the Church to look forward in time as well as to look back. Often Christians have given the impression that the Church is essentially backward-looking: that the Church's task is to be faithful to Christ and his instructions; so that the Church is seen as a custodian who has been given a treasure that is to be preserved for an indefinite future.

This backward-looking stance is often fostered by a view of New Testament fulfilment that sees the Old Testament as the time of hope awaiting the fulfilment of God's promises; and the New Covenant as their fulfilment. In fact, many of the Old Testament promises still await their earthly fulfilment. The coming of Jesus in the Incarnation did not totally fulfil all promises; but provides a deeper ground and stronger evidence for the fulfilment of what was not realized in the first coming but will only be fulfilled in the second.

The streams thus challenge the Church to recover the

fullness of her eschatological hope. They challenge the
Church in her established attitudes: that is to say, the
mentalities that forget that Christians are 'strangers and
exiles on the earth' (Heb 11:13). They confront us with the
ways that we are at home in this world, just as or even
more settled and permanent as political and educational
institutions.

The Gospel of Life

Streams of New Life
The evangelical, Holiness, Pentecostal and charismatic
streams are above all streams of new life. This is their
original calling and gift. While they all involve a re-
focusing on central truths of Christian faith, the streams
are not primarily theological currents: the pioneer figures
such as George Whitefield, Phoebe Palmer and William
Seymour were not primarily theologians or people with
new ideas; they were believers transformed by their
encounter with the Lord. The core truths they taught
were the convictions imprinted on their hearts; they in
their turn preached these convictions so as to bring life
to others. This was the whole context of the teaching of
Jesus and the apostles: 'I came that they may have life,
and have it abundantly' (John 10:10). When the streams
cease to be life-giving, they change their character and
lose their distinctive gifting.

Their primary challenge to the Church is to restore
to first place the life that is the Father's gift in Christ
through the Holy Spirit. The evangelical stream has
emphasized the Word of God and the personal response
of faith. The Holiness stream has added the link between
new life and sanctification through the Cross of Christ.
The Pentecostal and charismatic streams have stressed
the power of the Holy Spirit to bring life through anointed
preaching and through the gifts and ministries of the
Spirit.

The heart of the Church is communion with the Father
and the Son in the Spirit: 'That which we have seen

and heard we proclaim also to you, so that you may
have fellowship with us; and our fellowship is with
the Father and with his Son Jesus Christ' (1 John
1:3). The structures of the Church exist to serve and
channel this life. The streams thus remind the Church
that 'the sabbath was made for man, not man for the
sabbath' (Mark 2:27). So the Lord is Lord even of the
Church, as 'the son of man is lord even of the sabbath'
(Mark 2:28).

Preaching the Gospel
The life of the Spirit does not appear simply because we
desire life. People join many movements in their search
for life. What brings the life of God is the preaching of
the gospel of Jesus Christ. St Paul tells us that Jesus
has 'abolished death and brought life and immortality to
light through the gospel. For this gospel I was appointed
a preacher and apostle and teacher' (2 Tim 1:10–11).

The evangelical and subsequent streams have been
life-giving because they have had a focus on the gospel,
the saving message of the death and the resurrection of
Jesus. They challenge the Church to preach the gospel
with clarity: to rediscover the *kerygma*, the basic proclamation that has the power to pierce the heart and to
bring hearers to conversion.

Thus, the streams challenge the Church to identify and
liberate the life-giving centre that is present, sometimes
hidden, in the midst of its own official doctrine. The
Church's task is not simply to present its complete creed
in systematic fashion. It has to preach the gospel to
the unconverted. This requires a differentiation between
evangelistic preaching aimed at basic conversion (the
kerygma) from the formative teaching required after
initial conversion (the *didache*). In the early Church,
there was a clear difference between the pre-baptismal
formation and the post-baptismal, that was known as
mystagogy.

At the heart of this rediscovery of the gospel is the
power of the death and resurrection of Jesus. All authentic conversion involves a death and a resurrection, a

death to the old order centred on self and a rising to the
new life centred on Christ. Real transformation of lives
is linked to such preaching and teaching.

The Call to Evangelism
The streams have all had a strong missionary thrust.
People converted by a clear preaching of the gospel have
often received a clear call to go out and evangelize the
world. Thus the streams have given rise to many heroic
and exemplary missionaries, such as Hudson Taylor,
Amy Carmichael (1867–1951), C. T. Studd and Willie
Burton.
   The streams have all given a high priority to evangelism. The majority of the para-church organizations to
which they have given rise focus on evangelism and basic
discipleship. In this way they challenge the Churches to
overcome the institutional bias towards self-preservation
and maintenance, and to re-order their priorities and
resources so as to make the preaching of the gospel
the centre of the Church's activity. The streams thus
challenge the Churches to give the work of evangelism a
practical priority. The declining number of missionaries
and the lack of explicit evangelism in many places points
to a lack of spiritual vitality and the need for the life and
power that the streams represent.
   The challenge of the life-streams to the Church can be
further examined by taking up the four characteristics
of the streams that were identified in chapter seven:
Biblical, Lay, Inter-denominational and Modern.

The Centrality of the Bible

All the life-giving streams are unambiguously committed
to the Bible as 'the Word of life'. Particularly in their
phases of greatest vitality, they show a reliance on the
power of the Word, that is 'sharper than any two-edged
sword, piercing to the division of soul and spirit, of joints
and marrow, and discerning the thoughts and intentions
of the heart' (Heb 4:12). This is not to deny that there
are forms of naiveté and rigidity in the way that stream

participants often interpret and use the Bible. But it is to insist that, whatever these deficiencies, in the streams the Bible has become a source of new life.

Preaching and Teaching

When the Bible comes to life, it has a potential to affect all dimensions of the Church's life. Preaching is the ministry of the Word. As the Holy Spirit touches preachers, the Word comes to life: the power in the Word unites with the fire in the preacher to penetrate the hearts of the people. Thus ministers of the Word, who are fed by the Word and have a deep love and reverence for the Word, will show this depth and this love by the way they expound the Word, how they open up its meaning and invite their hearers to respond to this depth.

In the same way, the streams with their love of the Scriptures challenge every Christian with a teaching role to find their deepest inspiration and source in the Bible. It is the Bible that provides the divine perspective on the whole of creation; it is only by making the Bible central to Christian study that teaching will truly be grounded in divine revelation rather than in shifting human opinion. As Vatican Two stated: 'All the preaching of the Church, as indeed the entire Christian religion, should be nourished and ruled by Sacred Scripture.'[2]

Worship

Likewise, the preaching of the Word with power releases a new power in worship. The evangelical and Holiness streams have been particularly blessed with a great zeal for intercession, while the Pentecostal and charismatic streams have been characterized by a renewed emphasis on praise.

The streams thus challenge the Church to allow the Word of God to be the shaping instrument of preaching and worship through the action of the Holy Spirit. They remind us that the renewal of worship cannot simply be the work of parish committees or liturgical commissions.

It is necessarily the work of the Holy Spirit in association
with the Word of God.

The Laity

The streams all have a strongly lay character, at least
in their origins and in their periods of expansion. That
is to say, the freer working of the Holy Spirit in the
streams does not privilege the officially ordained and
the theologically qualified, but is manifest in the lives
of ordinary believers. God is no respecter of persons. God
fills and equips the lowly as well as the high-ups, the poor
and uneducated as well as the rich and the esteemed.
This egalitarianism of the Spirit has become most apparent in the Pentecostal and charismatic streams, no
doubt because of their more affective and demonstrative
character.

The streams thus challenge the Churches to recognize
the truly catholic and non-élitist character of the Holy
Spirit's work. As St Paul says, 'To each is given the
manifestation of the Spirit for the common good' (1 Cor
12:7). The Spirit is calling the Church to be a body in
which all members contribute actively to the health and
welfare of the whole.

Thus, the streams radically challenge all forms of
clericalism and élitism in the Churches. In Romans, Paul
paints a picture of a Church in which those with gifts
from God are encouraged to exercise them. 'Having gifts
that differ according to the grace given to us, let us use
them' (Rom 12:6). In the streams the Spirit activates the
people and in stream-settings the people often have more
freedom to take new initiatives. Evangelistic groups,
educational initiatives, youth-formation and training,
missionary societies: all these and more have flourished
where the streams have flowed.

In Latin America, one of the reasons why the Pentecostal Churches are growing so fast is their ability to
welcome all comers and encourage them to play their
full part in the worship and the evangelism of the local
Christian community. St Paul provides a model of this

'every-member' participation in 1 Corinthians: 'When you come together, each one has a hymn, a lesson, a revelation, a tongue, or an interpretation' (14:26). The outpouring of the Spirit abolishes any form of religious proletariat, who are just consumers and clients.

Inter-denominational

The life-streams have typically transcended particular denominational limits in touching Christians across the spectrum of the Protestant Churches. The inter-denominational character has only been lost when rejection and ridicule led to the expulsion or freezing out of the new stream with the inevitable formation of new denominations, as happened especially with the Pentecostal stream. The charismatic stream in many ways represents the recovery of this inter-denominational dimension, with the additional surprise of its spread to the Roman Catholic Church (and other milieux closed to the evangelical and Holiness streams). This inter-denominational character has been further expressed in the para-church movements and organizations in the evangelical and charismatic worlds.

Their inter-denominational character challenges the Church(es) to a greater inclusivity and a less possessive attitude towards participants. This facet has a strong appeal to young people whose reluctance to accept the inherited divisions and boundaries of the Churches cannot be wholly attributed to their ignorance and naiveté.

The inter-denominational dimension of the streams is closely linked with their focus on the life-giving centre that is Jesus Christ. The fact that what unites them as streams has a strongly existential and spiritual character often provides a depth of association that is less readily found in many formal ecumenical encounters.

Modernity

The modern character of the streams is evident in a variety of ways: obviously the most modern streams, the

Pentecostal and the charismatic, may be more modern than the evangelical, that is still marked in many respects by the rationalism and commonsense realism that characterized the eighteenth century.

Modernity is found in patterns of organization, communication and formation. This can be seen most clearly in the non-denominational sector of the charismatic stream. Here the formation of fluid networks, based primarily on relationships between leaders, mirrors the pragmatic patterns of the business world more than traditional patterns within the Churches. The ways of forming future leaders owe little to traditional patterns of seminary and theological college and much more to contemporary ad hoc methods of on the job training.

The new networks of charismatic churches represent a firm move away from a society based on status and privilege to a fully functional and participatory if not democratic pattern. Leaders lead not because they have been through a formal educative process but because they have shown their capacity to lead. This corresponds to the patterns operative – necessarily operative – in the professional and commercial worlds.

The challenge of modernity to the Church(es), particularly of the newest streams, is especially one of flexibility and effectiveness in the face of historic structures and models. The recent streams pose afresh the relationship between the structures of the Church on the one hand and the structures of contemporary society on the other hand. At issue here are elements that belong to the permanent God-given structure and those that rightly adapt to and reflect the norms of particular societies. On the one side stands the danger of perpetuating obsolete patterns that become an obstacle to the gospel; on the other side lies the danger of pandering to the Zeitgeist, the spirit of the age, and placing relevance above truth and revelation.

The Lordship of Jesus

The streams bring home very forcefully the claim of Jesus to be the Lord to whom has been given 'all authority in heaven and on earth' (Matt 28:18). The grace of baptism in the Holy Spirit first in the Holiness movement, but then (especially) in the Pentecostal and charismatic movements involves the revelation of the Lordship of Jesus and our submission of mind, will and spirit to that Lordship. Through the streams, the Lord seems to be saying: 'Allow me to exercise my Lordship. Let go of your own control. Let me restore my Lordship over my Church.'

The streams challenge the Church to be truly Christ-centred, to move from often being Church-centred to being Christ-centred and Church-based. In other words, there is a movement of renewal in all Churches from being centred on their own life, their own confessions of faith, their own traditions, their own norms to being centred on Jesus Christ and his life. This is not a movement from Church being central to Church being marginal, but a change of perspective concerning the Church. The call is to shift from a focus on Church to a focus on Jesus as the Lord, the head, and the life of the Church that is his body.

The streams challenge the Church to be the Church of history moving towards the climax of the Lord's return, to be a Church in movement, growing 'until we all attain to the unity of the faith and of the knowledge of the Son of God, to mature manhood, to the measure of the stature of the fulness of Christ' (Eph 4:13). They challenge the Church to be the bride, ready without spot or wrinkle, being prepared for the wedding feast of the Lamb. Then 'when all things are subjected to him, then the Son himself will also be subjected to him who put all things under him, that God may be everything to every one' (1 Cor 15:28).

Chapter Nineteen

The Church Challenge to the Streams

T he challenge of the Church to the streams is every bit
as important as the challenge of the streams to the
Church, but this challenge is rather less obvious, at least
to those tempted to live in the immediate present. For
the stream-enthusiasts with their effervescent vitality
can easily regard themselves as the real Christians
and the older Churches as the shrivelled husks of dead
religion. The first challenge then of historic Church
to stream-Christians (evangelical, Holiness, Pentecostal
and charismatic) is for the latter to see that the streams
are not self-sufficient and that they need the Church of
history and particular Church traditions for their own
calling to be fully realized.

We should remind ourselves that the life-streams have
existed and still exist both within historic Churches and
outside them. Clearly for those Christians receiving the
life of the streams within the historic Churches, the
challenge of Church to stream is an ever-present reality
(see chapter twenty). Then there are Christians who
live in modern denominations (particularly Holiness and
Pentecostal) for whom the life of their stream has been
channelled into a denomination. For these Christians,
their Church often represents a structuring of stream
life, bringing some advantages and some disadvantages,
rather than any stream-entry into the historic Christian
traditions of East and West. For them, the challenge of
the Church to the streams is similar to the challenge
to the new charismatic churches, namely the challenge
of the ancient liturgical and historic Church traditions
to the life-force of the modern streams.

Not the Totality

The Church of history challenges the streams to be what the Lord has created them to be, as impulses of new life, that are nonetheless not everything. To accept that a stream is a stream, not the ocean, requires humility of heart and a willingness to learn.

A stream within the Christian world is like an artery within the body. An artery is a channel of life-blood for the body, but it can never become a substitute for the body. A body without functioning arteries cannot survive. But a body is more than a network of arteries. Thus, each stream has a vital contribution to make to the living body of Christ, but no accumulation of streams can constitute a body. Streams enliven but cannot create the Church.

Each of the life-streams exists to bring life beyond themselves, to be like a blood transfusion for the body of Christ. The streams with their focus on the core of the gospel, the core that brings new life, need to be in interaction with the whole Church heritage for their purpose to be fulfilled. Let us look more closely at this challenge of the Church to the streams: the challenge to serve the fulness of God's purpose.

Each stream is both the bearer of a message and a conduit of new life. As we have seen, there is a close connection between the message and the life. The message of each stream is concentrated; it represents something central at the heart of Christian faith. That is why it is life-giving. The sharpened focus contributes to the energy of new life. This principle is in some ways carried further in the para-church organizations, whose message is often blended with a practical methodology that adds a practical focus to the focus of the streams that gave them birth. Here an increased and immediate efficacy is obtained through a greater sharpening of the message aided by modern methods of packaging, training and dissemination.

But the characteristic message of a stream, however important and life-giving, is never the whole of Christian faith. It draws from the heart of Christian faith, but is not its totality. It draws from the Scriptures, but is not the whole biblical revelation. It gives rise to distinctive patterns of prayer and worship, but these patterns are not the whole of Christian worship. It may develop particular styles and forms of ministry, but they are not the totality of Christian ministry.

The sharp focus of the stream messages is not given simply for the sake of the streams, but for the sake of the Church; indeed, the streams are gifts to the Church for the sake of the transformation of the world. Thus, for each stream to bear its appointed fruit, it has to become the instrument of renewal for the whole: for the whole Church, for the whole Christian tradition, for the whole biblical heritage.

The fulness of the tradition is borne by the historic Churches of East and West: the Oriental Orthodox Churches and the Orthodox Churches of the East, and the Catholic Church in communion with Rome, largely the Latin Church of the West. The proper understanding of the Great Church of East and West, that has to breathe with 'both lungs' as Pope John Paul II has said on several occasions, requires also an understanding of their rooting in the people of Israel, the original olive tree on to which the Churches of the nations are grafted.

I hope that this last paragraph can be taken by my Protestant readers, not as simply a statement of Catholic and Orthodox faith, but also as a recognition that the historic Churches have a radical need for what their Protestant brothers and sisters represent, both in the historic Churches of the Reformation and in the fruit of the life-streams with which this book is more directly concerned. For the claim that the ancient Churches of East and West represent a fulness of heritage is really saying no more than that they grew organically out of the full heritage of the two Testaments. They represent the only forms of Christianity that did not spring out of any subsequent movements of reform, renewal or revival. To make this claim is saying nothing about the extent to which these Churches have strayed or deviated from God's gift and call. Such a statement is compatible both with the ecumenical hesitations of conservative Catholics (and Orthodox) and with the most energetic of Reformation protests.

Thus the challenge of the Church to the streams involves a call for:

(1) an interaction between the message of the stream and the fulness of divine revelation (doctrinal–theological interaction);

(2) an interaction between the renewed life of stream milieux and the total life of each Church (practical-life interaction).

1. An Interaction between the Stream Message and the Fulness of Divine Revelation

This challenge at the level of teaching and doctrine has various levels of application. First, the usage of the Scriptures within the streams needs to be confronted with the whole of the Bible. The streams are typically strong on preaching, but their preaching tends to draw on particular themes and emphases within the Bible; evangelical preachers readily focus on the Pauline epistles; Holiness teachers often major on Romans 6 and 8, though many have explored the typological meaning of the ark and the tabernacle in the Old Testament; Pentecostals pay more attention to narrative books, particularly the Acts of the Apostles and books such as Samuel and Kings in the Old Testament. No stream seems to feed on the total revelation of the Scriptures.

Revivalist Christians may wonder at this point how the ancient Churches, which do not seem to them to have an overwhelming love for the Scriptures, can help them relate the part they love to the whole they may want to love. One of the answers is in the liturgical character of the ancient Churches, and the ways in which their worship draws on the Scriptures in a fuller and richer way than the non-liturgical denominations whose approaches are more literal and whose preachers select their own texts to expound. The importance of liturgical forms of worship has various facets, affecting for example both the content of biblical proclamation and the manner in which it is communicated.

In the liturgical traditions of East and West, both the lectionaries containing the biblical readings at the celebration of the eucharist and the texts used in the Divine Office that is sung or read in the monasteries,[1] are drawn from all the books of the Bible. These provide over time a reading of most of the Scriptures.[2] This liturgical practice is, whether or not participants realize it, a practical recognition of the authority of the Word of God, and facilitates, though it cannot compel, a submission of the Christian community to the full revelation of God in Christ Jesus to which the inspired Scriptures bear a unique testimony. There is a challenge here to non-liturgical Christian traditions, of which the life-streams form a large part, as to how they ensure a practical proclamation of and formation by the totality of the Scriptures.

Secondly, the historic liturgies are more than just collections of texts. They embody a whole way of relating to the Lord of the covenant that draws not just on biblical concepts but on symbolic actions that are deeply rooted in the biblical tradition. The Word of God is proclaimed is ways that are not just rational and logical, but imaginative and intuitive. This liturgical practice challenges stream Christians to overcome the rationalism of domination by scientific concepts that is a negative by-product of their modernity in the post-Enlightenment world.

Thirdly, the particular doctrines emphasized within the streams need to be related to and act upon the full teaching of the Christian Church. Here too the key doctrines of the streams (salvation through the saving death of Jesus, the necessity of repentance and personal conversion, the effects of the fall, justification and sanctification, the gift of the Holy Spirit) have to become life-giving for the full faith of the Church. This interaction can begin by the relating of key stream doctrines to the truths taught in the creeds. The creeds have a clear Trinitarian framework that can provide a firm context for the affirmation of the life-changing teaching of the streams. But this process needs to go beyond even the creeds, as the historic creeds did not mention the sacraments in their respect for the holiness of these enacted mysteries of faith, to which new converts were only introduced after baptism.

2. An Interaction between the Renewed Life of Stream Milieux and the Total Life of Each Church

Besides bringing a core-message, each stream brings new currents of life to the Church. This new life is not just for its own sake, but for the renewal and restoration of the Church. The new life has to pulsate through all the limbs, organs and tissue of the whole body.

It is characteristic of streams as streams that they can only flow where they are able to flow. Streams bring new life where new life is welcomed. But the Church is necessarily an assembly that is concerned with every dimension of life: family life from cradle to grave; education and formation; all forms of Christian worship; the fostering of ministries; evangelism and missionary work; forms of service to the Church and to the world; the care and defence of the poor and oppressed; the service of the mind through scriptural, theological and historical studies. The renewal of the Church means the re-centring of all these services and activities in the core-truths of the gospel rekindled in the streams.

These reflections can help us to see how the historic Churches and the streams need each other. Without the new life-forces represented by the streams, the Churches are in danger of having a complete system of doctrine and a full range of services that lack life and transforming power, and so they can fail to make any significant impact on our world. Without the fulness of doctrine and organic structure in the historic Churches, the streams run the risk of the new life failing to develop in a coherent way; they can then lack the capacity to shape the future to any significant degree.

194

The Strategy of the Spirit?

Not the Only Work of the Holy Spirit

The streams also need the wider context of the historic Churches to discover that there are other works and currents of the Holy Spirit at work in the Church and in the world. It remains true that the life-streams of modern times are of a particular importance in the Lord's purpose of revival and renewal. This is indicated by their focus on the central truths of Christian faith and by their life-giving power. However, there are other significant currents of the Spirit of God in the classical Protestant, Orthodox and Catholic worlds, as has been indicated in chapters eight to twelve. To ignore these other currents and to act as though the life-streams are the only show in town is not only to be guilty of self-absorption (never a Christian virtue) but to assure an unduly narrow vision of Church renewal.

Exclusive focus on the life-streams, which are more revivalist than intellectual in their thrust, will undervalue the role of movements of ideas in the Church. Important examples of major theological and ideational currents in modern times are the liturgical movement, the recovery of a communion-centred and organic understanding of the Church, liberation theology and, most importantly, the ecumenical movement. Not everything in all of these currents is necessarily of the Holy Spirit, but in each case a dimension of biblical faith and divine revelation is being rediscovered.

If stream-conscious Christians with their focus on new life in Christ feel uneasy with some of these more theological currents or with aspects within them, it may be because these currents are insufficiently in touch with the life-streams. The fault here can be on both sides! The life-streams and the renewing currents that are more theological need each other. Healthy interaction between the two can be seen in several movements within the historic Churches, whether in communities like Sant' Egidio in the Roman Catholic Church or the Iona Community in the Protestant world.

The ecumenical movement provides another example.

As briefly indicated in chapters two and three, there was an important contribution from the evangelical and Holiness streams to the original inspiration of the movement towards Christian unity. This thrust was soon lost, aided no doubt by the growing ecumenical involvement of the Orthodox and Catholic Churches as well as by liberalizing tendencies in the Protestant world to which the stream-adherents mostly reacted in defensive ways. Thus the stream-presence in the ecumenical movement of the late twentieth century has become rather modest, though a brave handful of convinced evangelical and Pentecostal ecumenists have made their presence known at the WCC assemblies.

The result of this narrowness (on both sides) has been the tragic failure to grasp the extraordinary importance and potential of the charismatic stream for Christian unity. On the one side, many charismatics dismiss the ecumenical movement as a merely human effort to achieve unity (a judgment that manifests a considerable ignorance of the movement's original inspiration), while on the other hand the majority of committed ecumenists have dismissed the charismatic explosion as irrelevant to ecumenism as they understand it, either seeing it as mere emotionalism or as yet another mutation of a conservative fundamentalism in which they see little that is positive.

The Need for Embodiment

The streams as streams of new life require embodiment if they are to survive and bear lasting fruit. This is part of the law of life in the physical world into which God has placed human beings as embodied spirits. It is for this reason that God's work of saving us from the divisive and destructive consequences of sin involved the Son of God, who is Spirit, taking on human flesh in all its physicality, dying on the Cross and suffering the separation of body and spirit, and then being raised as 'a spiritual body' (1 Cor 15:44), 'a life-giving spirit' (1 Cor 15:45).

Without the historic Churches, the streams remain impulses of new life that are not fully embodied. Indeed, without a truly Jewish base and a form of ingrafting into historic Israel, the historic Churches themselves are lacking a fulness of historic embodiment. It is true that the process of formation of stream institutions and even more of new denominations represents an element of embodiment. But few within the denominations that were formed out of the revivals of recent centuries would claim that the embodiment involved in this structuring process represents a work of the Holy Spirit, as clear as that is in the original springing forth of the streams.

What begins as an impulse of the Spirit has to become enfleshed both to survive and to bear fruit. Continuity over time is rooted in bodiliness. This principle was deeply embedded in the existence and memory of Israel, and was expressed in every biblical genealogy. The four life-streams are impulses of new life from the Holy Spirit; they are accompanied by certain basic faith convictions, that belong to the world of ideas. Both the new life and the idea-convictions need to be embodied to bear their appointed fruit.

The streams need the ancient Churches of East and West because these Churches did not begin simply as impulses of new life or as faith-convictions but as organic bodies that issued forth from the people of Israel through the labours of the Twelve and of St Paul. They are 'built upon the foundation of the apostles and prophets' (Eph 2:20). The attempts at stream-embodiment that scorn or ignore the ancient Churches are doomed to the perpetual process of creating new structures that reflect the organization of man rather than the creativity of God. As such, the new denominational structures lack the inner strength of the organic body and the intrinsic authority of historic apostolic succession.

The Constraints of Enfleshment

The taking on of human flesh by the Son of God has two important dimensions that are in some tension with each other: (1) the showing forth of divine life through Jesus' humanity; (2) the emptying (*kenosis*) that is involved in infinite majesty squeezing God's being not just into human nature but into our wounded human nature within the limitations of space and time. There is thus at one and the same time an element of **manifestation** and an element of **hiddenness** in the Incarnation. The emptying dimension is most graphically expressed in Paul's paean of wonderment in Philippians 2:5–11.

There is a similar process that is involved in the Church's reception of every move of the Holy Spirit – during the time of the Church's pilgrimage on earth. The Holy Spirit is infinite and unrestricted by nature, but the Spirit is sent to us humans, pilgrims in the flesh; the full reception of the Holy Spirit thus involves an element of emptying on the part of the Spirit, as the Spirit is limited by and constrained by the limitations of human and fleshly existence. There will always be in this world a disparity between the gift of the Holy Spirit and the bodily form into which the gift is received. That is why 'we do not know how to pray as we ought, but the Spirit himself intercedes for us with sighs too deep for words' (Rom 8:26).

The revivalist ethos of the life-streams tends to favour maximum manifestation now, and to emphasize the immediately realizable. Stream Christians are often impatient of routine and of delay, that seem to smack of dullness and complacency of spirit. The embodied mystery of the Church confronts the impulses of new life in the streams with the law of Incarnation. The element of constraint experienced as the new life becomes embodied is not simply due to 'old wineskins', or to rejection by the unenlightened; these factors may be involved, but there is a fundamental law of Incarnation and kenosis at work that is part of the very way that this new life is deepened and communicated. This theme is perhaps most fully worked out in 2 Corinthians. Paul speaks clearly there of this disparity between the gift and its earthly container: 'But we have this treasure in jars of clay to show that this all-surpassing power is from God and not from us' (2 Cor 4:7 NIV). The 'jars of clay' are not only our human bodies, but the embodied structural forms of the Church.

Thus the Divine Spirit coming into this human body marked with the signs of mortality is in constant tension with this deathward tendency. 'For while we live we are always being given up to death for Jesus' sake, so that the life of Jesus may be manifested in our mortal flesh. So death is at work in us, but life in you' (2 Cor 4:11–12). The outer and the inner are pulling in opposite directions: 'Though our outer nature is wasting away, our inner nature is being renewed every day' (2 Cor 4:16). However, this tension that results from Incarnation-enfleshment is only temporary; God is thus preparing for us the eternal dwelling where all dichotomy between outer and inner, spiritual and bodily, will be overcome. 'For this slight momentary affliction is preparing for us an eternal weight of glory beyond all comparison' (2 Cor 4:17).

Our present state of living this tension and of awaiting its final resolution causes us to **groan:** 'Here indeed we groan, and long to put on our heavenly dwelling, so that by putting it on we may not be found naked' (2 Cor 5:2–3). It belongs then to our present condition on earth to cry out to the Lord in groaning; the first instalment of the Holy Spirit has been given to us so that we can cry out for the Lord's work to be completed. 'For while we are still in this tent, we sigh with anxiety; not that we would be unclothed, but that we would be further clothed, so that what is mortal may be swallowed up by life. He who has prepared us for this very thing is God, who has given us the Spirit as a guarantee' (2 Cor 5:4–5).

It is then an intrinsic element of being an alive Christian to experience a suffering that results from the constraints of embodying the Holy Spirit within what as yet are still earthly vessels. This suffering has to find expression in a prayer of groaning in travail, like St Paul, in a prayer of anguish for our condition, and in a prayer of longing for the final resurrection, our full clothing with the body and the robes of glory.

Such suffering involves staying with situations that are difficult, provided that they are situations in which the Lord has placed us. It means working through difficult issues; it means facing the things inside ourselves that make us difficult to love, to respect, to listen to, to work with. It means facing the limitations to our understanding, allowing our prejudices to be exposed, letting the Lord teach us through those we find difficult and the situations from which we long to escape.

This does not mean that the Lord never calls people to move from one Church situation to another. But it does suggest that for committed Christians such moves are only appropriate after much prayer through the anguish and the sufferings of church tensions. To move at the first point of disapproval and difficulty is simply to give in to the immature pattern of running away from real life in search of a problem-free Utopia.

It is only in this way with a degree of suffering and a prayer of groaning that the new life of the Spirit will become embodied in any depth. This is ultimately the only answer to the problem of complacent and rather lifeless churches on the one hand and lively and enthusiastic but rather superficial charismatic assemblies on the other hand. These remarks are not a criticism of all new church leaders. In fact, because their networks are primarily based on personal relationships, some new church leaders have worked through more painful difficulties concerning personalities and doctrines than many leaders in the older Churches have ever done in their more protected situations.

Penetrating the Culture

A major strand in Catholic thinking on evangelization that marks it out from much evangelical debate is the emphasis on an evangelization in which the proclamation of the Christian gospel is aimed not solely at the conversion of individuals but at the penetration of the culture. Pope John Paul II has written of this process:

> Through inculturation the Church makes the Gospel incarnate in different cultures and at the same time introduces peoples, together with their cultures, into her own community. She transmits to them her own

values, at the same time taking the good elements
that already exist in them and renewing them from
within. Through inculturation the Church, for her
part, becomes a more intelligible sign of what she
is, and a more effective instrument of mission.[3]

Evangelical readers may fear that Catholic attempts
at inculturation too easily represent a form of religious imperialism in which the core gospel message
with its liberating power is not clearly preached. They
are concerned lest the gospel be compromised through
an unholy marriage with pagan cultures; some of
what evangelicals and Pentecostals have seen in Latin
America has heightened this fear. It was to guard against
this misconception of inculturation that Paul VI coined
the phrase 'the evangelization of cultures', meaning that
cultures have to be transformed, elevated and purified
through the proclamation of the gospel. While the life-
streams challenge the Catholic Church to preach the
full challenge of the gospel, the Church challenges
the streams to allow the sifting of the message from the
linguistic and cultural framework of the evangelists so
as truly to incarnate the gospel in other cultures. The
streams with their strong rooting in the Anglo-Saxon
world and their pragmatic tendency to value activity and
productivity over depth of reflection are more tempted
to take short-cuts in the process of taking the gospel to
foreign cultures. It is not that the missionary strategists
in the streams are unaware of the inculturation issue, but
more that their style and patterns, particularly perhaps
those of the international para-church movements, favour
immediate action and practical training more than the
long-term insertion of missionaries and evangelists into
a culture that they penetrate from within.

    The authentic penetration of cultures by the gospel also
involves a self-emptying on the part of the evangelists
and the leaders of the new communities of faith. For
those coming from another culture, it means taking on
all that is positive in the thought-forms, the lifestyle and
the sensitivities of the host-culture and letting go of these

values from one's own culture. Anything less represents
an evangelization that is weakened by elements of a
cultural imperialism. This process requires a profound
interior abnegation that is a sharing in Jesus' own
emptying in which he did not think 'equality with God
a thing to be grasped, but emptied himself, taking the
form of a servant, being born in the likeness of men' (Phil
2:6–7).

Chapter Twenty

Two Ways

We have argued that the streams of new life need the Churches and that the Churches need the streams of new life. We have argued that these statements apply particularly to the ancient Churches of East and West, the Oriental Orthodox, the Eastern Orthodox and the Catholic.

It will be seen from the historical summaries earlier that there are two different ways in which the Churches and the streams can interact and to some degree are already interacting positively. The first is the rise and reception of the streams within the life of existing Churches. The second is where stream-life has developed apart from the existing Churches, but has learned, early or late, to relate positively to them in a co-operative spirit.

Just as there are two ways of Church and streams relating positively, there are two ways of refusing to relate: the first is where Churches refuse to welcome the streams or at least to allow them any space to develop; the second is where streams that have developed apart from the Churches live in antagonism to them. Both then see themselves as opponents and rivals, the Churches being tempted to denounce the streams as sects and the streams to accuse the Churches of being dead or irrelevant.

1. The Reception of the Streams within the Life of Existing Churches

As outlined in chapters two to five, the streams have mostly found a degree of acceptance, though a limited welcome, within the historic Protestant Churches. Almost from the beginnings of Evangelicalism, there has been an evangelical presence in the Anglican Communion, one that has been increasing in recent times in the Church of England. There have been revivalistic strands of evangelical inspiration within the Reformed Churches, particularly those of Switzerland and France, and within Lutheranism, especially in Scandinavia. The Holiness stream has had considerable influence in many mainline Protestant circles, especially through the Keswick convention and in German Lutheranism, where it built on an older Pietist tradition.

By contrast, the Pentecostal stream was almost wholly rejected or ignored by mainline Protestantism. In the few circles where the Pentecostal fire was received into Church milieux, such as those associated with the Anglican Alexander Boddy in England and a handful of Lutheran pastors in Germany, indifference and rejection prevailed over time. One or two such Pentecostal circles survived, such as the Baptist Orebro mission in Sweden. However, it was basically with the charismatic stream that the Pentecostal new life penetrated the historic Churches. This time, besides the mainline Protestant Churches, the new life-stream entered the Roman Catholic Church.

Where the life-streams have been received into the mainline church circles that were open to them, there have been a number of patterns of reception. Sometimes a stream enters a Church tradition, and establishes itself as a distinctive grouping, perhaps a distinctive party, within that Church, as with the evangelical stream within the Church of England. The stream has been able to develop and be a force for spiritual revival, but its party character has limited its interaction with the rest of the Church. Though there was an evangelical influence on the founders of the Oxford Movement, the evangelical and the Catholic movements within the Church of England long saw themselves as opponents. Only with the arrival of the charismatic stream, which touched both parties, was a breach made in this wall – though by this time the Catholic wing of the Church of England had passed its zenith. However, total separation of parties within a Church communion is difficult to achieve, however strong the party spirit. Some interaction is unavoidable, even more since synodical forms of government were introduced in which all parties and currents were represented. This interaction has been carried further in the Anglican communion by the appointment of bishops from the evangelical and Catholic parties.

In another pattern of reception the stream-life acquired a legitimate space to exist, and avoided being an object of contestation or ridicule, but it did not exert much influence on the Church that received it. This seems to have been the case with some of the German Holiness movement, which inherited the inwardness of the earlier Pietist movement.

Another pattern was one of lengthy tension and conflict between the new stream and the milieu of the receiving Church. Perhaps the most obvious example here is the response of American Methodism to the Holiness stream of the nineteenth century. Thirty or more years of struggle and increasing tension led to many Holiness people leaving the main Methodist Churches and forming new Holiness denominations. Some, however, remained, but the stream-life then became more removed from the main thrust of those Methodist Churches.

Because the charismatic stream is more recent and has affected more Churches and on a more global scale, the patterns of interaction between Church and stream are less clear and perhaps have not yet resolved into patterns acceptable to Church and to stream participants. This is why the charismatic stream in the mainline Churches is the place where this issue of interaction is most relevant, and the interaction and integration between the charismatic renewal and the Roman Catholic Church is like the test case.

Catholic Charismatic Renewal

As a current of new life in the historic Church in communion with Rome, the Catholic Charismatic Renewal lives in the necessary tension between stream and

Church. This tension takes many forms: between the call
to affirm the prophetic distinctiveness of this stream and
the Catholic affirmation of it being one work of the Spirit
among many in the Church; between the upholding of the
ecumenical character of the stream and the need for it to
be integrated into Church life; between the free exercise
of the charisms distinctive of the charismatic stream
and their insertion into the received structures of the
Church, hierarchical, liturgical and educational; between
the call to a practice anchored in the distinctive biblical
convictions of the stream and the received patterns of
Church piety.

In this way, the charismatic renewal in the Catholic
Church is by its nature struggling to maintain its full
witness to the Spirit's gift in the charismatic stream
and to affirm its full Catholicity as an integral element
within the communion of the Catholic Church. If this
struggle is lived in full fidelity to the Holy Spirit, it
will lead to authentic renewal of the Church through a
process of enrichment, of enlivening and of purification.
If participants yield to pressures that are not of the Holy
Spirit, then either the charismatic will not permeate the
organic life of the Church and will become marginalized
and poorly embodied or it will be diluted in the interests
of easier acceptance leading to a reception by the Church
of something less than God's renewing gift.

Perhaps the issues at stake can be seen by the very
different histories of charismatic communities within the
Catholic world in the two countries where they have had
the biggest resonance, the United States and France. In
the United States, the charismatic communities, of which
the Word of God Community at Ann Arbor, Michigan was
the pioneer and model, had an explosive growth rate in
the early years, tended to have a centralizing pattern
drawing people to the community's geographical centre,
and have mostly run into serious difficulties in their third
decade. By contrast, the French charismatic communities
have maintained a steadily increasing growth rate over
three decades, have not centralized but have constantly
formed new branches in other locations and countries,

and have handled more successfully the transition from first generation enthusiasm and informality to a co-ordinated but flexible established community life.

The contrasts between the American and the French experience is not simply one of differing patterns of growth, distribution and success. It also concerns the intensity and depth of interaction between new charism and old Church. The American communities probably gave freer rein, at least in their early years, to the charismatic dimension, and their affinity with the wide charismatic stream was more readily acknowledged. It was in the United States that the bold experiment of covenant communities with both Catholic and Protestant members was launched. However, the links between the new communities and the Church institution were weaker than in France. This difference was due in large part to the highly critical situation of the French Church, with drastically reduced congregations and a severe shortage of priests; within this situation, the potential of the new communities with their appeal to youth was soon sensed by the bishops. Ancient church buildings, monasteries and convents that the old religious orders could no longer fill were made available to the new char-ismatic communities. These historic settings joined with the European sense of history and the Catholic reverence for tradition to cause the new charismatic communities to find their identity in relation to the rich French heritage of Catholic spirituality and scholarship.[1]

In comparison to France, the American communities have not been able to achieve a similar degree of rootage and stability. In part, this reflects the lesser degree of historical roots in American society. The American con-text allows a greater facility for creative experimentation, and so the rise of the American communities preceded by a few years the beginnings in France. Some of the French communities manifest an element of the harnessing of charismatic energy to forms of Catholic traditionalism, though it would be wrong to dismiss them in the manner of some critics as a wholly reactionary phenomenon. But what is clear is that the American–French contrast can provide a first-class case study of the issues of the prophetic and the institutional, of charismatic newness and creativity in relation to historic embodiment and Church integration.

Summary
An historical overview is likely to leave the impression that the interaction between stream and Church has generally been inadequate, that the streams have rarely or never had the impact on their Churches that their adherents hoped, and that when the streams have been granted a degree of legitimacy they can lose their cutting edge and become Church parties rather than streams of new life.

However, these conclusions refer primarily to the reception of the streams within the mainline Protestant Churches. As indicated, the penetration of the charismatic stream within the Roman Catholic Church is too recent to make more than very provisional comments. At this point, it would appear that the charismatic renewal has received a more generous official welcome within the Catholic world than any of the streams have received in mainline Protestant circles. However, the Catholic welcome has often been the granting of legitimacy and of a space for expression, more than it has been a reception of the challenge posed by the charismatic stream to the whole Church.

The question should then be asked of each stream and of each Church that it touches: has there remained a vision to be a leaven for the whole Church? This is closely related to the question as to whether there have been believers firmly committed to a travailing prayer for their Church.

2. The Development of the Streams apart from the Older Churches

As mentioned in chapters two to five, the new life-streams always had a trans-confessional character. They were never confined to any one tradition in their origins.

Some from their first years had an element that was not related to any one Church tradition. This 'outside the Churches' character developed in various ways: (1) Those (mostly small) congregations maintaining an independent stance; an obvious example are those evangelical assemblies in Britain that belong to an association such as FIEC but retain a strong congregational independence; French evangelicalism largely follows this pattern. (2) The groupings that formed themselves into new denominations with a stream identity, e.g. the Holiness and the Pentecostal denominations. (3) Those stream groupings that have formed themselves into identifiable networks that welcome trans-local forms of ministry (a major distinction from the first category) but which are determined not to become new denominations (their distinction from the second category). The obvious example here is found in the new networks of charismatic churches. (4) The formation of itinerant ministries that are stream-inspired but which are not affiliated to any denomination. This pattern is especially a recent development reflecting an entrepreneurial spirit and the ease of modern travel.

In general, the four types of stream expression apart from the older Churches have not shown great interest in positive interaction with the latter. Often these 'outside' stream-expressions have adopted hostile attitudes towards the older Churches, and have thus been seen as sectarian. This label may not always have been fair, because they have generally eschewed the severer expressions of sectarian exclusivism, as they have mostly accepted the fellowship of other participants in the same stream, whether 'inside' or 'outside' the Churches. These 'outside' expressions have normally shown little interest in positive relations with the older Churches, as they have mostly rejected the claims of these Churches to be truly Church, and they have often regarded themselves as the authentic Church, either the replacement for or the restoration of the true Church of Jesus Christ.

However, there are many more hopeful signs in recent years of the Holy Spirit opening up broader horizons among those outside the older Churches. Particularly significant here is the much wider collaboration being promoted and practised by the leaders of the new charismatic churches, especially in countries like Great Britain and South Africa.

Accepting Both Ways

Effective collaboration between Churches and life-streams requires an openness to recognize that the Holy Spirit is at work in both ways, in the streams within the historic Churches and in their expressions 'outside', whether in new denominations or in the other forms indicated. It will not be possible for Churches to relate properly to stream-expressions in their own midst, if they do not recognize that the streams there present are worldwide, inter-confessional and present in more ecclesial and less ecclesial forms. Without this understanding of the nature of the streams, Church leaders will be apt to think of stream expressions in their Church as simply 'home-grown'; this will immediately limit the prophetic challenge of the stream to the Church.

Both stream-expressions within the historic Churches and those 'outside' are likely to see their form, inside or outside, as the proper expression. This is not necessarily wrong in terms of what is understood to be normal or regular, but it easily becomes distorted when anything outside the normal or regular is automatically regarded in a negative way. Even when both sides are open to fellowship and co-operation with each other, the other form is easily seen as inferior and even perilous. Stream leaders within the historic Churches may recognize that the Pentecostals and new church people are moved by the Holy Spirit, but still see them as fringe, naive and to some degree deviant. Pentecostals and new church leaders may admit that the Holy Spirit is (surprisingly) at work within the older Churches, but regard this as exceptional and as having little to do with the Churches: so Catholic charismatics, for example, would be seen as 'Spirit-filled' *despite* their Church.

The Spirit's call is to recognize the work of the Spirit

wherever it is happening, whether in the places and ways that we expect or in those that we dismiss. This requires that we all want to discern, identify and welcome as much of the Holy Spirit's work as we can find. It does not require that we abandon our confessional or our 'non-denominational' convictions, whichever they may be. We are not called to abandon our beliefs concerning the normal or regular patterns of God's dealings with the body of Christ, but to allow them to be purified and deepened. Thus I, as a Roman Catholic, believe that it is through the historic Church in communion with the see of Rome that 'the fullness of the means of salvation can be obtained'[2] and that the Catholic Church has in a definite sense an official normative character.

However, we need to be open to the Holy Spirit giving us new and more flexible understanding of the relation between the regular or normative in our faith-convictions, and the ways in which the Lord works outside these forms. The Second Vatican Council recognized that other Christian communions 'have by no means been deprived of significance and importance in the mystery of salvation'.[3] While Vatican Two was talking about Churches and denominations, the principle adopted by the Council can be extended to the life-streams outside the Roman Catholic communion. From a Church-centred perspective as to what is normative, they will be seen as at best inferior and derivative, but from a Christ-and-Spirit-centred position they may be seen to have a major significance in God's purpose. This can only be determined by long and prayerful examination of the life-streams through all the criteria we have for discerning the presence of Christ and the working of the Holy Spirit.

It is the conviction of the author, expressed throughout this book, that the life-streams and the Churches are complementary in God's purpose. If this is so, it also means that the two ways of relating Church and streams are also complementary. We should accept both ways of positive relationship, welcoming them as different spheres of the Holy Spirit's action, seeking how they fit together in God's overall plan, but letting go of the urge to make judgmental comparisons that effectively relegate the others to relative insignificance.

Two New Factors

However, with the twentieth century, two new factors have emerged that touch on the permeation of the Churches by the new life of the streams: the first is the ecumenical movement, understood as the burden for and pursuit of Christian unity. I give this understanding, so that the ecumenical movement is not misunderstood as restricted to official forms of inter-Church relations and official ecumenical bodies. The second new factor is constituted by the world-wide para-church movements that have arisen from within the streams. Both of these factors have opened up the possibility of a more creative and fuller relating of Church and streams.

The Ecumenical Movement

While the streams always had in their origins and subsequently retained, with the exception of the Pentecostal stream, a trans-denominational character, there was minimal inter-Church exchange before the rise and acceptance of the ecumenical movement. This lack meant that the trans-confessional character of the streams remained largely at a personal level, and so the impact of their trans-confessional dimension on the Churches remained rather slight.

The growth of ecumenical relationships between the Churches now makes possible, if Church leaders and stream-participants are willing, a deeper and more penetrating interaction between the trans-confessional streams and the various Churches. The first condition for such an interaction to occur is that the stream-participants recognize that the streams are not ends in themselves but exist to serve, renew and restore the Church – not just one denomination, but all together. In other words, to see that a trans-confessional stream has an ecumenical calling to help renew the Churches and bring them into unity.

This ecumenical call applies both to stream-elements within the older Churches and to those outside. For the associations, networks and assemblies outside the historic Churches are also part of the Lord's purpose for the revival, renewal and restoration of the whole Church.

A second condition is that stream-participants understand themselves not just as stream-participants, but also as organically part of Church, whatever form this may take. Then they can begin to live their stream-participation as an element contributing to the life of the Church and tradition to which they belong.

A third condition is that the Churches take the streams with a new seriousness. This will be made easier if their stream-participants do not sit light to their Church traditions. For the Churches to take the streams with greater seriousness is to take their trans-confessional character more seriously too. Then they will be able to see the streams as part of the Lord drawing his people into the unity of the Church.

The Para-Church Movements

The new international para-church movements of the twentieth century are themselves trans-confessional. With their determination not to establish local churches in their own name, they are obliged to some degree to become servants of the existing churches. This is particularly the case with those movements, like YWAM, that move beyond the evangelism and discipleship of individuals to become involved in church planting and community-formation.

This development also creates the possibility of a deeper interaction between streams and Church. But this possibility can only be realized as certain conditions are fulfilled, similar to those for the ecumenical movement. For example, a deeper interaction would require that the Churches take the para-church movements more seriously, that they desire their assistance, that they welcome the trans-confessional exposure involved. For a greater openness of this kind to lead to regular co-operation requires that the Churches let go of their controlling tendencies, for the para-church organizations that draw participants from many backgrounds will refuse to be controlled by any one Church.

It is also necessary for the para-church movements to take seriously the Church affiliations of their members and to respect the rightful authority and leadership of the Churches. This presents greater difficulties, because their members are usually young and have less developed Church loyalties. This demand may then appear to be the imposition of the rigidities of the elders on the youth. These kinds of issues need to be addressed together by the para-church leaders and Church leaders.

We can see here a need for humility on both sides. Each side is tempted to regard itself as the show that counts. The para-church movements can see themselves as the action-spots, the people who have the know-how and the capacity to move from ideas to action in any part of the globe. The Churches can regard themselves as the only authentic representatives of Christ, the only bodies with the proper pedigree, and those whose approval is necessary for any Christian venture to be authentic.

A proper humility will seek first to accept and recognize the real gifts and call of the other. Church leaders will want to recognize the work of the Spirit in the para-church movements. Movement leaders will want to recognize the calling and responsibility of bishops and church leaders. Church leaders will want to give scope for the Spirit to work through inter-Church movements. Movement leaders will want to benefit from the discernment, the wisdom and support of bishops, moderators and other Church leaders.

The Way of the Cross

The two ways of relating positively the life of the streams with the historic Churches – as currents within them or as new groupings establishing co-operative links – are not simply methods or techniques to follow. The work of correlating the streams and the Churches is a calling of the Holy Spirit that can only bear fruit through the work of the Cross.

For new stream life to bear fruit within the life of any Church requires a dying to self and a willingness to suffer. New impulses of life from the Lord always call for such an interior purification if they are to bear lasting fruit. To urge the complementarity of the historic Churches and the modern life-streams is not to deny that there is in this world always a spiritual battle to be fought, but it is to refuse to see the battle in simplistic terms as 'us versus them', whether the new 'restoration' churches against the old dead denominations or the 'one true Church' against the sects.

To work to correlate the historic Churches and the life-streams is not inherently an act of compromise (to see it that way is too sectarian). It is to uphold and build on the work of the Holy Spirit and of Jesus Christ both within the older Churches and outside. It is precisely to refuse to reduce Christian discipleship to any kind of party loyalty; it is to submit all other genuine loyalties to the following of Christ. 'For while there is jealousy and strife among you, are you not of the flesh, and behaving like ordinary men? For when one says, "I belong to Paul," and another, "I belong to Apollos," are you not merely men?' (1 Cor 3:3–4).

Within the Historic Churches
Christians within the mainline Churches, whose faith has been enlivened by any of the life-streams, will seek to be faithful to the whole grace of God that they have received. They will seek to bear witness to the life of the Spirit in the life-stream that has touched them, and they will seek to bear witness to the grace of God in their own Church tradition. They will recognize their spiritual affinity with others in their stream, but they will also recognize its compatibility with full loyalty to their own Church and the heart of its tradition. This stance will not always earn them applause and appreciation, but this is part of the price to be paid for faithful discipleship.

In the Catholic and Orthodox traditions in particular,

there is a deep sense that the call to holiness of life
and to renewal of the Church will be costly, and that
a humble and obedient but persevering witness to the
Lord and his call is what will bear the most lasting fruit.
This stance cannot be imposed on other Christians. This
sometimes heroic call fits most readily with a sacramental
ecclesiology that makes greater claims for one's Church.
Changing one's church affiliation does not mean the
same in a Free Church context as in the Catholic.
Nonetheless, the speed with which some Christians leave
their churches when they encounter opposition is not
reassuring. It has to be asked whether this is part of
the anaesthetic culture in which no pain is tolerable, and
in which any real taking up of the cross is instinctively
avoided.

In New Stream-Denominations and in the New Churches

Here there is also a price to be paid for faithful witnessing to the work of God both in the renewal of the
historic Churches and in modern Holiness and/or Pentecostal denominations and new charismatic churches.
New groupings conscious of the Spirit's leading are often
tempted to become exclusive in their outlook, sometimes
urging other believers to 'come out of Babylon' and seeing
no value in fellowship with those in 'dead institutions'. To
take a stand for forms of fellowship and co-operation with
Christians within the older Churches may arouse ridicule
and opposition and be denounced as compromise. On the
contrary, it calls for a principled co-operation, that is not
just 'fellowship with anybody' irrespective of convictions,
but a discerning and open stance, seeking to recognize
the presence of the Spirit and of the Lord among all who
profess the name of Christ.

Either way, the call of the Lord to an authentic ecumenical stance involves the way of the cross. It is what
Paul writes about when he says: 'And those who belong
to Christ Jesus have crucified the flesh with its pas-
sions and desires' (Gal 5:24). It involves the rejection
of all judgmentalism, all pigeon-holing of the 'others'

in stereotyped and prejudicial ways; it involves being
purified of the human tendency to absolutize all differences and to prefer lazy and misleading generaliza-
tions to real discernment; it involves a call to mutual
love and respect of those who love the Lord Jesus and
value the work of the Holy Spirit, but have different
theologies, different church cultures, different value-
systems. Truly the way of true respect and of collaboration is a way to personal purification and to holiness of life.

Chapter Twenty-One
Repentance

In the last two chapters, we have examined the challenges posed by the new streams to the ancient Churches, and those posed by the Churches to the streams. These challenges are multi-faceted. These challenges require a questioning of attitudes, of doctrinal presuppositions, of philosophies, and of practice. For example, attitudes of superiority and of narrowness, whether sectarian or ecclesial; doctrinal presuppositions that are one-sided or rationalist; philosophies that are individualistic, clerical, Church-centred at the expense of being Christ-centred; practices that flow from any of these mentalities.

Wherever a challenge 'bites', and the Holy Spirit convicts us through a challenge, we are being given the grace of repentance and forgiveness. Whenever we see that the Church has not preached the saving gospel of Jesus with clarity, we need to grieve before the Lord for this failure. Each time that we see that we have acted as though our convictions were the whole of divine revelation or all that mattered, we should humble ourselves before the Lord and beg pardon for this arrogance. When we see that we have neglected the Word of God, and not made the Scriptures the basic diet of our church life, our theology and our piety, we should acknowledge this sin of neglect and ingratitude to the God who has spoken to his people through his Word.

As there has been sin in our separations, so reconciliation can only come from repentance for our sin. The ancient Churches and the new streams represent one of the major tension-points in the contemporary Christian world. This is where the most intemperate language is being used between Christians: whether the dismissal of

most stream-life as 'fundamentalist' or of their organizations as 'sects'; or the attacks on the ancient Churches as
dead or apostate, the mocking of liturgical rites as lifeless
rituals. This confrontation, with all its harshness and
mutual ignorance, can only be overcome by the convicting
and illuminating work of the Holy Spirit, and mutual
repentance for our hasty judgmentalism. 'If you do away
with the yoke of oppression, with the pointing finger and
malicious talk . . . Your people will rebuild the ancient
ruins and will raise up the age-old foundations; you will
be called Repairer of Broken Walls, Restorer of Streets
with Dwellings' (Is 58:9, 12 NIV).

The principle that real reconciliation of disputants
can only be achieved through mutual repentance and
forgiveness is widely acknowledged in relation to the
spiritual life and relations between Christians in general.
However, the Churches and Christian movements have
been slow to admit and apply this principle to their
mutual relationships.

The Obstacles to Corporate Repentance

Both the ancient Churches and the modern life-streams
have difficulty in receiving the challenges posed by the
Lord through the others and of coming to a corporate
repentance for their sin that is thereby exposed. Both
ancient Churches and modern streams share the difficulty that comes from their sense of being God's chosen,
and the inappropriateness of repenting to those who are
regarded as reprobate. But some of the other reasons for
their difficulties over corporate repentance are peculiar
to each group.

Catholics and Orthodox
The Catholic and Orthodox Churches both have a strong
sense of tradition and the importance of the past. They
also have a strong corporate sense of themselves as
Church, even though this has been diminished among
the Catholic people in the West by the pervasive individualism of modern Western culture. These positive factors

favour the possibility of corporate repentance for sins against Christian unity and for sinful responses to the work of the Holy Spirit in the streams.

The obstacles to such repentance by Catholics and Orthodox come much more from their sense of the holiness of the Church and of her infallibility or indefectibility. To say that the Church has sinned seems to go too far, and to threaten the Church's confession of faith in the Church as mystery and as the body of which Jesus Christ is the head. This reluctance should not be dismissed as wholly due to arrogance and smug superiority. In the Catholic and Orthodox understanding, the mystery of the Church as the communion of saints not only includes Jesus as head, but also the glorious Church of heaven and the assembly of the redeemed whose purification is being completed after death.

The ancient Churches need to find a way of expressing corporate repentance for the evils attributable to the Church on earth, as an institution of humans who have often failed the Lord, not simply as individuals but as structured bodies of believers. A cry of repentance has to rise from particular Church communities. Some of the clearest expressions of repentance for the sins of the whole Church can be found in a place where many would not look: in the liturgy of the Catholic Apostolic Church, formed in the 1830s, which sought to combine charismatic, sacramental and eschatological elements:

O Almighty God, who art greatly to be feared in Thy holiness; we are ashamed of our manifold iniquities; we confess unto Thee our sin. We offend continually and grievously in deed, in word, and in thought. Our fathers have transgressed against Thee; and we, our children, and our brethren, do fill up the measure of their iniquity. Thy people, from generation to generation, have resisted and turned from Thee. We have abounded in false doctrine, heresy, and schism. The priesthood have sinned, and all the people. We harden our hearts, and are impenitent; we are proud and rebellious; we are high-minded, and refuse to be

humbled. We have rejected Thine ordinances, and
have chosen paths of our own. We have lived in strife
and confusion; and have not desired peace.

We have loved lies and vanity, hypocrisy and
deceit. We covet and lust after the things which
perish, and seek not Thy heavenly kingdom. We
confess the sin of all Thy people, the members of
Thy One Catholic Church. We have received Thy
truth with our minds, but have closed our hearts
against Thee. We have sat in judgment on those
whom Thou hast set over us, and we judge not
ourselves. We have loved the ways of disorder in
which we have lived, and have been slow to learn
reverence and humility. We have caused Thy truth
to be rejected of the heathen by our foolishness and
our sin; and have brought reproach upon Thy holy
Name. By our hardness of heart and unbelief we
have grieved and quenched Thy Holy Spirit. We are
a burden unto Thee, hindering Thy purpose of grace
to others; and we have forsaken our own mercies.

We confess unto Thee, O God, the sin of all kings,
princes, and governors; the sin of all ranks and
estates of men. From the highest to the lowest, we
have all transgressed against Thee. And as dwellers
in this land, we especially acknowledge before Thee
the sin of this kingdom and people. For all these
our manifold offences and iniquities we do beseech
Thy mercy. We have sinned wilfully and grievously,
yet have pity on us. We have presumed on Thy
long-suffering, yet deal with us in mercy and in
truth, and forgive us our sins: through Thy Son
Jesus Christ, our only Redeemer. Amen.[1]

The Streams
Christians belonging to the life-streams have a different
difficulty in coming to corporate repentance for their sins,
particularly those against the older Churches and their
members. In general, stream Christians (evangelical,
Holiness, Pentecostal, charismatic) are more accustomed

than most other believers to repenting for their sins before others. However, they do not typically attribute great importance to tradition, and they tend to have more of an individualistic mentality than a strong corporate sense. These two factors militate against ready acknowledgment of shared sin.

It is difficult to own the past and to accept responsibility for the past if you do not value continuity with your spiritual forebears. But continuity with our forebears is precisely what tradition in the proper sense concerns. Because the streams are relatively new in Christian history, and it is of their nature to be more fluid than Church institutions, they might appear to have greater flexibility; but their identity also has less clear cut edges, and this can make acceptance of corporate responsibility more difficult.

Repentance First to God

Much of the difficulty in corporate repentance can be removed by reminding ourselves that repentance is first of all to God, as all sin is first an offence against God. As the son in the parable of the prodigal son says: 'Father, I have sinned against heaven and before you' (Luke 15: 18, 21). Conviction of sin means allowing the Holy Spirit to imprint our hearts with a sense of the injury done to God and of the affront to God's majesty.

When Churches have adopted attitudes of arrogance towards other groups of Christians, this grieves the heart of God. It represents a scorning of God's work in them, a denial of God's love for them. When the Word of God has been neglected, there has been a failure to acknowledge the full work and gift of God. There has been a preference for the human words of theological systems over the Word inspired by the Holy Spirit. The Holy Spirit will show us the grotesqueness of such a stance in face of the love, the holiness and the wisdom of God. When the work of God in ordinary Christians has been devalued by forms of clericalism, God is being offended. Those whom God has chosen and for whom Christ died are being treated

without respect for the presence and work of the Holy
Spirit of God.

Catholic Moves Towards Repentance

The Second Vatican Council in its Decree on Ecumenism,
Unitatis Redintegratio, took up and made central in its
vision of ecumenical practice the teaching of the Abbé
Couturier on 'spiritual ecumenism'. These principles can
be summed up as follows:

1. 'Every renewal of the Church essentially consists in an increase of fidelity to her own calling'
(para 6).
2. 'There can be no ecumenism worthy of the name
without interior conversion' (para 7).
3. 'This change of heart and holiness of life, along
with public and private prayer for the unity of
Christians, should be regarded as the soul of the
whole ecumenical movement, and merits the name,
"spiritual ecumenism"' (para 8).

Although the Catholic bishops emphasized spiritual
ecumenism in this way at the Council, the subsequent development of ecumenical relations has rarely
reflected this priority. While the Catholic 'conversion'
to ecumenism gave a major boost to the ecumenical
movement for a decade or more, ecumenical interaction
has largely taken the form either of theological dialogue
or of practical collaboration. The natural setting for
the former has been in bilateral dialogues between the
Churches, together with a multilateral expression in the
Faith and Order movement, and the primary setting for
practical collaboration has been in Councils of Churches
at whatever level.

Meanwhile, spiritual ecumenism has largely faded
from consciousness. Among the reasons for this would
appear to be: (i) spiritual ecumenism was a largely
Catholic contribution born in the years of adversity (see
chapter ten); (ii) the Council failed to make explicit that

the responsibility for conversion (and thus for repentance) was a corporate responsibility of the Church as well as of the individual Christian. A 'spiritual ecumenism' without corporate Church expression of repentance for sins against unity remains private and without real impact on public Church behaviour.

In consequence, the practice of ecumenism has involved very little expression of repentance by the Churches. This must surely be one of the major reasons for the sense of malaise and immobility in the ecumenical movement today. Thus, we have had a significant number of inter-Church theological dialogues that have produced results beyond most people's expectations. But the Churches, especially perhaps the Roman Catholic Church, have then had great difficulty receiving the results of these dialogues and allowing them to impact Church life and teaching. Is this not basically because there can be no real progress without repentance? If theological dialogues reach any form of consensus, they must at least implicitly be recognizing deficiencies in past understanding and practice. But if such recognition remains merely implicit and theoretical, and if it does not lead to expression of sorrow for our past failings and the asking of forgiveness from those who were hurt and scandalized by these faults, then the attitudes of our hearts are not changing and real reconciliation is no nearer.

It should be noted, however, that while Vatican Two did accept the concept of spiritual ecumenism from the teaching of the Abbé Couturier, the Abbé himself had taught and practised forms of repentance on behalf of his Church. This Catholic repentance of Couturier found particular expression in regard to the atrocity that historically has dominated the French Christian consciousness, the massacre of several thousand Protestants on St Bartholomew's Day, 24 August 1572. He acknowledged that the Protestants had been killed by the Catholics for wholly political reasons, that the news of the massacre was greeted with joy in Rome, with a commemorative medal being issued to celebrate the event. The Abbé requested that the Catholic hierarchy establish a day of penitence for the French Church in a spirit of reparation for this evil in all its dimensions, suggesting that this day coincide with the day observed each year by the descendants of the Huguenots in memory of the sufferings of their ancestors in the persecutions of Louis XIV following the Revocation of the Edict of Nantes in 1685. This request, which preceded official Catholic acceptance of ecumenism, was not granted.

While all sides are called upon to turn from sin and to repent in response to the grace of the Holy Spirit, the ancient Churches of East and West have a particular responsibility flowing both from their length of witness and from the high claims made on their behalf. The Roman Church has a great responsibility to lead the way in repentance, flowing from the claim of the Pope to a primacy of service, and because it existed and sinned before any of the Protestant churches came into being. If the Church of Rome 'presides in love' as St Ignatius of Antioch says, then it must be the first to repent for lack of that love.

Signs of New Hope

In recent times, there have been several encouraging signs of a greater willingness to move beyond a cerebral ecumenism to forms of Church repentance. The Groupe des Dombes, a group of Catholic and Protestant theologians originally convened by the Abbé Couturier in 1937, celebrated its 50th anniversary by producing a document on the conversion of the Churches.[2] They distinguish between Christian identity (the personal confession of faith in Christ within the Trinitarian framework made in the Church), ecclesial identity (formed by faith in the full catholicity of the Church yet to be realized) and confessional identity (shaped by the present self-understanding of one's own Church). Corresponding to each identity there is a necessary repentance and conversion. Christian conversion is rooted in the call of Jesus 'the kingdom of God is at hand; repent, and believe in the gospel' (Mark 1:15). Ecclesial conversion is the same response of Christian conversion, but at the collective and institutional level, turning from sinful attitudes and actions that have defiled the body of Christ. Confessional conversion is that part of ecclesial conversion that applies to one's own Church tradition, the repentance for the sins of our Church/tradition/denomination.

In November 1994, Patriarch Bartholomew I of Constantinople paid a visit to the Benedictine monastery of Chevetogne in Belgium to thank them for their work for Christian unity, especially between the Orthodox and the Catholic Churches. In the course of his address to the monks, the Patriarch said:

> The sins of one and the other side are more than simple theoretical errors in the formulations of the Gospel of the Church. They have produced a specific form of social life, that is to say a civilization of a certain type. The theological problems that we have together to confront are deviations from the purity of the Church's life. They have given rise to individualism, rationalism, legalism, positivism and the fruits of the anguish that torment the human race. Unfortunately, it was in Christian circles that there developed the first forms of totalitarianism, of the oppression of consciences, of systematic propaganda, of police repression. If contemporary civilisation, since the Age of Enlightenment, obstinately persists in the denial of the Christian roots of Europe, if it is a civilisation of physical power, of nihilism, and of the tacit violation of the natural rights of the individual, if it has become a society of asocial individuals, we bear the responsibility, especially we who have reduced the Gospel of the Church to an infantile religiosity.[3]

In his apostolic letter of November 1994 urging the Catholic Church to prepare for the third millennium, *Tertio Millennio Adveniente*; Pope John Paul II spoke of the need to repent for sins against Christian unity. 'Among the sins which require a greater commitment to repentance and conversion should certainly be counted those which have been detrimental to the unity willed by God for his People' (para 34). Further on, the Pope remarks: 'Another painful chapter of history to which the sons and daughters of the Church must return with a spirit of repentance is that of the acquiescence given, especially in certain centuries, to intolerance and even the use of violence in the service of truth' (para 35).

Six months later, Pope John Paul II issued an encyclical letter on ecumenism, *Ut Unum Sint*. The Pope here links dialogue with examination of conscience, a new point in official Catholic statements on ecumenism and on dialogue.

> If such dialogue does not become an examination of conscience, a kind of 'dialogue of consciences', can we count on the assurance which the First Letter of John gives us? 'My little children, I am writing this to you so that you may not sin; but if any one does sin, we have an advocate with the Father, Jesus Christ the righteous; and he is the expiation for our sins, and not for ours only but also for the sins of the whole world' (2:1–2) . . . Even after the many sins which have contributed to our historical divisions, Christian unity is possible, provided that we are humbly conscious of having sinned against unity and are convinced of our need for conversion. (para 34).[4]

The entire encyclical is strongly imbued with a spiritual understanding of ecumenism.

The instances cited of Church leaders calling for repentance for sins against unity all come from the context of reconciliation between the major Church traditions. The argument of this book urges that this call has to be extended to cover the relationships between the historic Churches on the one side and the modern life-streams on the other side. This need flows from three points in particular: (1) the life-streams reflect a particular work of the Holy Spirit in the last two and a half centuries that is central to the Spirit's summons to the Churches for revival and renewal; (2) the streams represent the cutting edge of Christian evangelism and expansion in the modern world; (3) the tensions between the Churches and the streams threaten if unaddressed to open up a new set of divisions in contemporary Christianity just as some older tensions and divisions are on the decline.

The challenges posed by the streams to the Churches (see chapter eighteen) and those posed by the Churches to the streams (see chapter nineteen) need to impact hearts as well as minds on both sides. The challenge to our hearts can lead to a mutual repentance to the Lord and to each other that will open the floodgates of divine grace in an unprecedented manner.

Chapter Twenty-Two

The Relevance of Israel

There has been a growing awareness among many Christians of the relevance of Israel for Christian unity. In this chapter, I want to look at the continuing theological importance of Israel and its implications for Christian repentance.

In modern times, there has been a revolution in Christian thinking concerning God's covenant with Israel. The enormity of the Holocaust, when six million Jews were eliminated through the systematic implementation of the Nazi ideology, has pricked the Christian conscience. The nagging question persists as to whether the Church's traditional stance towards the Jews had created the possibility for such an atrocity. Largely in consequence, the 'replacement' theology, that has dominated most of Christian history, is being increasingly abandoned. This theory asserted that the Old Covenant of the Lord with Israel had been abrogated as a result of Israel's rejection of Jesus as the Messiah and that in consequence Israel's place in God's promises had been taken by the Christian Church.

A Renewed Understanding of Israel

Both the life-streams and the Roman Catholic Church have been rethinking Christian attitudes towards Israel and the ongoing place of the Jewish people in God's plan. The streams as loci of new life have done most to seize anew the prophetic sense of the place of the people of Israel in God's plan. The Catholic Church with its detailed creed and formal liturgy has taken the most significant steps in terms of the correction of traditional teaching

concerning Israel and the elimination from the liturgy
of language offensive to the Jewish people, though the
extent to which popular Catholic attitudes to the Jews
have changed varies from country to country.

Evangelical

The greatest credit for Christian recovery of the ongoing
place of Israel in God's purpose belongs to the evangelicals. There were antecedents to faith in the restoration
of Israel in the Puritans, but the period of a strong
reaffirmation of the promises to Israel was the early
nineteenth century leading up to the pre-millennialism
of the Plymouth Brethren. This recognition is rather
difficult for many mainline Christians to accept because
of their visceral antipathy to all forms of literal and fundamentalist exegesis of the Scriptures. It is not necessary to
accept all the dispensationalist theories of Darby and the
Brethren to accord them the honour of taking seriously
the whole prophetic tradition of the Old Testament,
despite the weaknesses in their exegesis, at a time when
the greater part of Christendom was paying little or no
attention to wide segments of this tradition, particularly
those concerning Israel and the nations.

In the evangelical rediscovery of the place of Israel in
prophecy, the context was one of eschatological urgency
aroused by the Napoleonic wars. Evangelical students
of Scripture believed that the end was near, the Day of
the Lord was fast approaching, and one of the signs of
this approaching end would be the re-entry of Israel into
the divine plan. In the dispensationalist schemata, too
absolute a disjunction was made between the promises
made by God to Israel, that would be fulfilled on earth,
and the promises made by God to the Church, that were
being fulfilled in heaven. In this view, Israel's time-clock,
with the realization of God's promises to Israel, had been
stopped when the Jews had rejected Jesus, and it would
be re-started with the sudden rapture of the Church
from earth to heaven (according to Luke 17:34–35 and
1 Thessalonians 4:17). It was this new hope of the
imminence of the rapture that spurred much evangelical

missionary activity and underpinned their interest in
Israel that sprang up in the nineteenth century.

Despite the theological weaknesses in this innovative
form of pre-millennialism,[1] it did make several generations of evangelical believers highly conscious of the
ongoing role of Israel in God's plan. In the twentieth century, this heritage was communicated to the vast majority
of Pentecostals. The political developments involving the
Jews in this century – first, the Balfour declaration about
a Jewish homeland in 1917, then the creation of the state
of Israel in 1948, and the Israeli capture of the West Bank
(Samaria) and the whole city of Jerusalem in 1967 – have
been seen by the majority of evangelicals as the fulfilment
of biblical prophecy. Modern history has thus served to
underline the wrongness of 'replacement' theology and
the necessity of understanding that God's promises to
Israel still hold.

It is worth noting too the recovery of belief in Israel's
ongoing place in God's plan in the Catholic Apostolic
Church dating from the 1830s. One of their restored
apostles, Drummond, wrote a detailed paper in 1844
(*Tracts for the Last Days*, No. XXII) entitled 'The Restoration of the Jews'.

Catholic

Renewed Catholic interest in the Jewish people goes
back to the nineteenth century with the conversion of
two Jewish brothers, both sons of a rabbi, who were
subsequently ordained as Catholic priests: Théodore
Ratisbonne (1802–1884), converted in 1827, and his
younger brother, Alphonse (1814–1884), converted in
1842. In 1843, Théodore founded an order of nuns, the
Congregation of Notre Dame de Sion, later helped by his
brother, and in 1852 they founded its male counterpart,
the Fathers of Sion. The call of these congregations is to
witness in the Church and in the world to the faithfulness
of God in his love for the Jewish people. 'We know how
much the Heart of Jesus Christ loved the sons of Israel
. . . This love that he bore them then he bears for them
always.'[2] Although Théodore Ratisbonne did not seem to

have any premonition of the return of the Jews to the land, he did have a sharp sense that the French Revolution had been a decisive step in the history of the nations, inaugurating an age of Gentile apostasy, that heralded the hour of Israel, when the children of Israel would turn to Jesus as their Messiah.

A major leap forward happened at the Second Vatican Council with its statement on the Jews, originally intended for inclusion in the Decree on Ecumenism, but eventually inserted in the Declaration on Non-Christian Religions (*Nostra Aetate*). The paragraph on Israel, the longest in the document (para 4), states:

> (i) The Jews remain very dear to God, for the sake of the patriarchs, since God does not take back the gifts he bestowed or the choice he made (ii) even though the Jewish authorities and those who followed their lead pressed for the death of Christ (cf John 19:6), neither all Jews indiscriminately at that time, nor Jews today, can be charged with the crimes committed during his passion. (iii) It is true that the Church is the new people of God, yet the Jews should not be spoken of as rejected or accursed as if this followed from holy Scripture. (iv) She [the Church] deplores all hatreds, persecutions, displays of antisemitism levelled at any time or from any source against the Jews. (The ennumeration is mine)

Pope John Paul II has carried further this affirmation of the ongoing importance of Judaism and the people of Israel. In 1980, he told German Jewish representatives in Mainz that the Old Covenant was 'never revoked by God' citing Romans 11:29. In April, 1986, John Paul II was the first Pope in history to visit a Jewish synagogue, telling the Roman Jews that

> the Church of Christ discovers her 'bond' with Judaism by 'searching into her own mystery'. The Jewish religion is not 'extrinsic' to us, but in a certain

way is 'intrinsic' to our own religion. With Judaism
therefore we have a relationship which we do not
have with any other religion. You are our dearly
beloved brothers, and in a certain way, it could be
said that you are our elder brothers.[3]

The deploring of anti-Semitism was repeated in the accord
establishing diplomatic relations between the Vatican and
the state of Israel in December 1993. The Holy See
'deplores attacks on Jews and desecration of Jewish synagogues and cemeteries, acts which offend the memory of
the victims of the Holocaust, especially when they occur
in the same places that witnessed it.'[4]

The Importance of Christian Repentance for Sins against Israel

The last chapter examined the role and the necessity of
repentance for all sins against Christian unity. While this
obligation falls on all Christians, it was argued that the
greater responsibility lies on the ancient Churches, precisely because they were the first to offend and because of
the high claims they make for their apostolic character.
These considerations have a particular application to
Israel and Christian attitudes towards the Jews.

Christian repentance for sins against the unity of the
Church needs to begin with repentance for sins against
the Jewish people. First of all, anti-Semitism is at root an
expression of human anger at the idea of a chosen people,
a rebellion against God's particular love for Israel. Israel
is in this intra-historical sense God's first love, preparing
for the entry into history of God's eternal first love,
his only-begotten Son. In many ways anti-Semitism is
a symbol of all sin, representing human rebellion against
the will and plan of God.

The original sundering of the Church came through
the division between Church and synagogue, which led
to the demise of Jewish Christianity. It was the nature
of the Church to be the union of Jew and Gentile, made
'one new man in place of the two' (Eph 2:15), so that the

Gentiles became 'fellow heirs, members of the same body, and partakers of the promise in Christ Jesus through the gospel' (Eph. 3:6), the 'wild olive shoot' grafted on to the 'cultivated olive tree' (Rom 11:17–24). The mutual rejection of Church and synagogue represents the root sin against unity, from which we still suffer.

At the heart of the sin of the Christian Church was the rejection of any ongoing validity of the old covenant between God and the people of Israel. Out of this rejection came the teaching, common though never given credal status, that the Church had replaced Israel in God's purpose; thus the as yet unfulfilled promises to Israel in the Old Testament now apply to the Christian Church, not to Israel. As a result, the Jewish Christian Church, that at the origins was the trunk of the tree, came to be rejected by both Church and synagogue, and its demise was virtually assured. This teaching of rejection and replacement also created the possibility for Christians in subsequent centuries to use these notions against the ancient Churches, arguing for their rejection by God and their replacement by new and pure bodies of believers.[5]

A Mystery not a Rejection

A constant re-reading of Romans 11 is vital for deepening Christian repentance for our sins against Israel. Paul says there: 'I want you to understand this mystery' and he wants this 'lest you be wise in your own conceits' (11:25). This mystery is the answer to the question posed by his people's refusal to accept Jesus as the Messiah, a question Paul must first have posed to himself: 'I ask, then, has God rejected his people?' (11:1). His answer is that God's dealings here form a **mystery**, which means they are a part of God's plan formed from all ages that could not be known until the chosen hour of its revelation in Christ. This mystery is that 'a hardening has come upon part of Israel, until the full number of Gentiles come in, and so all Israel will be saved' (11:25–26).

In fact, the Christian Church through most of its history has not heeded this word of St Paul. We have done

what Paul told us not to do, namely be wise in our own
conceits, which is to conclude that Israel and its covenant
had been rejected by God and that the Church had taken
Israel's place. Israel was not rejected as God's people,
but a **part** of Israel has been **set aside** (the meaning
of *apobole* in Romans 11:15[6]) for a **time**; but this setting
aside is an essential element in God's plan of salvation for
the Gentiles and for the ultimate salvation of 'all Israel'
The replacement–substitution theory concerning Israel
and the Church is the very opposite of divine mystery; it
reflects the false simplicity of human arrogance.

The Appalling History of Contempt and Persecution

A respected Jewish scholar with a sympathy for Christianity, the late Jules Isaac (1877–1963), has insisted that
Christian anti-Semitism has been worse than previous
pagan forms because of its content, its coherence, its
variety of themes and its continuity. Moreover, the sins
of the Church against the Jewish people have been
worse and have been sustained over a longer period
than any of the sins committed against Christian groups
seen as heretical or schismatic. The anti-Semitic themes
whose variety was noted by Isaac are: the theme of a
degenerate Judaism, the theme of a sensual people, the
theme of Christ misunderstood and rejected by a blind
and refractory people, the theme of the people reproved,
degraded, denounced by God, the theme of a deicide
people, the theme of the dispersion of Israel, and the
theme of the Synagogue of Satan.[7]

The separation of Church and synagogue intensified
after the destruction of the Temple in Jerusalem in AD 70
and probably reached its completion with the Christian
refusal to participate in the rebellion of Bar Kochba in
the year 135 that was so catastrophic for the holy city of
Jerusalem. The replacement concept that the Christian
Church has now become the 'true Israel' appeared in
apologetic works against the Jews from the second century, but it was only with the conversion of Constantine

and the Christianization of the Roman Empire that anti-Jewish attitudes hardened among Christians and led to the deliberate cultivation of contempt towards the Jews. Many of the Fathers of the Church used intemperate and unseemly language about the Jews, one famous bishop likening the synagogue to a brothel. The legal codes in force progressively diminished Jewish rights; the Theodosian code forbade Jews from holding public office, owning land or possessing Christian servants, and the Code of Justinian called for the death penalty for any Jew who tried to persuade another Jew not to become a Christian or who tried to convert a Christian to Judaism. Though these laws were not always enforced, they witnessed to the strength of Christian antipathy towards the Jewish people.

The more violent persecution of the Jews and the arousal of popular hatred against them belongs however to the second millennium. The movement for reform within the Church from the time of Hildebrand (c 1021–1085) drew renewed attention to the patristic hostility to the Jews, and led to renewed efforts to expel them from the land. The rise of the medieval guilds as Christian bodies reduced Jewish opportunities for employment, and tended to push Jews towards the despised role of money-lender, forbidden by Church law to the baptized. This promoted hatred of the Jews, particularly among the knights and the 'middle class' of the time. The launching of the first Crusade occasioned attacks by such groups on the Jews in several German cities and in Rouen in 1096, and when Jerusalem fell to the Crusading army in 1099, the Jews were massacred, including hundreds who had taken refuge in a synagogue. Peter the Venerable, the Abbot of Cluny (1092–1156), wrote of the Jews: 'God wishes them not to be killed or wiped out but to be preserved in a life worse than death, in greater torment and humiliation than the fratricide Cain.'[8]

The thirteenth century saw an intensification of ecclesiastical and popular oppression of European Jews. By this time, accusations against the Jews of desecration of the eucharistic host and of ritual murder of Gentile infants were becoming common. One of the worst massacres of Jews by Christians occurred at York in 1190. Strangely, the new renewal movements of the friars were to the fore in promoting anti-Jewish sentiment.

From the Middle Ages until modern times, there have been European countries – hardly ever all at the same time – within which the Jews were consistently ostracized, herded into ghettos, and denied full participation in civic life. Often they were attacked, tortured and killed; at other times they were forced to profess faith in Christ, or expelled from a country (England was the first to do so in 1290). The expulsion of all Jews from Spain in 1492 was followed by the efforts of the Inquisition to root out all lingering attachment to Judaism among the Marranos, the Jews who had accepted baptism rather than enforced emigration. Appalling things were done to them, often in the name of Christ and under the sign of his cross. The Orthodox Church and lands of Eastern Europe have no better a record in this than the Catholic Church and the nations of the West: since the Reformation in fact, the treatment of the Jews was generally worse in Eastern Europe, both Orthodox and Catholic, than in the West. The term **pogrom** used of massacres of Jews is a Russian word. In the Protestant Reformation, the diatribes of Martin Luther (1483–1546) against the Jews played a major role in perpetuating and fomenting anti-Semitism in Germany.[9]

Historical studies show that the contempt for and persecution of the Jews by the Church and by Christians had its ups and downs. There were often bishops and kings who defended the Jews and condemned the atrocities committed against them; St Bernard of Clairvaux (1090–1153) journeyed to Germany near the end of his life in response to an appeal from the Archbishop of Mainz to restrain a fellow Cistercian monk who was inciting the killing of Jews. However, it has to be conceded that such protests remained within a theological framework that denied or prevented respect for the Jewish people.

The Importance of Joint Acknowledgment of Responsibility

Since Catholic, Orthodox and Protestant Christians have shared in the oppression and persecution of the Jews, there is a particular appropriateness in their coming together to repent and to ask forgiveness of their Jewish brothers and sisters. However, the Catholics and the Orthodox need to recognize their greater responsibility for they practised centuries of persecution and humiliation of the Jews before the existence of Protestant Christianity.

This can also be a step towards taking responsibility for our collective histories, and for Protestants to get beyond saying that past Catholic behaviour had nothing to do with them, and vice versa. Joint Christian (Orthodox, Catholic and Protestant) self-humbling before the Jewish people will also recognize in an unprecedented way the debt owed by every Christian and each Christian body to the people of the old covenant. In God's providence, it may be that such a common confession before the Jews may facilitate and deepen our mutual confession to each other as Catholics, Orthodox and Protestants.

Christian repentance to the Lord and to the Jewish people for all the manifold forms of anti-Semitism in thought and practice needs to include:

1. Repentance for the **contempt** of Christians and the Church for the chosen people of Israel to whom the Lord God showed a particular love. For this people whom the Lord 'kept . . . as the apple of his eye' (Deut 32:10) and whom the Lord loved 'with an everlasting love' (Jer 31:3), the Christian Church has for many centuries shown and even cultivated a contempt. As Gentile Christians, we have to confess that we have not obeyed the injunction of St Paul in Romans 11:18 not to 'boast over the [natural] branches'. 'So do not become proud, but stand in awe' (Rom 11:20).

2. Repentance for not honouring the full Jewishness of Jesus Christ. Not to love the Jewish people is to fail to love Jesus fully.

3. Repentance for the theology of 'replacement' or of 'substitution' that has been the underlying motor for Christian contempt and persecution of the Jewish people. Part of this repentance would be for the rejection of the possibility of a Jewish Christianity and the requirements that Jewish converts abandon all Jewish practice and Jewish identity. This was particularly the decision of Church authorities and calls for a Church repentance.[10]

4. Repentance for all the stereotyped forms of Christian prejudice against the Jews that are perhaps epitomized in Shakespeare's Shylock in *The Merchant of Venice*. It is here that it should be easiest to persuade all Christians that they bear a degree of responsibility for the appalling treatment accorded to the Jewish people by Christians throughout the centuries. This stain on the Christian conscience is perpetuated in all forms of anti-Semitism among Christians, whether overt or latent, much of which lies deep in the Christian psyche. It is manifest in anti-Jewish humour, in our stereotypes concerning Jews which are generally much more negative than positive (much more about Jewish love of and skill with money than about the qualities of Jewish family life), our Gentile aversion from distinctively Jewish patterns of dress.

5. Repentance for the failure of the Churches to recognize the significance of Messianic Judaism in our day and to seek together to find ways of enabling Jews who accept Jesus as the Messiah to continue in their Jewish identity. It is true that Messianic Judaism constitutes an obstacle for Jewish–Christian dialogue, but it is unjust to present it as equivalent to or worse than a form of 'Uniatism'.[11] But whatever one's evaluation of Uniatism, Messianic Judaism is something quite different: it represents the reconstitution to some degree of the form of Christianity that preceded all Gentile expressions of faith in Christ.

Chapter Twenty-Three

A Day of Fasting and Prayer?

Any serious examination of the issue of the modern life-streams and the historic Churches necessarily leads into the question of repentance for our sins and failures, not just as individual Christians but as Churches and as fellowships. Recognition of the need for repentance brings us face to face with the fact that there is no structure or mechanism to express such a repentance in our own Church circles, let alone to do so together as an act of ecumenical humility.[1] So I ask: is the Holy Spirit calling us all to a joint acknowledgment of our sins against each other as Christians and our sins as Christians against Israel? Do we need a day each year when we come together from every kind of Christian background, Church and stream, to confess our sin and to beg the loving mercy of our God?

The Precedent of the Jewish Day of Atonement

Even though the Christian Church has never had a universal day for the common confession of sin, the Jewish people already had such an observance for several centuries before Christ. This is **Yom Kippur**, the Day of Atonement, celebrated on the tenth day of the seventh month of the Jewish year, that is in our autumn or fall season in the northern hemisphere. When the Christian Church developed out of first-century Judaism, the Gentile Christians continued to celebrate the ancient Jewish feasts of the Passover and of Weeks, but not those of the Day of Atonement and the feast of Tabernacles.

The Feasts of Israel

It is clear from the Torah, the books of Moses, that
the earliest pattern of feasts in Israel involved three
celebrations each year: of Unleavened Bread (Passover),
of Harvest (Weeks or Pentecost) and Ingathering (Tabernacles). These feasts alone are mentioned in Exodus
23:14–17; 34:18–23; Deuteronomy 16:1–16. The first list
is prefaced with the words: 'Three times in the year you
shall keep a feast to me' (Ex 23:14). Only in Leviticus
(16 and 23:26–32) and Numbers (29:7–11), texts of later
origin, is there mention of the Day of Atonement.

The original three feasts structured the annual life of
Israel. Each feast involved the linking of events of salvation history to the agricultural cycle of a rural people.
The Feast of Unleavened Bread was the celebration
of the first sheaf (Lev 23:10) and the commemoration
of the deliverance from Egypt (Ex 23:15; 34:18; Deut
16:3). The Feast of Weeks was the celebration of the
first fruits of the wheat harvest (Ex 34:22) and came
to be associated with the gift of the Law at Sinai.[2] The
Feast of Tabernacles celebrated the ingathering of the
full harvest; this was later associated with the making
of booths to commemorate the time in the desert (Lev
23:40–43).

These three feasts have a salvific meaning. The first
sheaf is Jesus Christ, risen from the dead at Easter. The
first fruits fifty days later are the first Christians filled
with the Holy Spirit at Pentecost. The final harvest will
be the ingathering of all the saints at the Day of Christ
Jesus. So not only did these three feasts structure the
annual life of the people of Israel, but what they represent structures the life of the Christian Church, that is
established by the Passover of Jesus, and exists between
the first fruits of Pentecost and the full ingathering of
the Parousia.

In parenthesis, it may be remarked that the two major
Jewish observances that did not find their way into the
Christian liturgical year, the Day of Atonement and the
Feast of Tabernacles, correspond to real weaknesses of
the Church, at least since the victory of Constantine

in the fourth century: the absence of any framework for expressing the sins of the Christian people and the feebleness of our hope for the Coming of the Lord.

The Origins of the Day of Atonement

Most biblical scholars recognize that there are primitive elements in the practices prescribed for the Day of Atonement in Leviticus 16. The selection of the scapegoat to send into the desert is a practice that is unlikely to have arisen once the people were established in the land. However, it seems that the origins of the total observance described in that chapter must have been later than the time of Nehemiah. For Yom Kippur is observed on the tenth day of the seventh month, and Nehemiah gathered the Israelites for a penitential ceremony ('fasting and in sackcloth, and with earth upon their heads' Neh 9:1) on the 24th day of that month, that would hardly have happened in this way had there been a Day of Atonement two weeks before.

However, it seems likely that the Israelite confession of sin led by Nehemiah described in Nehemiah 9 played a part in the rise of Yom Kippur and its establishment in the seventh month. It makes most sense, both historically and spiritually, that the establishment of a Day of Atonement to confess the sin of the whole people arose out of the humiliation of the Babylonian exile and the prophetic reflection on the exile as a punishment for Israel's rebellion and infidelity.

We are likely to be on the right track then in seeing the establishment of Yom Kippur as a liturgical expression of the spirit expressed in the book of Lamentations and in Psalms 74 and 79. The faithful Jew, devastated by the ruin of Jerusalem and the destruction of the Temple, laments: 'the LORD has made her suffer for the multitude of her transgressions' (Lam 1:5); 'Jerusalem sinned grievously, therefore she became filthy' (1:8); 'Behold, O LORD, for I am in distress, my soul is in tumult, my heart is wrung within me, because I have been very rebellious' (1:20). 'The Lord has scorned his altar, disowned his sanctuary' (2:7). 'Your prophets have seen for you false and deceptive visions; they have not exposed your iniquity to restore your fortunes' (2:14). 'This was for the sins of her prophets and the iniquities of her priests' (4:13).

In other words, the need to have a ritual to deal with the sins of the people as a whole, as distinct from rituals for individual sin, arose out of the corporate humiliation of the exile, and the interior work of the prophetic Spirit in leading a remnant of pious Jews, such as Nehemiah and the author of Lamentations, to see and confess the sin of the people. In this confession, they were especially conscious of the sins of those appointed to lead the people, the kings, the prophets and the priests; this links up for example with the words of the Lord through the prophet Ezekiel against the shepherds of Israel (Ez 34).

This process highlights something that it is difficult for evangelical Protestants to understand, namely the essential link between a priestly ritual and the profound interior experience of the Spirit's work in the people. The observance was not simply decreed in every detail in a moment of revelation, but arose out of the working of the Spirit in the interaction of God's persistent call and the constant wavering in the people's response.

A Day for Confession of the Sins of the Churches

There is much to suggest that now is the time for all the Churches and every Christian body to set aside one day a year to humbly acknowledge their sins against each other and against the Jewish people. What are these indications that this last decade of the second millennium might be the right time to inaugurate such an observance?

First, the end of a millennium is an appropriate time to reflect on the history of the two millennia of Christianity. Pope John Paul II has invited such a reflection in his letter *Tertio Millennio Adveniente* in which he notes that the last millennium has been especially marked by Christian division. 'In the course of the thousand years now drawing to a close, even more than in the first millennium, ecclesial communion has been painfully wounded, a fact for which, at times, men of both sides were to blame' (para 34). In chapter twenty-two, we noted that the Christian persecution of the Jews intensified markedly in the second millennium.

Secondly, recent years have seen a growing Christian reflection on the Holocaust, and a willingness to accept the Christian responsibility for the systematic extermination of six million Jews by Hitler and his minions. More and more Christians are coming to realize that such an atrocity could not have been possible without the long-standing stigmatization of the Jews as rejected by God and as the killers of Christ. Moreover, the fact that the roots of Christian anti-Semitism go back deep into the patristic era calls for at least some qualification of the deeply-held Catholic image of this period as the golden age of the Church.

Thirdly, the last decade has been steadily stripping us of our naive optimism in imagining that the world is steadily advancing into a new age of harmony and peace. The horrible genocides in Bosnia and in Rwanda have, under the glare of modern publicity, appalled us with the depths of inhumanity and degradation there displayed. Not only do these horrors bring shame to the whole human race, but they particularly disgrace the Christian Churches: in former Yugoslavia, because of the role of the Orthodox and Catholic Churches, and in Rwanda because this was nominally one of the most Christian nations in Africa. There is much evidence to suggest that this twentieth century that has witnessed such wonderful movements of the Spirit of God is also producing a crescendo of evil. This is also the reflection of Pope John Paul II.

Fourthly, the consideration of the relationship between the historic Churches and the life-streams of modern times directs our attention to the sins of the Churches. It is surely only because of the sins and failures of the historic Churches that the Holy Spirit has been poured out in the life-streams that are only partially within the Churches and often in competition with them. The

increasing spread of the streams in our day underlines
further the weakness and inadequacy of the Church's
witness. The signs of renewal in the historic Churches
are a wonderful testimony to the generosity of the Lord,
but they should not be used as an argument against the
Lord's work 'outside the city'. For it is far from clear
that the renewal within is stronger and more powerful
than the revival without. Rather the fact that the Lord
is working both inside and outside is a sign both of the
depth of God's love and of God's judgment on our sin.

An Expression of the Church's Sin

A day of repentance for the sins of the Christian people
against each other and against the Jews will need, like
the Day of Atonement, to arise out of a deep interior
conviction of our responsibility for our divisions, for the
weak condition of our Churches, and for the poverty of
our witness to the world. Pope John Paul II has stated:
'On the threshhold of the new millennium Christians
need to place themselves humbly before the Lord and
examine themselves on the responsibility which they too
have for the evils of our day.'[3] We need to groan before the
Lord: 'My eyes fail from weeping, I am in torment within,
my heart is poured out on the ground because my people
are destroyed, because children and infants faint in the
streets of the city' (Lam 2:11 NIV). 'How the gold has
grown dim, how the pure gold is changed! The holy stones
lie scattered at the head of every street' (Lam 4:1).

Any Christian initiative in this matter needs to have
a great sensitivity to the Jewish practice. First, that we
do not cause unnecessary offence by appearing to imitate
an observance that is deeply etched into the Jewish consciousness and that has particular associations for them
with the horror of the Holocaust. Secondly, that deep
appreciation is expressed for the tradition of Yom Kippur
and, thirdly, that the Christian maltreatment of the Jews
is made central to the observance, with a recognition that
this was the beginning and root of persecution of fellow
believers in the One God of Abraham, Isaac and Jacob.

Preparing for the Parousia

A day of corporate repentance by the Churches would have an eschatological significance. In fact, the Jewish Day of Atonement was placed immediately before the feast of Tabernacles, that foreshadows the final ingathering of the Lord's harvest.[4] This timing signifies that there has to be repentance by the people of God before they can welcome as a people the return of their Lord in glory.

In several places in the New Testament, there is mention of the role of repentance in preparing for the Day of the Lord. 'Repent therefore, and turn again, that your sins may be blotted out, that times of refreshing may come from the presence of the Lord, and that he may send the Christ appointed for you, Jesus' (Acts 3:19–20). The same message is found in 2 Peter 3: 'What sort of persons ought you to be in lives of holiness and godliness, waiting for and hastening the coming of the day of God' (3:11–12). This exhortation echoes the constant admonitions to be blameless in waiting for the Day of the Lord's return (1 Cor 1:8; 1 Thess 3:13; 5:23).

There is then an essential inter-connection between the issues of renewal and evangelism, Christian unity, the role of Israel, and the second coming of Jesus. The outpourings of the Spirit are to prepare for the final great work of the Spirit in the resurrection of the dead and the establishment of the new heavens and the new earth. This preparation involves a power for the proclamation of the gospel to all tribes and nations before the end comes, the turning of Israel to Jesus as their Messiah, and the reconciliation of the divided Christian Churches. Only then will the Bride be ready for the returning Bridegroom.

Chapter Twenty-Four

Mary, the Mother of Jesus

In this chapter I want to tackle directly the highly sensitive question of the mother of Jesus. The various designations by which she is known by Christians – Mary; the Virgin Mary, the Blessed Virgin, Our Lady – themselves express a range of sentiments. Even though it may seem rash to venture on this difficult terrain, the issues concerning Mary between the Catholic Church and the life-streams must be addressed. The argument of this book about the complementarity of Church and streams in God's purpose and their need for each other would be seriously weakened if the major difficulties posed by the Marian question were simply ignored. Such an omission could give the impression that the whole book is hopelessly Utopian, the ecumenical dream of an enthusiast out of touch with reality.

In this chapter, I shall not attempt a full presentation of Catholic faith concerning Mary,[1] nor will I attempt to examine all Protestant objections. My more limited goal is to approach this difficult topic, so as to help move us beyond a Catholic triumphalism that is indifferent to Protestant sensitivities and an evangelical indignation that dismisses Marian piety as simply the survival or infiltration of paganism. For there to be progress between Church and streams on this issue, there has to be a listening to each other and a willingness to ask the Holy Spirit for light on what is valid and authentic in the witness or the complaint of the other party. It is not sufficient to do what both sides have customarily done: to evaluate the other from our present standpoint, assuming our side is totally in the right and the other is totally in the wrong. To seek agreement when there is widespread outrage and disdain is quite unrealistic. To seek to move a few steps towards each other is possible. Those few steps will then show us how to take a few more.

Movement on this matter and other issues in contention is important if there is to be growing co-operation and respect rather than increasing confrontation and suspicion between Church and streams. The person and subject of Mary is a particular instance of the challenges that the streams pose to the Church and that the Church poses to the streams. In fact, not only are the difficulties greater concerning Mary, but the challenges that each side poses to the other are greater too. This is to say that the great differences represent differing strengths and different weaknesses, and that there is in the differences a significant challenge of the Holy Spirit from each side to the other.

Mary As Symbol

It has been remarked by a number of theologians, especially by Karl Barth (1886–1967), that Mary is symbolic of Roman Catholicism as a whole, and that differences concerning her are symptomatic of all Catholic–Protestant disagreement. In particular, Mary is a symbol of human co-operation with God's redemptive work: she who said, 'Behold, I am the handmaid of the Lord; let it be to me according to your word' (Luke 1:38), is the one who co-operates with God by faith and so conceives the eternal Word in her womb. Catholic doctrine affirms the necessity of human co-operation, that nonetheless is only possible with God's grace; Protestant teaching, especially of the more evangelical type, is very chary of affirming any human co-operation lest there be any 'Jesus plus' understanding of salvation or any claim to human achievement and merit. In this sense the *solus Christus* (Christ alone) of classical Protestantism is one with *sola Scriptura* (the Bible alone), *sola fide* (faith alone) and *sola gratia* (grace alone).

By contrast, the Catholic tradition instinctively says 'and . . . and' where the Protestant says 'either . . . or'.

So the Catholic says 'Christ and the Church', 'Jesus and Mary' and 'Christ and us', along with 'Scripture and Tradition' and 'Faith and Works'. In fact, Catholic teaching does not affirm the equality of both poles in these twosomes: we are saved by Christ alone, but the saved have to co-operate; Scripture alone is inspired by the Holy Spirit, but it is handed down to us, i.e. traditioned, by and within the framework of the Church; we are saved by faith, which has to bear fruit in works. However, in practice the Catholic danger, particularly at the level of popular attitudes, is to put the two poles on the same level, and not to grasp sufficiently the total dependence of the second on the first: of all believers, including Mary, on Christ, of tradition on Scripture, and of works upon faith.

The issues at stake are enormous. Threaten the uniqueness of Jesus Christ, the uniqueness of the Scriptures, and the uniqueness of faith, and the very sources of Christian life are endangered. On the other hand, to remove human co-operation, to deny a significant role to tradition in relation to the Scriptures and their understanding, and to devalue the performance of works of righteousness risks making the uniqueness of Christ, of the Bible and of faith inoperative. From the Protestant angle, Mary is the biggest threat to the uniqueness of Jesus as mediator and Saviour. But from the Catholic side, she is the link with Jesus that earths him in our world, and she is the first-fruits of faith that shows the fullest fruit of Jesus, of the Scriptures and of faith.

The only way that progress can be made is to enter more deeply into the mystery of the dealings of the infinite God with finite humans. The concept of a covenant between God and human beings cannot be easily assimilable for anyone who grasps who God is. Yet such a covenant elevates God's 'partners' to a new dignity beyond anything that can be imagined or deserved, even in the Old Testament. This generosity and delicacy of the Lord God in some way reaches its climax in the message of the archangel Gabriel to the Virgin of Nazareth.

This way of progress requires the constant and vigilant

maintenance of two apparent opposites: the transcendent uniqueness of the absolute and sovereign God; and the real participation in God's eternal life that the Father offers freely to humans. The divine activity and the human response remain on two quite different levels, of which the lower always remains totally subject to and derivative from the higher. From this angle, the Catholic affirmation of God plus is absolutely correct: for God's plus is the whole creation, and the whole redemption that cleanses and raises the whole creation to the glory of the new heavens and the new earth. But this Catholic affirmation always requires the Protestant protest that guards against every blurring of the line between the Creator and the creature, between the inspired Word of God and all other writings, and between the divine gift of faith and all other virtues. Without this protest, Church life can slide into the Jesus and the Church, Scripture and tradition, faith and works, Jesus and Mary, where the totally subordinate character of the second element is blurred or forgotten.

The Challenge to the Streams

The challenge of the Church of history to the streams and particularly to all expressions of evangelical Protestantism centres on doing justice to the biblical data concerning Mary. It can be succinctly expressed by asking whether these Christians are among those of all generations who will call Mary blessed (Luke 1:48). To what extent do they recognize the 'great things' that the Lord had done for her (Luke 1:49) on account of which she would be called the **blessed** Virgin Mary?

The challenge of the Church concerning Mary can be put in another way that may be less easy for Protestant Christians to hear, but which is important to ponder. How is it that all the ancient Churches of East and West, not simply the Roman Catholic Church, but also the Orthodox Churches in communion with Constantinople and all the smaller Oriental Orthodox Churches of Armenia, Iraq and India, as well as the Copts of Egypt and Ethiopia, give high honour to Mary? If this witness came only from one or two old traditions, then it might be plausible that their doctrine had departed from the gospel or become unbalanced. But that all the ancient Churches, even those largely cut off for centuries from the rest, should have deviated in the same way seems highly implausible. These are mostly highly conservative bodies, that have fought to survive through many centuries of trial and suffering, often as minorities in the midst of Islam. There has been then for three-quarters of the Church's history a consensus that Mary's role in salvation history is of unique and lasting significance, and that she is worthy of honour as the most blessed of all creatures.

Arguments of this type will only have any persuasive power if stream-Christians can be helped to see that there is a biblical basis and foundation for the honouring of Mary that is common to all these ancient Christian traditions. Here the witness of the ancient Churches of the East is particularly important, because as 'fellow-Easterners', mostly from similar Semitic cultures less influenced by Western history, they tend to be closer in their forms of thinking and of interpretation to the world of the Bible and its authors. This perspective forces us to face the question: how much of Protestant objections to the honouring of Mary as 'unbiblical' come from modern Western ways of reading the Bible that miss much of the richness of ancient Semitic thought? It also makes Roman Catholics ask how much of Catholic piety in the West reflects patterns of Western thought and culture (individualism, rationalism, romanticism) that are equally foreign to the thought-world of the Scriptures.

Contemplation and Mary
The Christian traditions that honour Mary are those that have developed forms of contemplative life, especially the monastic calling. The deep respect and veneration for Mary that characterized the patristic era came from prolonged reflection on the marvel of the Incarnation, and what it means that the eternal Son of God was

born of the virgin, drew life and sustenance from her, and became man in the family of Joseph of the tribe of Judah.

When I was giving some workshops recently at a conference for leaders in a major para-church movement, I deliberately grasped the nettle posed by the question of Mary. After a presentation and some discussion, a Protestant made the perceptive comment: 'What I am hearing is that for Catholics Mary is a person whom they love, but for Protestants Mary is a doctrine that they deny'. It is the life of contemplation that produces a depth of appropriation of faith that moves from texts and doctrines to persons. It is part of the challenge of the Church to the streams to make place for a more contemplative dimension to temper an activism, that both grounds their real achievements but threatens their depth and durability. It is no accident that Luke's Gospel presents Mary as the exemplar for this reflective wonderment at the great and mysterious workings of the Lord: 'But Mary kept all these things, pondering them in her heart' (2:19), and 'and his mother kept all these things in her heart' (2:51).

The Challenge to the Roman Catholic Church

This section will consider the challenge concerning Mary to the Roman Catholic Church, since the Catholic Church of the West has the most developed Mariology and Marian piety among all the historic Churches. Clearly the heart of the challenge of the streams is for the Church to be Christocentric, biblical and life-giving.[2] Since the streams all emphasize the life-giving gospel and the urgency of evangelization, a major point of interrogation for the Catholic Church is the primacy of evangelization. Several Catholic leaders, including Cardinal Suenens, have acknowledged that many Catholics have been sacramentalized but not evangelized. A corollary of this lack is that many have been taught and recommended patterns of piety and devotion that have not been grounded in a grasp of the gospel. The post-conciliar currents of renewal have been rediscovering this priority of explicit evangelization, strongly supported by Paul VI's document *Evangelii Nuntiandi* (1975), and see clearly that the gospel of salvation is the foundation of all Christian life. This rediscovery then points to the problematic character of the promotion of Marian devotions among those who have never been properly evangelized. Here the challenge from the streams to a reordering of Church priorities has major implications for popular piety in the Catholic Church.

The Hiddenness of Mary

When we seek a renewal of Church life through a deeper rooting in the Scriptures, we will have to pay attention to all the biblical data concerning the person and role of Mary. There is a challenge here that comes from the relative infrequency of direct mention of the Lord's mother, but that is offset by her presence at key moments in the unfolding of God's work of salvation through her Son. Obviously she is present at his birth, but she is also present at the beginning of his public ministry (Cana in John 2), at the foot of the cross (John 19) and apparently on the Day of Pentecost (Acts 1:14; 2:1). This combination of infrequency and important moments has to be taken seriously. It points both to her significance and her reticence. The reticence means that her significance is not blazoned forth; her significance is 'suggested' rather than 'proved' or 'demonstrated'. In other words, there is a hiddenness about Mary's role in the New Testament that is not always noticed by Protestant dismissal or by Catholic enthusiasm. This hiddenness is typified by the narrative of the miracle at Cana that illustrates the discretion of Mary: she simply says to her son 'They have no wine' and does not try to tell him what to do, and says to the servants 'Do whatever he tells you'. These words are full of faith, full of faith in Jesus, but they are delicate and not intrusive.

The hiddenness of Mary is also illustrated in her role at the foot of the cross. 'When Jesus saw his mother, and the disciple whom he loved standing near, he said to his mother, "Woman, behold, your son!" Then he said to the disciple, "Behold, your mother!" And from that hour the disciple took her to his own home [*eis ta idia*]' (John 19:26–27). Since John presents fewer episodes than the Synoptics, and chooses those he includes for their soteriological significance, it is highly improbable that Jesus is merely making domestic arrangements for his mother after his death. There is a wealth of meaning hidden in these verses, suggested particularly by the words 'that hour' that in John refer to the passover of Jesus to the Father (see John 13:1). Catholics have come to understand them in terms of the spiritual motherhood of Mary in relation to all disciples of her Son, yet the allusiveness of such texts remains important. Important progress will be made when Catholics and evangelicals can together reflect, with reverence and without fear, on these and other passages, bringing simply a desire to hear and penetrate the Word of God, that cannot be encapsulated in merely human categories.

The biblical renewal of the Catholic Church calls for a more thoroughly biblical form of honouring Mary. This kind of purification can be seen in a number of recent Catholic writings. This biblical reflection needs to learn how to respect this hiddenness or discretion of Mary in the New Testament, while telling forth the glories of the Lord in his servants. This hiddenness is not properly respected in the kind of deductive Catholic Mariology that is based on human logic and focused on Mary and her privileges in separation from the biblical context.

Here we can sense a tension within Catholicism between the more restrained and contemplative reflection on Mary in the monasteries and the more exuberant and demonstrative Marian piety of the masses. This tension is also manifest in the sphere of art between the great artistic masterpieces that have drawn heavily on the Infancy narratives and the tawdry mass-produced objects on sale in many Catholic stores. The fact that popular piety manifests tendencies towards doctrinal imbalance and a cheapening of the holy is not however just a problem for the Catholic Church, but has its very different expressions in the Pentecostal and charismatic worlds. There is a need here to steer the difficult course between forms of spiritual snobbery on the one hand and of excessive tolerance on the other.

The Catholic Church, that has always had a capacity to shape popular culture, seems to be much less tolerant towards deviations on the secularizing and irreligious side and quite indulgent towards deviations on the side of popular religiosity and superstition. If there is to be movement towards each other, there has to be a greater willingness on the Catholic side to recognize excess and abuse in the sphere of Marian piety. Part of the challenge to the Catholic Church is to develop clearer criteria for what is healthy and what is unhealthy in popular piety.

Increased Sensitivity Towards One Another

However, the sharpness of the challenges of the life-streams and the Roman Catholic Church to each other can be formulated in terms of mutual sensitivity. Part of the process of meeting and sharing with Christians of very different theological and cultural backgrounds is that we begin to learn what spirit and what love animate their faith and their practice. Such knowledge leads to respect and sensitivity. In turn, this respect and sensitivity have to lead to modifications in forms of behaviour (on both sides) that cause shock and scandal. There is something shocking and scandalous in our indifference to the disturbance each side arouses in the other. There is Catholic indifference to the shock and scandal provoked by some Catholic expressions and practices concerning Mary among evangelical, Pentecostal and charismatic Christians. There is Protestant indifference to the shock and disgust felt by devout Catholics in the face of evangelical attacks on Marian devotion.

Both sides have to address this challenge. The deepest scandal is that we are indifferent to the deepest sensitivities of brothers and sisters who love Jesus Christ and seek to be open to the movement of the Holy Spirit. We

have to listen to each other's hearts. We do not have to
agree with everything the other holds. But we do have
to listen; we have to sense what committed Christians of
other traditions find offensive in ours. Do some Catholic
expressions offend against the biblical witness concerning the uniqueness of our Lord Jesus Christ? Do some
Protestant utterances manifest an irreverence for the
mysterious and gracious workings of the Lord in the
Incarnation? It is only as such a sensitivity grows that
we will acquire the love and the sympathy that can
bridge the abyss of misunderstanding and disdain that
remain a grave scandal to non-Christians. The growth of
this respect and sensitivity is essential if the relatively
recent forms of sharing and co-operation are to have any
real chance of long-term survival.

An Approach to Receiving these Challenges

Any approach to the question of the Blessed Virgin Mary
that can commend itself to evangelical and Pentecostal
Christians has to be demonstrably biblical and Christocentric. It is clear also that any approach that is to
convince Roman Catholics and Orthodox that their faith
concerning the Mother of God is not being compromised
has to be deeply grounded in the historic tradition. One
possible approach that could satisfy both requirements
is to focus on two dimensions of Christian faith that the
Holy Spirit has been bringing to the fore in the streams of
revival and renewal: the relation of Israel to the Church,
and Christian eschatology.

Israel and the Church
Mary is the link between Israel and the Church. Because
of the virginal conception of Jesus, it is only through
Mary that Jesus belongs physically to the house of
Israel. Jesus is not only Son of God, but son of David
and son of Abraham: 'who as to his human nature was
a descendant of David, and who through the Spirit of
holiness was declared with power to be the Son of God,
by his resurrection from the dead' (Rom 1:3–4 NIV).

It is thus through Mary that the eternal Son of God
enters human history, and takes on human flesh. The
history that he enters is the history of humanity, but
specifically the history of Israel, and the tribe of Judah.
'The sceptre will not depart from Judah, nor the ruler's
staff from between his feet, until he comes to whom it
belongs and the obedience of the nations is his' (Gen
49:10 NIV).

It is central to the calling of Israel to prepare for
the coming of the Messiah, to be the instrument that
brings to all peoples the Saviour of the world. In this,
Mary is like a personification of Israel. Here she, a
woman, joins the representative figures that shaped
the life and history of Israel: Abraham, Jacob, Moses,
David, the suffering servant. That which the people of
Israel have been bearing and preparing for centuries,
laying the foundation for the coming of the Messiah, in
type and in figure, in promise and in faith-expectation,
Mary now does as the instrument of the Spirit and the
handmaid of the Lord. She conceives and gives birth to
the Messiah-Saviour, and gives him in faith to his mission
first to the people of Israel and then to the world.

Mary is then the climax of faith of the people of Israel,
believing in the promise, and she is the beginnings of
the faith of the Church, of those who believe in Jesus,
his person, his identity and his mission. She is wholly
to be understood within the framework of Israel and
the Old Testament, and she is wholly to be understood
within the framework of the new covenant. Seeing her in
this full biblical context of Israel and the Church avoids
the dangers of any 'non-historical orthodoxy' that would
place her uniquely alongside Christ rather than as the
pre-eminent figure in Israel and the Church.

Eschatology
Most biblical exegetes would agree that there is a relationship between Genesis 3:15 and Revelation 12. Both
speak of the hostility of the serpent to the woman and
her seed and of the ultimate defeat of the serpent.
Catholic exegetes tend to see a Marian reference in the

'woman' of both passages, though in recent times they
have increasingly seen the woman as having a double
or multiple reference in both places: a reference to Eve
in Genesis as well as to Mary, and a reference to Israel
in Revelation as well as to Mary as the mother of the
'male child' (v 5). These are examples of the hiddenness
of Mary in the Bible, which is not a devious way of making
nothing into something, but rather real references and
allusions that are deliberately not spelled out in logical
systematic form. Catholics need to exercise a restraint
that respects this allusiveness, while Protestants need
to overcome their inhibitions to consider in freedom and
truth the fuller implications of such passages.

The close links between Mary and Israel themselves
have an eschatological dimension. The theme of the
Daughter of Zion in the Old Testament is related to
the Day of the Lord: see Zephaniah 3:14; Zechariah
9:9 (see also Zechariah 2:10). Mary is the embodiment
of the Daughter of Zion who will rejoice and magnify
the Lord at his coming. But his first coming cannot be
totally separated from the second, least of all in the
Messianic prophecies of the Old Testament. Mary's song
of rejoicing in the *Magnificat* is the song of the Anawim,
the poor of the Lord; she is an exemplar of the lowly
who are exalted (see Luke 1:52). The Catholic doctrine
of Mary's bodily assumption into heaven is not biblical
in the ordinary evangelical sense of what is biblical; but
I suggest that it has definite biblical roots in a less literal
and proof-text sense. Not only was the concept of bodily
assumption congenial to Jewish understanding (see the
biblical instances of Enoch and Elijah and the reference
to the dispute about 'the body of Moses' in Jude 9), but
it represents in the case of Mary the fullest application
of God's exaltation of the humble, of which the vision of
Revelation 12 is not a strict proof, but an imagery that
dramatizes this exaltation.

If however any progress is to be made on this most
difficult and emotive of topics, Catholics have to grasp
the nettle of addressing those expressions and practices
regarding Mary that are not fully compatible with or

which in any way obscure the uniqueness of Our Lord
Jesus Christ in his roles as Lord, Saviour and Mediator.
Mary is not the topic to take up when we first meet
brothers and sisters from the other side of the Catholic–
evangelical divide; but if we do not begin to address this
matter when we have established respectful relations,
then there will remain lingering doubts of the viability
of such co-operation.

Chapter Twenty-Five

Towards the Coming Fulness

In this final chapter, I want to summarize the main conclusions of this book. Its main contention is that the historic Churches and the modern streams of new life need each other. There are several grounds for this assertion, and we will examine them briefly in turn.

1. The Holy Spirit of God is demonstrably at work in both sectors

If the Holy Spirit is at work in both the historic Churches and in the life-streams, then the two must be complementary, for there must be a unity and coherence between all the work of the Holy Spirit of God.

2. Sharp Focus and Organic Fulness are complementary.

The sharp focus of the streams that is tied to their vitality and impact is complementary, not opposed, to the concern for catholicity and organic fulness of the ancient Churches of East and West.

3. Streams Outside the Churches are Part of God's Judgment and Mercy towards the Churches.

The rise of streams not integrated into the historic Churches is a consequence of the sin of the Church communities. While this is a form of judgment, it is also an expression of mercy, because the new life of the streams is not given **against** the Churches (though some have misunderstood stream-life in this way) any more than the grace of God to the Gentiles was given against Israel. As the gift of life to those God longs to save and renew, the streams are held out to the Churches for the upbuilding of the one body of Christ.

4. The Complementarity of Church and Streams

can only be realized through Repentance.

Because of sin in the Churches, the streams have
appeared and developed in a significant way outside
the Churches. Because of the mercy of God, they have
appeared within the Churches. Reacting to the sin in
the Churches, evangelical, Pentecostal and charismatic
believers have sinned in their disdain, not just for the sin
but for the substance of the historic Churches. Mutual
sin has resulted in outright opposition between 'Church'
and 'sects'. As sin is only dealt with through repentance,
first Church and then streams have to repent for their
own sinful attitudes towards each other. Only with such
repentance is any real co-operation possible, for without
repentance there is no real respect for the presence and
the work of the Holy Spirit in each other.

**5. Repentance for Sins against Israel is Essential
for Church-Stream Progress**.

The first sin of rejection of the covenanted people was
by the Church of the Gentiles, and this opened the door to
subsequent 'sectarian' rejections of the Catholic Church.
Repentance for the sins of the Church against the Jews is
then dealing with the roots of all 'replacement' ideologies,
that replace the Lord's chosen of the past with ourselves
as the new family of God. Dealing with the issue of
Israel is thus fundamental for getting to grips with the
Church-and-election issues between the Churches and
the streams.

**6. Church-Stream Correlation and Co-operation
is Needed for Christian Preparation for the Second
Coming**.

This point is a consequence of (i) the Holy Spirit being
at work both in the streams and in the renewal of
the historic Churches and (ii) the whole work of the
Spirit of God in the period of the Church being directed
towards the completion of the Father's plan in Christ
at the Parousia. The New Testament suggests that the
Parousia is hastened or delayed by the obedience or the
disobedience of God's people (2 Pet 3:11–12); the Father's
mercy holds off the day of judgment until the gospel has
been preached throughout the world (Matt 24:14) and

until all have had the opportunities they need to repent and believe (Rom 2:4; 2 Pet 3:9). The obedient co-operation of all moved by the Holy Spirit in Church and stream will advance the evangelization of the world, hasten Israel's welcome of the Messiah and the return of the Lord in glory. In this build-up to the completion of history, both Mary and Israel have key roles that should not be seen as unrelated.

The Issues at Stake

Immense issues are at stake for Christianity itself in the way that the life-streams and the historic Churches relate to each other. In particular, the four modern streams on the one hand, and the ancient Churches of East and West, Orthodox and Catholic, on the other hand, comprise together a high percentage of the world's believers in Jesus Christ. Each side has a choice how to relate to the other side. They can choose mutual rejection or mutual acceptance.

Mutual rejection is simple: that leads to increasing confrontation and greater misrepresentation. The rejection of the grace, truth and light present in the other produces distortion in one's own grasp of the gospel and of divine revelation. Evangelical–Pentecostal rejection of the ancient Churches heightens the sectarian tendencies present within the streams, leading to more rigid formulations of doctrine that then threaten the flow of new life that is the very essence of the streams. Catholic and Orthodox denunciation of the streams as sects, seeing them as quite different from mainline Protestant Churches with whom manageable ecumenical relations are possible, fails to identify the gospel focus at their heart and makes more difficult truly evangelical renewal within the ancient Churches. This in turn renders much more difficult any effective evangelization of the modern world.

Mutual acceptance is more complex. It has to involve a recognition of the presence and work of the Holy Spirit in each other. It does not mean recognition of everything

on the other side as of the Holy Spirit, but it means
acknowledging and affirming what is seen to be of the
Spirit of God. It is discerning faith replacing sheer
prejudice. The principle of discerning mutual acceptance
leaves open what forms of interaction and co-operation
are possible or desirable, but it means that some must
be possible – on the basis of what is recognized to be of
the Holy Spirit.

Some Issues At Stake

One issue is **Life** and **Depth**. The streams are currents
of new life. They are outpourings of the Holy Spirit of
God from the throne of the Father. Like the river that
flows from the Temple in Ezekiel 47, the streams bring
life and healing wherever they flow. (This is not to
deny that they can also bring problematic elements.) By
themselves, they tend towards activism and immediate
results, lacking the more reflective-contemplative dimension that is particularly related to depth. But without
the streams, the depth within the Churches seems to be
the preserve of the few. Without the coming together of
Church and streams, we are likely to see great numerical
and territorial expansion of the streams bringing new life
across the world, but in a way that does not put down
deep roots and that will be plagued by a lack of depth,
sometimes a superficiality, that is vulnerable to the latest
fad and to the spirit of the age.

Another issue is **Heavenly** and **Worldly**. The streams
have helped to restore an eschatological awareness that
the Kingdom of God is not of this world, and that
Christians 'desire a better country' that is 'heavenly'
(Heb 11:16). But their acceptance of Enlightenment-type
division between the spiritual and the physical causes
this awareness of the heavenlies to be understood in
opposition to the physical order. This leads, despite a
real recovery of eschatological hope, to a loss of the New
Testament vision of the new heaven and the new earth (2
Pet 3:13) and of the Holy City, the new Jerusalem, 'coming
down out of heaven from God' (Rev 21:2). By contrast, the

Churches have become too established and at home in this world, losing their longing for the return of the Lord and rather hoping that he will not come too soon. It is only the renewal of the Church incarnate in this world, but now seated with Christ in the heavenlies (Eph 2:5–6) that will restore the right balance between the inheritance in heaven (see Phil 3:20) and the salvation of the whole created order that 'has been groaning in travail together until now' (Rom 8:22).

Towards an Evangelical–Charismatic–Catholic Fulness

What then is at stake in the relationship of Church and streams is the realization of the fulness of the body of Christ. It would seem that the Churches without the life-blood flowing in the streams will lack the concentrated focus and the transforming power of the Holy Spirit. But it would also seem that the streams without the Church cannot become one body, and will lack the capacity to translate their new life and energy into the coherence and depth of the body of Christ.

The letter to the Ephesians is the place in the New Testament that speaks most of the fulness of the body of Christ. The Church, the body of Christ, is 'the fulness of him who fills all in all' (1:23). The gifts and ministries of the Spirit are poured out 'for the equipment of the saints, for the work of ministry, for building up the body of Christ, until we all attain to the unity of the faith and of the knowledge of the Son of God, to mature manhood, to the measure of the stature of the fulness of Christ' (4:12–13). Christ has loved the Church as a bridegroom loves his bride 'that he might sanctify her, having cleansed her by the washing of water with the word, that he might present the church to himself in splendour, without spot or wrinkle or any such thing, that she might be holy and without blemish' (5:26–27).

This fulness will be evangelical, because it flows from the atoning sacrifice of Calvary and is rooted in repentance and conversion. The fulness will manifest Holiness,

for the fruit of the cross is death to sin and resurrection
to a life of holiness in union with Jesus. The fulness will
be Pentecostal and charismatic, because it is the fruit of
Jesus' gift of the Spirit, poured out initially at Pentecost
by the risen ascended Christ from the throne of God, and
because it is the role of the Spirit to fill believers with
divine life, love and power. The fulness of the body of
Christ will be Catholic because there is only 'one body
and one Spirit' (Eph 4:4), because in this body all things
are united in Christ (Eph 1:10) and because this one body,
'joined and knit together by every joint with which it is
supplied . . . makes bodily growth and upbuilds itself in
love' (Eph 4:16).

This last passage makes clear that the fulness of the
body of Christ will only be realized through love, through
the sacrificial self-giving that is called *agape* in the
New Testament. While the first stages of evangelical–
Catholic contact are bound to be cautious, they have to
lead through mutual respect to mutual love. This love,
that is totally the gift and the presence of the Holy Spirit,
should arise as we learn to recognize the work of the Holy
Spirit in each other and to rejoice in it.

In this *pleroma* or fulness of the body of Christ, Israel
will have her place as she recognizes her own Messiah;
the gospel will lead into the mystery of Christ; the gifts
and ministries of the Spirit will visibly yield the fruit
of the Spirit; the power of the Spirit will be seen to be
the power of love that flows from the heart of Jesus, the
Church on earth will herald the coming of the glorious
Church of the Parousia.

Notes

Introduction

1 *One Lord One Spirit One Body* (Exeter: The Paternoster Press, 1987) and *The Glory and the Shame* (Guildford, Eagle, 1994).
2 Exeter: Paternoster Press, 1986. A revised edition is in course of preparation.
3 The European meeting in Vienna, Austria in October, 1991 and the Latin American meeting in Quito, Ecuador in June, 1992.

Chapter One

1 Word Publishing, Dallas and London, 1995.
2 J. I. Packer,'Crosscurrents among Evangelicals', in Charles Colson and Richard John Newhaus (eds.) *Evangelicals and Catholics Together: Toward a Common Mission* (Dallas and London: Word Publishing, 1995) 147–174.
3 *The History of an Encounter: Roman Catholics and Protestant Evangelicals*, 81–114.

Chapter Two

1 D. W. Bebbington, *Evangelicalism in Modern Britain: A History from the 1730s to the 1980s* (London: Unwin Hyman, 1989) 271.
2 The Scofield Bible was not a new translation, but a version of an existing translation, originally the Authorized or King James version, provided with ample footnotes interpreting the biblical text on the basis of Darby's teaching on successive dispensations, each of which replaced its predecessor and during which God dealt with humanity on a different basis.
3 From his introduction to *The Lausanne Story* (Charlotte, NC: LCWE, 1987) 4.

Chapter Three

[1] Phoebe Palmer, *Selected Writings* (ed.) Thomas C. Oden (Mahwah, NJ: The Paulist Press, 1988) 109.

[2] M. E. Dieter, *The Holiness Revival of the Nineteenth Century* (Metuchen, NJ: The Scarecrow Press, 1980) 21.

[3] The Pilgrim Holiness Church merged with the Wesleyan Methodist Church in 1968 to form the Wesleyan Church.

[4] The *Gnadauer Verband* (Gnadau Association) was named after the place where the conference establishing it was held, Gnadau near Magdeburg in the week after Pentecost in 1888.

[5] Hudson Taylor and the faith missions are discussed in more detail in chapter six.

[6] J. E. Church, *Quest for the Highest* (Exeter: The Paternoster Press, 1981) 99.

[7] *The Message of Keswick and Its Meaning* (London & Edinburgh: Marshall, Morgan & Scott, 2nd edn. 1957).

Chapter Four

[1] The title of the book on US Pentecostal origins and pioneers by Robert Mapes Anderson (New York: Oxford University Press, 1979).

[2] Tomlinson later became the founder of the Church of God of Prophecy, also based in Cleveland, Tennessee, when conflicts arose concerning his leadership of the Church of God.

[3] It is also strongly presented in a recent book by Jean-Jacques Suurmond, *Word and Spirit at Play* (Grand Rapids: Wm B. Eerdmans, 1995).

[4] David Reed, one of the few scholars specializing in Oneness Pentecostalism, has described it as a form of 'simultaneous modalism'.

[5] Related to the Church of God (Cleveland, Tennessee).

[6] 'Are we too "Movement" Conscious?' *Pentecost* 2 (Dec. 1947, inside of back cover).

Chapter Five

[1] Michael Harper joined the Antiochene Orthodox Church in March 1995, and has since been ordained to the Orthodox priesthood.

[2] Neither term is wholly satisfactory. The problem with 'Messianic' is that expecting a Messiah characterizes all Jews, who are then Messianic believers, even if they do not accept Jesus as the Messiah.

The term 'completed' avoids the de-Messianizing of other Jews, but it is, shall we say, eschatologically crude, for the language of completion belongs to the final consummation at the Second Coming of Christ.

3 Attitudes towards the charismatic stream among Southern Baptists were vividly illustrated in the sharp questioning of Dr Jerry A. Rankin before his appointment in 1993 as president of the Southern Baptist Foreign Mission Board concerning his views on spiritual gifts and his acknowledgment that he had 'prayed in the Spirit' in his private prayer.

4 See Peter Hocken 'The Charismatic Movement in the United States', *Pneuma* 16/2 (1994), 191–214.

5 See the article by Reinhard Hempelmann, 'Protestant Charismatic Renewal in Germany', *Pneuma* 16/2 (1994), 215–226.

Chapter Six

1 The CIM was the first of what have come to be called 'Faith Missions': see Klaus Fiedler, *The Story of Faith Missions* (Oxford: Regnum Books, 1994).

2 Not non-denominational. 'They avoided all non-denominational concepts, which the Brethren offered. Equally, they refused all offers of integration, whether from denominations or from supra-denominational organizations. They had to do this if they wanted to survive' (Fiedler, op. cit., 183).

3 Fiedler, op. cit., 33.

4 Grattan Guinness lived from 1835 to 1910, and Fanny Guinness (née Fitzgerald) from 1832 to 1898.

5 Fiedler has a big chart listing the faith missions that have led to the formation of new denominations in the receiving countries (*op. cit.*, 92–101), and illustrates the process of eight stages by which the Mission Philafricaine became the Evangelical Church of south-east Angola (ibid., 90–91).

6 Norman P. Grubb, *The Four Pillars of WEC* (London: WEC, 1963).

7 J. I. Packer 'Crosscurrents among Evangelicals' in Charles Colson & Richard John Neuhaus (eds.) *Evangelicals and Catholics Together: Toward a Common Mission* (Dallas & London: Word Publishing, 1995) 166.

8 The roots of the Navigators go back to the 1930s, but their organization and structure really dates from the period of the Second World War. See B. Skinner, *Daws* (Colorado Springs: Navpress, 1974).

9 *Operation World* (ed. P. Johnstone), 1993 edn., 636.
10 Law One: God Loves You, and Offers a Wonderful Plan for Your Life. Law Two: Man is Sinful and Separated from God. Therefore, He Cannot Know and Experience God's Love and Plan for His Life. Law Three: Jesus Christ is God's Only Provision for Man's Sin. Through Him You Can Know and Experience God's Love and Plan for Your Life. Law Four: We Must Individually Receive Jesus Christ as Saviour and Lord; Then We Can Know and Experience God's Love and Plan for Our Lives.
11 *Operation World* (ed. P. Johnstone) in its 1993 edition lists CCC as having 11,043 missionaries in 105 countries (633).
12 *Operation World* (ed. P. Johnstone, 1993) lists YWAM as having 7,076 missionaries in 106 countries (640).
13 According to *Operation World*, OM had 2,234 missionaries in fifty-seven countries (637).
14 Mooneyham was succeeded by Ted Engstrom (1982–1984) and Tom Houston (1984–1989).
15 According to the 1993 edition of *Operation World*, WV has 1,287 missionaries in thirty-two countries (640).
16 World Vision International, *Corporate Policy Manual*, 11.1.3.
17 Other agencies also come under Robertson's umbrella, such as AIMS.

Chapter Seven

1 'Do Tongues Matter?' *Pentecost* 45 (Sept. 1958) inside of back cover.
2 The Pentecostal and charismatic streams are here considered together, as the differences between them concern, not the specific focus, which is basically the same, but the milieux in which this message is given and built upon.
3 Especially the father, Johann Christoph Blumhardt (1805–1880), but to a lesser degree his son, Christoph Friedrich Blumhardt (1842–1919).
4 One does not have to agree with the Pentecostal Holiness theology to recognize the importance of baptism in the Spirit being built upon conversion to Christ and a dealing with basic patterns of sin in one's life.
5 See, e.g.: 'The Cross and the Spirit: Towards a Theology of Renewal' in Tom Smail, Nigel Wright and Andrew Walker, *Charismatic Renewal: The Search for a Theology* (London: SPCK, 1993) 49–70.
6 Glenn Myers gives a description of a network: 'The analogy is a

net: the knots in the net are autonomous organizations like local churches, mission agencies and denominations. Shared information is what links them together ... True networks are loose, open, non-threatening, non-bureaucratic. They enhance our individual efforts, setting them in a wider context.' ('The Network Revolution', *Renewal* 214, March 1994 14–15).

Chapter Eight

1 From Pusey's first speech at the English Church Union, cited by Peter G. Cobb in his article 'Leader of the Anglo-Catholics?' in P. Butler (ed.) *Pusey Rediscovered* (London: SPCK, 1983) 354.

2 R. W. Church, *The Oxford Movement* (London, 1892) 191–192.

3 Cited from A. Perchenet, *The Revival of the Religious Life and Christian Unity* (London: A.R. Mowbray & Co., 1969) 247.

4 Perchenet, op. cit. 249.

5 Cited from F. Biot, *Communautés Protestantes* (Paris: Editions Fleurus, 1961).

6 St John of Kronstadt, *My Life in Christ* (Jordanville, NY: Holy Trinity Monastery, 1984) 2, 496.

7 See the Thailand Report, *Christian Witness to Nominal Christians Among the Orthodox*, a report on a 1980 consultation sponsored by the Lausanne Committee for World Evangelization.

8 See Sergey Chapnin, 'St Tikhon, Moscow, Russia: The Orthodox Charitable Brotherhood' in Gerhard Linn (ed.), *Hear What the Spirit Says to the Churches* (Geneva: WCC Publications, 1994) 30–33.

Chapter Nine

1 G. M. da Masserano, *The Life of St Leonard of Port Maurice* (Philadelphia, 1909) 88.

2 It is important however not to exaggerate the limitations of post-Tridentine Catholicism, as would be the case if the culture of Catholic Europe since the sixteenth century were represented as simply defensive and inward-looking. The clearest evidence against such a view is provided by the extensive missionary work of the Catholic Church from the time of St Francis Xavier (1506–1552) that astonishingly preceded Protestant missionary endeavours by some two hundred years.

3 Antonio Rosmini, *The Five Wounds of the Church* (Leominster: Fowler Wright Books, 1987) 17.

4 Rosmini says of the seminary textbooks: 'I believe that in centuries

to come, which contain the hopes of the imperishable Church, these books will be judged the most miserable, feeble works written in the eighteen centuries of the Church's history' (ibid., 37).

5 Ibid., 34.

6 John Henry Newman, *On Consulting the Faithful in Matters of Doctrine*, J. Coulson, ed. (London: Geoffrey Chapman, 1961) 106.

7 Elena Guerra was beatified by Pope John XXIII in 1959.

Chapter Ten

1 The English translation of the French original was first published by the University of Notre Dame Press in 1956, but was later re-printed by Servant Books of Ann Arbor, Michigan in 1979.

2 Thus, for example, Daniélou has three chapters on the types of baptism in the Old Testament: one on creation and the deluge, one on the crossing of the Red Sea, and one on Elias and the Jordan.

3 *Exégèse Mediévale* (1959).

4 The English translation from Bruce of Milwaukee, Wisconsin, appeared in 1938.

5 The English translation appeared from MacMillan in 1948.

6 It is not known whether this letter ever reached the Pope. There was no reply.

7 Lilian Stevenson, *Max Josef Metzger: Priest and Martyr* (London: S.P.C.K., 1952) 47, 49–51.

8 This book was never translated into English.

9 A revised edition, with addenda, was published in 1965 (London: Geoffrey Chapman).

Chapter Eleven

1 The Catholic Church had long recognized that non-Catholics could be saved, but this was because of their sincerity and **invincible ignorance** and in spite of their Church belonging. Pius XII had in fact disciplined an American priest, Fr Leonard Feeney, who had taught that non-Catholics could not be saved.

2 The liturgy first of the Roman rite.

3 'Sacred Scripture is of paramount importance in the celebration of the liturgy. For it is from Scripture that lessons are read and explained in the homily, and psalms are sung; the prayers, collects, and liturgical songs are scriptural in their inspiration, and it is from Scripture that actions and signs derive their meaning. Thus if the restoration, progress, and adaptation of the sacred liturgy are to be achieved, it is necessary to promote that warm and living

love for Scripture to which the venerable tradition of both Eastern and Western rites gives testimony' (para 24).

4 'The rites should be distinguished by a noble simplicity; they should be short, clear, and unencumbered by useless repetitions; they should be within the people's powers of comprehension, and normally should not require much explanation' (para 34).

5 Of the two Vatican documents on liberation theology, the second entitled *Christian Freedom and Liberation* (Sacred Congregation for the Doctrine of the Faith, 1986) is the more positive. The most positive Church statement on women is Pope John Paul II's recent letter to women, dated 29 June 1995.

Chapter Twelve

1 Chiara Lubich, *That All Men be One: Origins and Life of the Focalore Movement* (London: New City Press, 1969).

2 Quoted in R. Lombardi, *Hope for a Better World* (Langley: Society of St Paul, 1958), 21.

3 The three parts were sub-divided into nine points, of which I cite only three: '4. The present state of the world, and the mentality of the masses, is supremely materialistic. 5. 'Revolt' of the sons of God against this intolerable state of things. 6. This is the hour of the Gospel – of Christianity socially applied (liberalism and Communism have both failed) – it is time to build the age of Jesus.' (Op. cit., 25).

4 Cursillo means 'little course'.

5 There are now several studies of Marthe Robin available in French; the only one so far translated into English is Raymond Peyret, *Marthe Robin: The Cross and the Joy* (New York: Alba House, 1983).

6 It is interesting that this prophecy was received about two or three weeks after the prophecy about a coming great Pentecostal-type revival that David du Plessis reported to have been given him by Smith Wigglesworth in South Africa.

Chapter Thirteen

1 In the teaching of Vatican Two, this manifestation of the Church reaches its fullest expression in the eucharist, especially the eucharist celebrated by the bishop (Constitution on the Liturgy, para 41). The ecclesiology of the Orthodox Church is even more strongly eucharistic.

2 The use of the term 'Renewal' rather than 'Revival' by the

proponents of the 'Toronto blessing' reflects a rather different rationale: since this outbreak had not yet reached the level of Revival in terms of its impact on the unconverted, a different designation had to be found. The choice of 'Renewal' points to this move being experienced as a renewal of the Pentecostal and charismatic streams.

[3] See Peter Hocken, *The Glory and the Shame* (Guildford: Eagle, 1994) Chapter 11.

Chapter Fourteen

[1] While some individual Catholics were baptized in the Spirit previously, February 1967 did represent the beginnings of a visible movement within the Catholic Church.

[2] Not to be confused with the Plymouth Brethren.

[3] See the article by the author on 'The Charismatic Movement in the United States' in *Pneuma* 16 (Fall 1994) 191–215.

[4] C. Norman Kraus 'Evangelicalism: A Mennonite Critique' in Donald W. Dayton and Robert K. Johnson (ed.) *The Variety of American Evangelicalism* (Downers Grove, Illinois: InterVarsity Press, 1991) 189. By 'prophetic witness' Kraus is not referring to Evangelical interest in the subject of prophecy, which has been considerable in modern times, but to the prophetic witness of a counter-cultural way of life.

[5] The oral post-modern character of Pentecostal practice has been repeatedly urged by Walter J. Hollenweger and its playfulness has been emphasized in Suurmond's recent study (see note 3 to chapter four).

Chapter Fifteen

[1] Protestant denominations can of course be organized in very different ways at national level, reflecting different theologies of the Church.

Chapter Sixteen

[1] The Catholic theologian who has done the most important work in reflecting theologically on contemporary developments in the Church and their importance for systematic theology has been the German Jesuit, Karl Rahner (1904–1984).

[2] Official Catholic teaching, particularly since Vatican Two, does

recognize a normative role for the Scriptures, but this is still far from permeating all Catholic thinking and behaviour.

[3] In June 1995, during the visit of Patriarch Bartholomew I of Constantinople, Pope John Paul II asked that the traditional Catholic doctrine of the *Filioque* be clarified to show that it is not in contradiction with the original wording of the Creed of the Council of Constantinople in the year 381. In response, the Pontifical Council for Promoting Christian Unity issued a statement on the Greek and Latin traditions concerning the procession of the Holy Spirit. This statement says that Catholic teaching just be given in such a way that 'it cannot seem to contradict the monarchy of the Father nor the fact that he is the sole origin (*archè, aitia*) of the *ekporeusis* of the Spirit'. There have also been a few occasions on which the Pope has celebrated a liturgy and recited the Nicene Creed without the added *Filioque* clause, that is in the form used by the Orthodox Church.

[4] Para 702. Throughout this section on the Holy Spirit, the Catechism speaks of the 'joint mission' of the Son and of the Spirit rather than of two missions.

Chapter Eighteen

[1] The Second Vatican Council recognized this in principle: 'Moved by that faith it [the people of God] tries to discern in the events, the needs, and the longings which it shares with other men of our time, what may be genuine signs of the presence or of the purpose of God' (*Gaudium et Spes*, para 11).

[2] Constitution on Divine Revelation, *Dei Verbum*, para 21.

Chapter Nineteen

[1] The divine office comprises Morning and Evening Prayer, a service of Readings, three shorter services during the day, and Night Prayer or Compline.

[2] In the Divine Office, the whole psalter is sung or read thus bringing forward the whole inspired prayer of Israel expressing their longing for the Messiah and the coming Kingdom. This central, even dominant, use of the Old Testament psalms by the Christian Church flows from and promotes a Christ-centred understanding of the Old Testament and the sense that Jesus Christ is both object and subject of the psalms, the one to whom they point and the one who utters them.

[3] Encyclical letter, *Redemptoris Missio*, (1988) para 52.

Chapter Twenty

1 A French sociologist of religion, Martine Cohen, has noted that the four major charismatic communities in France all correlate with a particular strand in French Catholic history: the Emmanuel Community with the French school of Monsieur Olier and Cardinal de Bérulle; the Chemin Neuf Community with the Jesuits; the Community of the Beatitudes with the Carmelites, and the Pain de Vie Community with the Franciscans.

2 Second Vatican Council, Decree on Ecumenism, para 3.

3 Ibid para 3.

Chapter Twenty-One

1 *The Liturgy and other Divine Offices of the Church* (London: H.J. Glaisher, 1925), 121–122.

2 The French original *Pour La Conversion des Eglises* (Paris, Centurion) was published in 1988; an English translation has since appeared.

3 Translated by the author from the French text published in *Irénikon* 68/1 (1995) 110.

4 Similar sentiments were expressed by the Pope earlier in May 1995 in his Apostolic Letter *Orientale Lumen* on the Eastern Churches (see paras 17–18).

Chapter Twenty-Two

1 Among the problems raised by the absolute disjunction between Israel and the Church in dispensationalist thinking are: the fact that many of the facets of the life and history of Israel in the Old Testament prefigure the life and history of the Christian Church in the new covenant; the fact that in Christ the physical order as chosen by the Lord (in the election of Israel and shown forth in the physical sign of circumcision and the promise of the land) is not replaced but is raised up as a spiritual body (see 1 Cor 15:42–49); the teaching in Romans 11:26 that 'all Israel will be saved'; the New Testament teaching that it is of the nature of the Church to be the union of Jew and Gentile in the one body (Eph 2:15–16; 3:6); the fact that in the heavenly Jerusalem, the gates have above them the names of the twelve apostles of the Lamb, who were Jewish Christians (Rev 21:14).

2 Interestingly an exact Jewish contemporary of Théodore Ratisbonne's, also the son of a rabbi, followed a very similar path.

Jacob, later François, Libermann (1802–1852), converted in 1826 and ordained a priest in 1841, had founded a small missionary congregation, that in 1848 joined up with the Congregation of the Holy Spirit, of which Libermann became the superior. Libermann was a pioneer in mission work among the black people of Africa, seeing the poor of the Lord, the *anawim* of the nineteenth century, as the black slaves, and seeking before its time a Church led by Africans for the Africans.

3 *Information Service* (The Secretariat for Promoting Christian Unity) 60/I–II (1986) 27.

4 Art 2, para 2.

5 I owe this point to M. Fadiey Lovsky, a French church historian, who has written profoundly insightful books on Israel and Christian unity.

6 The translation 'rejection' used in many English translations (RSV, NIV, REB, NJB) contradicts Paul's formal answer in Romans 11:1 that underpins the whole argument of the chapter.

7 Jules Isaac, *Has Anti-Semitism Roots in Christianity?* (National Conference of Christians and Jews, New York City, 1961).

8 Letter 30, written on the occasion of the Second Crusade in 1146.

9 Calvin was much more moderate in his teaching about the Jews.

10 The (Evangelical) Lausanne Consultation in a statement on Jewish Evangelism dated June, 1995 noted 'the skepticism of many churches towards Jewish believers in Jesus who maintain their Jewish identity'.

11 Uniatism is a term that refers to those Churches and people who observe the liturgical and other traditions of the Eastern Churches, but accept the primacy of the Pope in Rome. They are seen by the Orthodox Churches as a form of proselytizing aggression by the Roman Catholic Church. A joint Catholic–Orthodox document on this highly sensitive subject was drawn up at Balamand in Syria in 1993.

Chapter Twenty-Three

1 There has been such a day in Lutheran Germany for the last century, ironically established by the State, and now being abolished by the State.

2 This association was made possible by the description of the Israelites reaching Mount Sinai in 'the third month' after they left Egypt (Ex 19:1) and the requirement to celebrate the Passover in the first month (Ex 12:3, 18), which would make the fifty days

from Passover fall at the beginning of the third month; note 'on the very day' of Exodus 19:1.

3 *Tertio Millennio Adveniente*, para 36.

4 The Day of Atonement is celebrated on the tenth day of the seventh month, and the feast of Tabernacles begins on the fifteenth day of the same month.

Chapter Twenty-Four

1 The best place to find this is in *The Catechism of the Catholic Church*.

2 In his Apostolic Exhortation on Mary, *Marialis Cultus* (1974), Pope Paul VI gave guidelines for the renewal of Marian devotion under the headings: biblical, liturgical, ecumenical and anthropological (II, 2, paras 29–39).